LEADing Small Business

Best

Steve Futer

Smith

LEADing Small Business

Business Growth through
Leadership Development

Stewart Barnes

Founder and Managing Director, QuoLux Ltd, UK

Steve Kempster

Professor of Leadership Development and Director, Lancaster Leadership Centre, Lancaster University Management School, UK

Sue Smith

Director, Centre for SME Development, University of Central Lancashire, UK

Cheltenham, UK • Northampton, MA, USA

Published by
Edward Elgar Publishing Limited
The Lypiatts
15 Lansdown Road
Cheltenham
Glos GL50 2JA
UK

Edward Elgar Publishing, Inc.
William Pratt House
9 Dewey Court
Northampton
Massachusetts 01060
USA

A catalogue record for this book
is available from the British Library

Library of Congress Control Number: 2015933452

This book is available electronically in the **Elgar**online
Business subject collection
DOI 10.4337/9781783475506

ISBN 978 1 78347 549 0 (cased)
ISBN 978 1 78347 550 6 (eBook)

Typeset by Servis Filmsetting Ltd, Stockport, Cheshire
Printed and bound in Great Britain by T.J. International Ltd, Padstow

Contents

Figures

Notes on the authors

Stewart Barnes is founder and Managing Director of QuoLux, which is a privately owned company that is a specialist in leadership and strategic development working closely with small–medium sized enterprises (SMEs), improving their productivity and profitability. Stewart has over twenty-five years' experience of leading, growing and developing a variety of private businesses in different markets in different countries, transforming organizations and their performance. QuoLux delivers the LEAD, GOLD and GAIN programmes to owner/managers of SMEs. Stewart is a Board director and trusted advisor to a number of SMEs.

Stewart is researching his PhD on the Leadership of Innovation and has an MBA with Distinction from Lancaster University Management School where he first became involved with LEAD. Stewart is a guest speaker at various universities on leading change, employee engagement, innovation, positive psychology and strategic planning. His work on transformational change has been featured in a number of books, articles and Government best practice guidance documents. He is a regular blogger, sharing his insights and passions on his key areas of interest.

Steve Kempster is Professor of Leadership Development and Director of the Lancaster Leadership Centre at Lancaster University Management School, Visiting Professor at Bristol Leadership Centre, UWE and a Board Director of the International Leadership Association. Originally an owner/manager of a surveying practice, Steve joined Lancaster University in 1992. With a PhD in Leadership Learning, Steve has published many articles and chapters on leadership and leadership development. In particular Steve's work has explored how managers have learnt to lead, captured in his book of the same title. In this work he illustrated the fundamental difference in leadership learning required for owner/manager development compared with employed managers. This research led to the joint design and development of the LEAD programme at Lancaster with Sue Smith.

Steve has been invited to give talks on leadership and leadership learning in the UK and various parts of the world including Lisbon, Brisbane and Gold Coast, Auckland, Montreal, Copenhagen, San Diego, INSEAD at Fontainebleau and Singapore. He has advised the Australian Centre for

Family Business on the design of a national programme for small business development.

Sue Smith is Director for the Centre for SME Development at the University of Central Lancashire where she is responsible for developing and delivering the business engagement strategy. Prior to this, Sue was Assistant Dean for Business Engagement at Teesside University and before that led SME growth programmes at Lancaster University Management School where she was the Director of LEAD and co-founder of LEAD along with Steve Kempster. During her tenure at Lancaster University, Sue led the roll-out of LEAD across England and Wales to over 2000 SMEs.

Sue has an extensive track record of university business engagement. She is passionate about how people learn to lead and manage and the real impact this can have on a business. Sue has designed and taught on many leadership development and entrepreneurship programmes for diverse learners in Higher Education from undergraduates and postgraduates to post-experience adult learners who do not traditionally engage with universities.

Her academic research focuses on two areas. The first is using social theories of learning to look at the impact of SME peer learning. The second is the relationship between universities, business and government and the impact this can have on the regional economy.

Foreword

Running a successful small–medium sized enterprise (SME) is no picnic. For those in charge it can be a hostile and often lonely environment. Surviving and staying afloat is challenging enough. The marketplace presents difficulties and opportunities that may lead to growth where growth in turn demands change. Change too early and you could end up with excessive overhead and waste. Change too late and you risk losing competitiveness.

There is also the problem of which change to adopt. There are literally hundreds of alternative routes espoused by enthusiastic academics, consultants and self-styled gurus. There will be no shortage of conviction or advocacy from often conflicting sources. The options facing the owner-manager, director, partner or senior manager (hereafter described as owner/manager) are often bewildering but choices have to be made to sustain and achieve success.

I first encountered this dilemma in 1999 when I was asked to chair a series of failing Business Links in Lancashire, North West England and create a viable and effective entity from the ashes of their predecessors. I had successfully transformed and run a large business as a Chief Executive, so my forte was mainly with the SMEs' bigger siblings. I thought it useful, therefore, to spend my early days talking to lots of SME leaders. It was only then that I began to appreciate the challenge. At that particular time, funding for business support was actually quite generous. However, the complaint made to me repeatedly was that supply was largely related to funding availability rather than to the specific needs of the client base.

In terms of more generic provision, particularly leadership development, similar arguments were trotted out. Whilst personally enrolling on a prestigious business course may be both satisfying and enriching, in most instances the owner/managers in question had neither the time nor the resources to go down that particular path. They want immediate guidance related to immediate problems.

I found this to be intractable, a problem without a practical solution. Everybody had issues but by and large they were different, or certainly they seemed so. Designing a support system to be entirely bespoke would be both excessively expensive and probably highly inefficient. Fortunately there were people about with better imagination than me: specifically my dynamic Chief Executive, Clive Memmott, who decided to tackle the problem head on and enlisted the support of Lancaster University Management School (LUMS). Thanks to the energy and foresightedness of Sue Cox, Ellie Hamilton, Al Mather, Steve Kempster and Sue Smith, together, they came up with the idea of the LEAD programme.

By sheer coincidence I soon found myself on the periphery of the £1 million pilot and £15 million LEAD dissemination programme as a Masterclass speaker for many of the deliverers across the North West of England. I began to marvel at how LEAD had such a positive impact on owner/managers across the region. If only we could bottle it, I wondered to myself repeatedly.

After the demise of the regional development agencies, Sue Smith obtained part funding, charged the SMEs and continued to make LEAD sustainable at LUMS. She also worked with the University of Swansea to leverage nearly £10 million to roll it out across Wales and has leveraged funding to run a similar programme in the North East of England. In parallel, as a private provider, Stewart Barnes has run LEAD on a self-financing basis in the South West of England and Steve Kempster is internationalizing LEAD.

The outcome has been quite spectacular for the business community. For the mercenary:

- average company size grew by 27 per cent;
- average employment increased by 13 per cent;
- 59 per cent of participants now trading with each other, raising millions in new business.

For the broader minded:

- 100 per cent felt themselves to be better leaders;
- 100 per cent felt more effective and confident;
- 97 per cent had grown their companies or felt confident of doing so;
- 83 per cent recorded improvements in their personal lives.

My personal preference is to major on the second set of outcomes. Enhancing self-esteem and confidence is the greatest contribution any leadership programme can give to the SME community. However, the financial benefits should not be underestimated. We all know that the UK has suffered from poor productivity over decades. The country is 17 per cent behind the G7 average and 30 per cent behind the US and Germany. That this should continue to go on for so long is a national disgrace but it still doesn't seem to be high on the political agenda. The methodology espoused by the authors could be the key to future success for the nation. Any doubters should read David Macleod and Nita Clarke's inspirational report[1] "Engaging for Success" which recommends LEAD.

Each time I come away from a LEAD programme, I am thrilled by the transformational impact it has on participants' lives. The energy and enthusiasm in the room is always quite startling as is the way peers relate to each other. This approach does seem to fill a void in the lives of SME leaders and helps them resolve so many of the challenges they constantly face.

I do hope you will explore everything this book has to offer as it attempts to bridge the gap between academia and practice. It provides a real-life narrative encapsulating the development of three owner/managers on LEAD whilst explaining the key theories, models and techniques that underpin the leadership methods and approaches deployed.

The authors have created a unique opportunity for you, the reader, to sample some of the joys and benefits of this extraordinary approach into leadership learning in the SME context.

As a reader, you may be an academic, undergraduate, postgraduate or doctoral student. You could be a policy-maker or a leadership development practitioner. You may be an owner/manager: part of the alumni from the 2000 plus participants who want to compare their experiences and learning with aspects highlighted in the book; or a delegate undertaking the programme; or an owner/manager intrigued to explore the topic of leadership and its impact on growth in the small business. For those in SMEs, my recommendation would be to tackle it as a team, either with other members of your management group or alternatively with peers from elsewhere.

The single most impressive dynamic of LEAD in general has been the power of solving problems by close networking, using simple approaches to diagnose and resolve. The process is infinitely variable, totally relevant and life enhancing. Yet, when stripped back, many of the issues that are faced are common to all. You are not alone, there is support out there!

Enjoy.

Professor John J. Oliver OBE
Team Enterprise Solutions

---

[1] Macleod, D. and Clarke, N. (2009), 'Engaging for success: Enhancing performance through employee engagement,' available at: Department of Business, Enterprise and Regulatory Reform, www.berr.gov.uk/files/file52215.pdf.

Preface: background and introduction to LEAD

Leadership is all around us and is one of the most talked about subjects in business. A search on Amazon.com in April 2015 revealed over 137 000 results on leadership alone, and this number has grown exponentially over the last two decades. With so many books already published, what is the need for another leadership book and why write it?

There are many different categories of leadership book ranging from weighty academic tomes and colossal handbooks that are not easily accessible to the practising leader, through to authors who write about their experiences of leadership and the "how to" guides which break complexity down into simple approaches and solutions but lack rigour when examined.

This book attempts to bridge the gap between academia and practice. It provides a real-life narrative encapsulating the development of three business people on a leadership programme whilst explaining the key theories, models and techniques that underpin the leadership methods and approaches deployed. Each of the key chapters is split into two parts. First, the personal stories are written in the style of a novel, allowing ease of access for the reader to associate and empathize with the situations of the real-life leaders. At the end of the dialogue there are a few questions (in *italics*) for the reader to reflect on to assist them with their own personal leadership development. Secondly, the reader can read the academic underpinning of the leadership learning journey. The reader thus can read the book in a normal linear manner or can read the story without the theory and vice versa.

The primary purpose of our book is to provide a research-based examination of leadership learning in the small–medium sized enterprise (SME) context. Yet the unorthodox approach to this examination is intended to enable readers to stand in the shoes of the owner-manager, director, partner or senior manager (hereafter described as owner/manager). Such readers could be academics, undergraduate, postgraduate and doctoral students. They could be policy-makers and leadership development practitioners. However, we also hope they could be owner/managers: alumni from the 2000 plus participants who want to compare their experiences and learning with aspects highlighted in the book; or as a companion for people undertaking the programme; or they could be owner/managers intrigued to explore the topic of leadership and its impact on growth in the small business. It may not be the normal bedtime read . . . but for the millions of owner/managers surviving against all odds it could be a useful companion that may just help them to sleep.

BACKGROUND TO LEAD

Small firms, virtually no matter how they are defined, make up at least 95 per cent of enterprises in the European Community. Within the UK, small–medium sized enterprises (SMEs) account for 99 per cent of all businesses (Carter and Jones-Evans, 2006). Today even the casual newspaper reader knows about the key role which small firms play in employment creation, their overall importance in the economy, their role in innovation and the importance which government attaches to "enterprise" (Storey, 1994, p. 1). By just about any measure the contribution small firms make to the economy of any country is increasing and their importance is now fully recognized (Burns, 2007). A flourishing small business sector is central to economic growth.

The leadership of the owner/manager is seen to have an impact on the performance of the business. The management and leadership capability is thus a key factor in SME survival and growth.

The LEAD programme (hereafter referred to as LEAD) was developed by the Institute for Entrepreneurship and Enterprise Development within Lancaster University Management School in 2004. At this time, policy was recognizing and pushing for the need for universities to support SMEs and develop their leadership. One of the government's key aims as outlined in the Skills White Paper is to improve leadership and management capability: "Effective leadership and management are key to the development of competitive businesses" (DfES, 2003, chapter 2, 2.14).

The Framework for Regional Employment and Skills Action identified the need to take action to address regional management capability, not only because it affects performance and productivity of individual companies, but also because it impacts on the ability of business leaders to address the skills gap by managing wider skills development within these businesses (Framework for Regional Employment and Skills Action, 2002).

LEAD was designed to benefit the region's micro companies by providing access to the highest quality leadership development to individual owner/managers.[2] The SME sector is under-represented in training programmes with most, if not all, other training programmes being designed for and marketed to managers within larger companies (Smith and Peters, 2006). The main objective of LEAD (a key objective still today) was to raise regional productivity, competitiveness and skills by addressing issues of leadership within the context of the SME sector generally and in particular within the owner/manager's business.

Although initially born out of Lancaster University, LEAD has over the past ten years been delivered across the United Kingdom by other Higher Education Institutions, Further Education Colleges and private training companies to over 2000 SMEs. Steve has provided guidance to the Australian Government linked with the Australian Family Business Centre at Bond University to design a similar programme. Finally the programme is being designed for delivery in partnership with Porto Business School in the spring of 2015 with discussion on-going with many other partners.

Whilst leadership is all around us, it is a subject that arguably means little to the person or persons running a small business even though they are "doing" leadership each and every day.

The challenge for the small business leader is whether to work "in" the business, providing day-to-day management support or "on" the business, providing strategic leadership, to enable growth. Research shows most do the former, finding it difficult to remove themselves from the operational concerns to focus on longer-term strategy (Jones et al., 2007).

LEAD is a research-led programme, based on extensive research into entrepreneurial leadership learning in SMEs (Kempster and Watts, 2002; Cope, 2003). The major contribution of this research was the identification that owner/managers are structurally disadvantaged in their leadership learning (Kempster, 2005; Smith and Peters, 2006; Kempster, 2009a; Smith, 2011) as a consequence of the small business context and the antecedent lived experience of the owner/managers such as feelings of isolation, limited confidence, distant relationship with leadership, prominent patriarchal style, control and limited role models (Perren and Grant, 2001; Smith et al. 1999). Stewart and Alexander (2006, p. 143) argue that the isolation of the enterprise owner/manager is a barrier to learning because they may be the only person within the company concerned with strategic decision-making, yet it is precisely the competencies of the owner/manager that directly impact on the survival and success of an enterprise.

Burgoyne and Stewart (1977) identified the notion of naturalistic

---

[2] Lancaster University Management School is one of two six star rated management schools in the UK.

learning as formative in shaping leadership learning and that leadership is primarily learnt through experience (Kempster, 2006) by actually trying to lead (Jackson and Parry, 2011). The design of LEAD responds to this.

The fundamental assumption made by LEAD is that any process for the leadership development of the owner/manager must be integrated with the business. This is because the senior management in SMEs typically *are* the business and the business reflects the senior management. Leadership is learnt within organizational contexts and leaders learn through the everyday activities they participate in. Yet because it is everyday life, leaders often cannot put their finger on how they have become the leaders that they are.

There is often a major disconnect between "what someone thinks leadership is" – their intent – and "how a person learns to practise leadership" – their impact. LEAD seeks to bridge this disconnect by connecting the awareness of leadership and learning with leadership practice, that is, how a leader leads within their business.

LEAD was designed on the premise that business growth and business development would occur if leadership became more salient to the owner/manager and the sense of leadership identity of owner/managers would become enriched, nuanced and relevant in the context of their own business and own lives (Kempster, 2005).

LEAD combines formal input and experiential learning within a peer group of other SME leaders. A "LEADership Learning Cycle through Lived Experience" is proposed (Figure P.1) integrating a combination of formal and situational learning to develop the owner/manager and the business through a variety of management and leadership development activities. This integrated process of "lived experience" over a ten-month period has been found to be critical to the success of LEAD as business people in SMEs do not typically identify themselves as a "leader" (Kempster and Watts, 2002).

From the outset, LEAD explicitly makes leadership highly salient to delegates in their organizational setting, building on the notion of learning about leadership as a deepening cycle of experience as the delegates shape and are shaped by the situation. It is also essential that the owner/manager be given the tools and transferable skills, for example coaching, to be able to develop and instil leadership within their teams, shaping both their own learning and that of others in the organization.

The cyclical model commences, if a starting point could be so easily identified, with reflection-on-action (Schön, 1983) which makes sense of an experience from which knowledge conceptualization follows. Experiences of leadership generate knowledge and understanding of leadership. Such

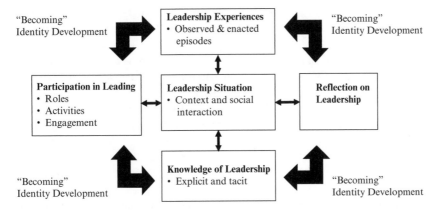

Source: Adapted from Kempster (2009a). Used by permission of the publishers, Palgrave Macmillan.

Figure P.1   LEADership Learning Cycle through lived experience

understanding relates to the situation from which it is drawn. This stimulates reflection from which knowledge is constructed. This knowledge, in the form of a personalized understanding of leadership, is subsequently applied and generates further experiences through participation that through reflection refine, elaborate or confirm knowledge of the experience. There is a move from understanding leadership to participating in leading and how lived experience is central to leadership learning.

This book seeks to outline why LEAD has been successful, establishes the context for small business leadership development, and describes the key dynamics of leadership learning and why it is different in the SME context.

Throughout, we explore the learning journey of three SME business leaders through a series of in-depth, semi-structured interviews aided by formal outputs of LEAD produced by the interviewees during and after the programme, and we draw on their reflective online forum blogs (an integral part of the programme design).

The approach to this research draws on a research method called "co-constructed autoethnography" (Ellis and Bochner, 2000; Boyle and Parry, 2007). Although it is not a common method in management research, Kempster and Stewart (2010) have argued that it is most relevant to the study of leadership learning as it allows the connection of context, historic antecedent influences and relationships to be examined in-depth to both describe and explain the manifestations of particular social processes (Atkinson et al., 2003). Such detailed qualitative research is argued to be a highly appropriate approach for explorations of leadership processes (Bryman, 1996, 2004; Parry, 1998; Day, 2000; Conger, 2004; Kempster, 2006).

It may seem odd that somehow good research can be achieved by examining case study stories of three owner/managers. However, Van Maanen wonderfully captures the essence of the approach: "the universal can be found in the particular" (2011, p. 229). Further, Boyle and Parry suggest that research needs to give more emphasis to relevance and connectivity of ideas and insights that resonate with readers' lives. "We would suggest that the critical 'n' factor is the number of people who read the research, rather than the number of people who are the subjects of the research" (2007, p. 6).

Similarly Ellis and Bochner (2000) suggest that generalization is tested by readers as they determine if it speaks to them about their experience or about the lives of others they know. Stake (2005) interprets such generalization as naturalistic: "a sense of empathetic appreciation from one world to another that provides a vicarious experience for the reader" (Kempster and Stewart, 2010, p. 210). With respect to the discussion in this book, we are seeking to provide a sense of an appearance of authenticity through rich insights into leadership learning of three owner/managers coping with the challenges of leader becoming (Ibarra, 1999).

When we speak of becoming, we are giving emphasis to notions of a relational sense of the self that is emerging through participation. The participation with others shapes us and others so that our becoming is inextricably linked to others in terms of being, knowing and doing (Shotter, 1993; Chia and MacKay, 2007). In this way we depart from an attention to becoming associated with essentialist qualities of an individual – such as traits. For example, the knowing, doing and being associated with becoming a leader is informed by historic practices and constructed through what others do, say and respond to; it is an on-going dynamic of becoming rather than a static sense of being (Alvesson and Sveningsson, 2003; Sveningsson and Larsson, 2006).

In brief, autoethnography examines the *ethno*, the three owner/managers in the context of being a delegate on LEAD and situated in their businesses. While the *graphy* describes the social engagement on LEAD integrated with the on-going leadership of their businesses for a period of ten months from March to December. If it was each of the owner/managers examining their experiences and distilling social theory this would be autoethnography – their accounts. Co-constructed is where we examine, interrogate and critique in depth what has occurred in greater depth. We bring the theory to be applied to what is happening to extract the social processes occurring. In this way the theory becomes relevant in the examination. Ellis describes this process as a "theory sandwich" (2004, p. 198) – a sense of a continual re-appraisal and interpretation of the story through theorizing (Kempster and Stewart, 2010, p. 210).

The layout of the book reflects this theory sandwich. We first provide the story from the three cases of Freddie, Jane and Bill. Then we subsequently examine the stories using selected and relevant theory.

Data was collected through access to over 150 pages of data regarding Freddie, Jane and Bill. This was from: online LEAD Forum notes, learning logs, contemporaneous notes from coaching and action learning, outputs from the Shadowing/Exchange and Learning Days. Additionally we examined their own meta-reflections contained in their 8000-word submissions of their Work Based Learning when they had their Master's level learning assessed. Using the findings from the data as a guide, semi-structured interviews were held with the three owner/managers in their offices, lasting twelve hours in total, where they each reflected on what they experienced, how they felt, what changes they were making in their business at each stage and what changes in themselves they were beginning to experience. The interviews were recorded and transcribed into 92 pages containing over 62 000 words which were compared to the other data collected and used in the narrative in each chapter to describe their unfolding stories. Notably the vocabulary of the three interviewees changed during LEAD as they adopted and applied some of the language learned in their everyday conversations. For example, the delegates spoke to their staff about "open questions" from "Action Learning Sets" and imagining a "Future Perfect" state which is from Coaching.

Our research approach to examining this data sought a combination of both evocative and analytic autoethnography. Evocative autoethnographic research seeks to "[move] the reader to feel the feelings of the other" (Denzin, 1997, p. 228). We see much value in enabling a reader to stand in the shoes of the interviewees to gain a deep insight into the experience, a sense of believability. Analytic autoethnography (Anderson, 2006, p. 376) seeks to go beyond the individual's experience and look for social processes and influences that are common in shaping leadership learning more generally. We hope the approach of the theory sandwich as research enables a deep sense of standing in the shoes of these three owner/managers and also gives a sense of the theory that explains the social processes occurring. We have sought to keep the theory to a minimum so that the sandwich does not end up feeling like having a dried out tough bit of meat ruining the sandwich. We hope we have struck the right balance.

LEAD has made a hugely positive impact on the business for the vast majority of participants. Three large-scale evaluations of LEAD have been conducted looking in particular at the personal, business and economic impact of the programme (Wren and Jones, 2006, 2012; Gill and Harris, 2014). The assessments identified an overwhelmingly positive set of statistics. Among these, significant increases in annual sales, employment and profitability or profits were reported by 97 per cent of participating firms with an average increase in turnover of 27 per cent and an increase in employment of 13 per cent. Delegates also reported increased confidence in and awareness of: individuals' leadership roles; elevated abilities to delegate effectively, leading to staff empowerment; and a wider approach to innovation as evidenced by expansion, relocation, diversification and acquisition activities.

The result of all this has been to free up time for owner/managers to work more *on* their businesses, and less *in* their businesses.

We conclude the story of LEAD with the policy implications of the programme in terms of economic growth through the dynamo of an economy – small business and the owner/manager. If policy-makers are committed to the growth of SMEs, then we argue that they need to make a commitment to developing the leadership of SMEs through the promotion and part funding of programmes such as LEAD. Economic payback in such short periods demonstrably drives growth and employment.

Finally, in an epilogue, we share how the business leader can continue their development journey on the subsequent GOLD and GAIN programmes and we also discuss how the owner/manager, through Work Based Learning, can progressively achieve a Postgraduate Certificate, Diploma and Master's degree by having their learning recognized to essentially obtain a Master's in running their own company.

INTRODUCTION TO LEAD

At the beginning of LEAD it's all a bit strange and different for delegates. LEAD is not a conventional taught "training" course; it is about the development of the leader and the development of their business. Delegates are encouraged to "trust the process" and to give themselves time to reflect, time to learn and time to enjoy the programme.

LEAD lasts for approximately ten months and delegates need to commit an average of two days a month (or part thereof).

LEAD employs the LEADership Learning Cycle through Lived Experience integrating a number of key elements that combine both formal (that is, taught) and informal learning, allowing for a high level of interaction between delegates and the LEAD team and, crucially, between delegates and their fellow cohort members. The key elements are:

1. Overnight Experiential
2. Masterclasses
3. Action Learning Sets
4. Coaching
5. Business Shadowing and Exchanges
6. Online LEAD Forum
7. Learning and Reflection Days

The programme commences with an Induction and concludes with a Graduation.

LEAD is rooted in a participative teaching methodology. It supports a social view of learning that relies upon peer-to-peer learning to make sense of the different learning interventions. This pedagogy is based on constructionist views of knowledge which requires the delegates to engage with the ideas that come from the different elements of LEAD and to develop skills and capabilities relevant to their own situations back in their businesses. This pedagogy includes learner-directed styles of learning and interactive approaches for the delegates to learn from each other and the knowledge they have about running small businesses.

LEAD uses a range of delivery approaches:

- Leadership situation – the *context* of a real, lived and situated experience is placed centrally as both a catalyst of available learning opportunities and as a filter shaping a delegate's learning. In essence, this is where the delegate "does" leadership on a daily basis.
- Knowledge of leadership – understanding of leadership becomes interrelated with the situation and subsequently allows the delegate to interpret the situation to provide guidance or prompts to leadership approaches.
- Participation in leading – engagement with leadership is within situations. Participation through roles and associated activities creates opportunities for experiences of leading and, through participation, knowledge of detailed nuances of leading in a particular situation may be absorbed both explicitly and tacitly.
- Leadership experiences – the variety and difference of experiences of leading drawn from situations enable greater development to occur through learning from observation and enacting leadership.
- Reflections on leadership – the overt role of reflection as a continual conscious process enables the delegate to surface and make sense of their activities which develops their individual leadership.

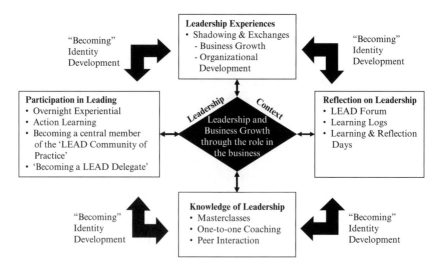

Figure P.2   Structure of the LEAD programme – "becoming" a leader

Each of the above five dimensions of the LEADership Learning Cycle is the basis of at least one of the elements of LEAD (see Figure P.2).

This is the central model that runs through the book – like a red thread – connecting the theoretical understanding together alongside the examination of leader becoming of the three owner/managers. For us it is much more than a set of individual aspects. We outline in the Chapter 10 theory sandwich the metaphors of marbles and a bird's nest. We would recommend jumping ahead to this theory sandwich to get an understanding of the metaphor. It speaks to the importance of a holistic appreciation of how the learning is integrated and reinforces each aspect rather than stand-alone elements.

The delegates' everyday social setting, their workplace, is situated at the centre of the LEADership Learning Cycle – Lived Experience. This *leadership situation* is the crucible of leadership (Bennis and Thomas, 2002) where their identity as a leader has been formed and where it unconsciously continues to develop in the everyday happenings of business. On LEAD, delegates are encouraged to consider how the range of delivery approaches – Participation in Leading, Knowledge of Leadership, Leadership Experiences and Reflection on Leadership – impact on them and the Leadership Situation in the context of their business.

There is a strong emphasis on reflective learning over the duration of the programme. LEAD encourages delegates to implement new ideas in their businesses and bring their experiences of this back to share with their cohort. Thus, delegates bring to the learning table both their experience of practice and their experience of themselves in that practice.

Throughout LEAD, delegates are asked to keep a learning log, which is a private and confidential record for them to plan and document their own personal development and the changes they implement in their business while they are on LEAD. It gives delegates the opportunity to record, review and plan what they do during their time on LEAD; it demonstrates examples of how delegates are putting skills into practice; it provides an insight into the delegates' preferred ways of learning and increasing subject knowledge; it encourages a greater sense of confidence, self-awareness and identity; it acts as a benchmark throughout LEAD on where delegates are in achieving their learning objectives.

Acknowledgements

We would first like to thank Edward Elgar Publishing for engaging us and then being open to a new style of book on leadership that transcends the business world and academic audiences.

We would like to thank Freddie, Jane and Bill for their contributions and for sharing their gripping story of their personal journeys and the development of their businesses.

Stewart would especially like to acknowledge his co-authors. First, to Steve who was the first to capture Stewart's attention on the importance of leadership, firing his imagination and prompting a thirst to learn more about the subject. This has directly led to Stewart creating a business in his quest to become an academically-influenced practitioner assisting other business people to improve their leadership. Secondly, to Sue and her husband Laurie, who initially coached the QuoLux team on the facilitation and delivery of LEAD. He would also like to acknowledge all the business leaders who have shown great faith, belief and trust in QuoLux and in becoming involved with LEAD. Thanks also go to his business partner, Rachael, who has brought LEAD alive, playing a major part in its success locally. Finally, Stewart would like to thank his wife, Polly, for her dedication in transcribing all the interviews, reading and checking drafts and for her unwavering and loving support across the many months it has taken in researching and writing this book.

Steve would like to give thanks to both co-authors. To Stewart, who has the ability to stand astride academia and practice with astonishing skill and whose energy and drive has made this book happen; and to Sue, who has been a leadership learning companion for over ten years to become world leading in the application of communities of practice in the entrepreneurial context. The debt we owe to participating owner/ managers and, more importantly, the debt that society owes more generally cannot be overstated. To my sons, Chris and Rob, I get more proud of you both every day. Finally to my wife Sarah . . . "you had me at hello".

Sue would also like to thank her co-authors: Steve, for the inspiration to begin LEAD back in 2004 and for unending support since then and Stewart, for his dedication to LEAD and the pedagogy and for making it such a success with some wonderful SMEs. Sue would also like to thank all the SMEs who have taken a leap of faith to participate in LEAD for the benefit of their businesses. Finally, Sue would like to thank all teams across the UK who have rolled LEAD out in their own institutions, and her husband, Laurie, who has expertly supported these teams to practically input a programme that isn't a traditional learning experience.

1. Does everyone feel this way? Loneliness, uncertainty, self-doubts and a distinct lack of time

It is lonely running a business, a company, an organization. I feel that the problems I face are unique to me and my company. How could someone else possibly understand my products, my services, my markets, my staff, the issues I face and all the things that make me and my business what we are? After all, I have spent years getting to where I am today.

Even inside my company I feel that I have no one I can openly turn to. I can't talk to those around me as they expect answers from me, not doubts, not questions. They want answers! Indeed, some of the issues that the organization faces have been caused by them. How can I talk to them about problems that I believe they are part of or that they have caused?

Deep down, I know I can't do it all on my own. I try and involve others in running the business but too regularly they let me down and I end up doing the work myself. In any case, it's quicker if I do it myself as it gets done correctly. If not, then I only have myself to blame. Yes, that's the best way to keep things in control, for the time being at least.

Dare I ask myself whether the same managers who have grown up with the business can take the company to the next level? I just don't know. And it is not easy hiring new people either. I've employed "wrong 'uns" before. CVs are all too similar, no one gives poor references and it's difficult to truly see what an individual is like from an interview. Psychometric testing? "That's not for us." Maybe it is best sticking with those that I know well? But plodding on will not bring the success that I want, that I crave, that we deserve. Something will have to change. But what? And how? Let alone in what order!

And where do I get new inputs, insights and innovation from? Effectively I have had to learn on the job. No one has prepared me for the role. There has been no training course and there has been little or no personal development. Leadership does not apply in my firm. It's only for "large" companies. Isn't it? Well, whatever leadership is or is not I am unaware of people who do it well in my circle of friends or business networks. And as for business networks, how can I possibly admit my doubts and concerns to strangers, some of whom may even be competitors?

Yes, my wits, drive and knowledge of my industry have carried us a long way so far. But as the company grows and we employ more, I have less and less time to spend with customers, with the employees that I have known for years – I simply cannot get around the organization to see what is really going on. Control, it seems, is slipping away like grains of sand between my fingers.

The company has never been as big, I've never run an organization so large and the pace of change is unrelenting. I have doubts on how to grow it further. There are no certainties. My overwhelming feeling is one of isolation leading to more self-doubts draining my already fragile self-confidence. Not that I'll admit that to anyone.

Time. I could do with more of that. I never seem to have enough. I can never really get to do the things I know need to be attended to, the priorities, as I am endlessly consumed by all the urgent things that continually drop on my desk or arrive in my inbox. Business seems to be 24/7, absorbing more and more of my time and energy.

* * * * *

Like many business leaders, Freddie Porter, Jane Bishop and Bill Richards felt all of the above. They had no one to turn to despite an ever growing number of business support organizations and consultants offering a confusing battery of similar services.

Freddie, Jane and Bill all ran businesses in the same part of the country and unknowingly had much in common though they had never met. They had survived the recession and despite the difficult trading conditions, all had opportunities to consider.

All three business people had concerns about the performance of their very different companies. Due to various factors, their enthusiasm and confidence were privately waning under their self-doubts. They had no training to lead their respective businesses.

* * * * *

FREDDIE PORTER

With his dark hair, light stubble beard, permatan and rakish frame, Freddie was a fun-loving and fashionably dressed husband and father of two young children. In his early thirties, the dark sports car parked outside his office reinforced the fast, racy image he liked to portray. Quick-talking Freddie was someone in a hurry, out to prove himself and make his own mark. He frequently used his cheeky smile, the twinkle in his eye and his sheer energy to move things in his direction to get his way.

As the oldest son, Freddie inherited the century-old family-owned building materials company together with its history and traditions from his recently "retired" father. Freddie worked alongside his two younger brothers but their relationship was a stormy one, not helped by the father who often sided with the brothers. Freddie's wife worked part-time, helping out in the office.

Freddie's father had ruled with an iron fist, controlling all aspects of the business and his sheer will and determination drove the organization. Not only had Freddie inherited the company, he had unknowingly inherited some of his father's rather direct ways though he was trying his best to adopt a more inclusive style. Distributing components to construction companies meant that as a supplier you must always deliver when customers demanded. The task is all-important. Freddie knew that, as did the 82-strong staff. Also, his father, "The Boss", despite being retired, would still come in most days, count the lorries in the yard and make his way to Freddie's office then slate him on the lack of sales, the cleanliness of the wagons or something else that *wasn't quite right*.

After leaving school, by his own admission, Freddie was not the most confident as he did not enjoy the experience of school. Leaving home, he went to university 90 kilometres away, far enough to be away from home yet near enough to come back when needed. There, he did a sandwich programme which meant he had to spend six months overseas. It was this experience, where he had to stand on his own two feet, that brought him out of his shell. After graduating, he did not join the family firm. Rather, he went to work for another company in the industry, picking up valuable experience of different business practices.

After a few years, an opportunity presented itself to join the family firm as Operations Manager. Freddie did not want to get the job because of his surname. He wanted to obtain the job on merit. He also did not want to be interviewed by his father who was the Managing Director so he went through a robust, three-hour interview with the Financial Director. A short while later, Freddie officially started within the firm. He had no job description, no induction, there would be no personal development, appraisals or direction as to what to do. His first year in the family business was a *wasted year*.

Nevertheless, Freddie had always looked up to the Financial Director who went on to become Managing Director, moving Freddie into different roles before Freddie became head of the retail division – an opportunity that he was to seize and make a success of. Still, at no stage were objectives agreed with Freddie.

Old business methods and models had remained unchanged over many decades, with personnel and systems left to stagnate. The mentality embedded at management level within the business was one of "the company can run itself, we don't really need director intervention". This was probably true to an extent; however, it meant the company would not grow and would progressively worsen over time. With no succession planning, the external accountants and bank managers were increasingly worried about the direction of the business, especially during the recession.

The business had had no one driving it forward and although some of the traditional methods to run a business that were employed were still working, which included relationships built with clients over many years, a good delivery service and good stocks of materials, a severe lack of communication and planning was preventing the company from moving forward.

Eventually the Managing Director retired and Freddie, who had just entered his thirties and become a father for the first time, was appointed to the role of Managing Director with his father as Chairman.

The next generation had arrived.

Freddie knew he had an enormous challenge to turn the company around to be a successful organization.

Again there was no handover. Freddie was full of trepidation, scared of the responsibility. Although it said "Managing Director" on his business card, he did not feel like one. He had the job responsibility but did not know how to do the role. It felt like the blind leading the blind. The management team were not up to standard and the family were all on top of each other, resulting in ill-feeling.

The company had laboured through the last ten years led by an autocratic Board with poor leadership and ineffective communication. The predominant leadership style or management style was autocratic and highly directive. Being told what to do was common. Communication was one-way, top-down. Senior managers felt battered and bruised.

The culture was one of "just do enough to get through" and until Freddie took control, "change" and "succession planning" were words that had never been broached in a generation. It was very challenging for Freddie working with family members on the Board who had very different viewpoints on all manner of ideas and issues surrounding the company. This also had an adverse impact at a personal level on the immediate family members who were not connected to the business.

Freddie knew he had to change "the way we do things around here". In short, he knew he had to change the culture, starting with the leadership style.

JANE BISHOP

In sharp contrast, bespectacled Jane was the embodiment of a demure, well-spoken and considered business person. Conservatively dressed with matching pearl earrings and necklace, Jane's preference for comfortable flat shoes underscored her average height and stature. Trusting, loyal and hard-working and now in her late forties, Jane was Managing Director of a marketing company with a local and regional reach, where she had a small shareholding.

The company was established 35 years ago and during the last two decades it had seen many transformations in the disciplines and services it offers and its ownership – always privately owned by its directors but Board members had come and gone. The company's two major shareholders were accountants and were both involved part-time in the business holding the main financial levers. Jane left the finances to them to manage and accordingly she lacked financial knowledge.

Jane had worked for six years under the owners and was well-liked, but although she knew the technical side of the business inside out and was respected by the staff, the owners did not trust her enough to run the firm unfettered, despite appointing her as Managing Director two years ago.

Jane had made a work–life balance adjustment to join the smaller, independent company as a director. Indeed, she took a pay cut to come aboard as it appeared a stable firm – a blessing after the continual ups and downs in her previous high pressure role. Her long daily commute of over an hour each way had thankfully gone too. She satisfied herself that she would have more time to spend with her husband of two decades and perhaps even write some poetry – a long-held ambition. Jane believed that she had joined an organization where she could influence change, be listened to and feel valued.

That was true for almost four years but at the onset of the recession, the then Managing Director left and the Board asked Jane to take on the role. Whilst being initially excited, Jane had no experience at Board level and she felt she was not equipped to do the job and lead the business out of difficulties.

To survive the downturn, the firm had to cut costs, close a loss-making division, shed overheads, including making staff cuts, and relocate to smaller, more affordable offices. All these things had taken Jane out of her comfort zone but she diligently worked alongside the owners, making the necessary but unpleasant cuts. The Board believed that the business was now in a much stronger position to move forward and be profitable again. The Board thus shifted its focus from fire-fighting and survival to preparation for growth. The company now had ten employees, down from the hundred plus at its zenith two decades ago, and was on the cusp between a micro and a small business.

Having gone through this dramatic change, Jane felt a sense of responsibility to help her company achieve more and release its latent potential to deliver success. She believed she needed to be "fully equipped" in order to fulfil that responsibility. Jane had reached the point where she was looking for ideas and for tactics to try, to grow in confidence and to turn these ideas into action in the business that would have a positive impact.

Somewhat poetically, Jane saw her role as one that *orchestrated* the talents of others towards a common goal and to choose the right *score* – one that made the best of her organization's capabilities and that an *audience*, the customer, would want *to pay to hear*. She knew she had to be clear about her expectations and make timely decisions.

However, Jane understood that *holding a really good practice session* was one thing and recognized that she didn't bring every aspect together to reach the company's performance goals. Inwardly, her confidence as a leader fluctuated wildly and mostly she felt her performance was below par. Typically she would lose herself in the day-to-day tasks and deadlines and then be on the back foot when she realized she had not progressed the more strategic aspects of the business.

Jane did satisfy herself that she was good at building up the confidence of her team but noted she lacked assertiveness, not always following her instincts and then regretting it. Part of Jane felt that she had reached a position of responsibility through "default" – promoted when "someone's got to step in" and where she was the most economic and viable option. While she knew she was supported, she didn't always believe she had earned the right to lead, which of course further undermined her self-confidence.

Jane had carried the burden of the past for too long: the experience of downsizing, closing operations and making people redundant weighed heavily. This led to a sense of failing despite creating an opportunity for the firm to improve and go forward. But she was ready for a fresh beginning. She had no formal leadership training. She wanted something personal that would address her needs.

Jane reasoned that something had to change if she was going to be able to influence the success of the company as fully as she needed to and wanted to. She didn't feel that she had many great leaders as role models to learn from through her career, so she really wanted to meet others to help guide her. She also needed the time to gain perspective away from daily activities.

BILL RICHARDS

Lively, energetic and effusive, Bill never seemed to run out of words but he wouldn't waste them either. He was considered, yet prided himself in getting straight to the point. Highly self-critical, Bill would continually drive self-improvement. He was a taskmaster, tough on himself and was very hard-working, often taking on what others would be able to do, if he gave them the chance, to ensure things got done to the correct standard.

This all-consuming approach had taken its toll. Now in his mid-forties, he had two broken marriages behind him. He was close to his four children, both emotionally and physically, as they lived nearby, but he did not see them as much as he would have liked. This led to a natural sadness that any parent separated from their children can identify with. He had since had a few relationships but none had lasted for one reason or another. This stoked his fieriness, inflaming his ruddy faced complexion. He was also recovering from a major health scare, an experience he did not want to repeat and one which understandably had set him back.

Bill was an extremely well-dressed, dapper individual, which signalled his colourful character. Dark tailored suits, brightly striped ties and highly polished shoes were his uniform and he wore it well. He would even be spotted wearing spats at formal business evenings. Bill was a confident individual. At two metres tall, muscular and well-built, the fair-haired, blue-eyed Bill had a commanding presence, a natural air of authority with a disarming smile.

Bill ran a professional services company and was one of four equal partners employing 55 staff in three offices in small neighbouring towns in the county. A high street presence was important to the firm as many customers would walk in to seek advice. All three offices had different cultures and an aging workforce. Bill worked at the major office, the most progressive and profitable office, and rarely visited the others. He had other priorities, mostly around workload and meeting clients.

In truth, Bill became Managing Partner as no one else wanted to do it. He was well-liked and respected by his partners. They trusted that he could deliver in the elevated role and acknowledged that he was the best person to do the role.

Bill's natural direct style was diametrically opposite to the machinations of a partnership. He knew he had to listen to his partners, ensuring everyone's thoughts and concerns were heard and considered. But this was very time consuming, and in his profession, time was money. All the partners were specialists working in their own areas and only occasionally came together to discuss the overall direction of the organization. Trying to make decisions for the good of the firm was not easy as everyone had to be consulted. Everyone had an opinion and often these were not always helpful, which slowed progress and frustrated the Managing Partner.

Bill had been with his company for over twenty years. When he joined he was given a free hand in his department and he enjoyed the autonomy and self-determination. Essentially he was his own boss and became a partner a few years later before his career drifted for a handful of years. In his early thirties, he stepped up his own performance to become the driving force behind the business. He led on restructuring and succession, then asked to become Managing Partner, knowing that no one else wanted to do the role. Previously, whoever had been the most senior had been given the role by default.

Bill could do things his way now. He saw the writing on the wall for the traditional business model and forecast that the sector would undergo major consolidation. He knew the company needed radical change. It needed to be a business as well as a profession; it needed a modern decision-making process in which he could lead, not consult, and be bold. He saw that he would fill the vacuum of leadership that existed. Bill had a vision for the firm and for his future in that vision. It was now time to take the first steps towards that mental picture.

Bill believed he was the lightning rod for change and certainly he was a force of nature as he set out to grow the business to achieve a critical mass through mergers. Quickly, other businesses would contact him to become part of his expanding organization. Within a few short years the firm doubled in size. The strategy was working. However, Bill's "one-dimensional approach" had led him to plateau. He now felt he'd lost his way a little.

By his own admission, his leadership style was mixed. He was good in a crisis, performing well and driving projects towards agreed goals, but on matters that held little interest for him his attention was prone to drift and he would not follow through. Staff morale suffered as a result.

Whilst the mergers had been successful, Bill observed that there was a lack of ambition within the firm amongst partners and staff and that organic growth was not being achieved. This was borne out in the review of management accountants and staff appraisals. Bill believed that there was a lack of leadership at various levels within the firm and that staff were acting within their own comfort zones. He recognized that the lack of key performance indicators, both financial and non-financial, did not help either, compounded by the absence of effective communication up, down and across the organization of any meaningful business information.

Bill knew he had to "find time for me" and to get out of the office. He recognized that he did not have the skills to "take the company to the next level".

Today, Bill found himself gazing into the distance and pondering, "*Where do I want to take my business? To what extent am I a significant constraint on the growth of the business? Where do the opportunities lie? Where does growth lie for the business?"*[3]

THEORY SANDWICH 1   THE OWNER/MANAGER,
                    LEADERSHIP AND BUSINESS
                    GROWTH

Here we outline what is understood in terms of how small business growth is inter-related with the owner/manager's leadership aspirations and practices. We show how growth can be stifled by the owner/manager and why leadership development is critical to the survival and growth of small firms.

The ability to learn through gaining and applying new knowledge is of significant importance for enhancing SME performance (Jones et al., 2010). Leadership has been identified as an important factor in the success and failure of SMEs and is crucial to national and regional economies of most developed countries (Anderson, 2002; Thorpe et al., 2009).

The owner/manager is the major influencing factor in determining the culture within an SME (Schein, 1992) and in shaping the way that things are done in an organization. Leadership is strongly argued to be a process of sense-making (Smirich and Morgan, 1982; Pye, 2005). Kempster (2009a) goes further, suggesting leadership is a process of "sense-giving" seeking to shape the sense-making processes of others. Viewing leadership as sense-giving points to leadership as also being an outcome (Drath et al., 2008). Drath et al. (2008) suggest that leadership as an outcome should be considered as a combination of direction, alignment and commitment. In this way an owner/manager is the dominant process of shaping colleagues' sense of the direction the business needs to travel in, how to align efforts and galvanize commitment to the direction and aligned efforts.

SMEs are dependent on the owner/manager's insight, leadership skills, training, education and the background of the company's leader. Often, lack of these characteristics shaping the process of leading is the cause of small business' lack of success (Gaskill et al., 1993), that is, the process of leading is weak and thus direction, alignment and commitment are similarly weak.

Leadership within SMEs has certain challenges. SME owner/managers

---

[3] These are questions explored at the different stages of a LEAD delegate's journey from before coming on the programme, through the induction and onto LEAD itself. During the ten months of the programme, the questions come mainly from the Masterclasses or are wider leadership development questions. We hope that these questions allow the reader to reflect on their own personal leadership development.

have very different career aspirations from those in larger organizations and do not typically identify themselves as a leader (Kempster and Watts, 2002). There is general acceptance that social phenomena such as leadership are learnt most notably through the process of observation (Bandura, 1986; Kempster, 2009a) and this is the dominant process of social learning.

In SMEs, the opportunity for owner/managers to observe leadership is reduced as the owner/manager is often alone and isolated or unable to bounce ideas off and confide in their management team, if they have one (Smith and Peters, 2006). Often they are without peers and have limited role models (Perren and Grant, 2001; Smith et al., 1999; Kempster and Cope, 2010) and often have bad bosses (Kempster, 2009a). There is a lack of in-house training, appraisals and development (Kempster and Smith, 2014). The leadership career pathway is restricted in SMEs for owner/managers and in many ways the SME context stifles leadership learning but this does not mean the owner/manager is not leading – far from it (Kempster and Cope, 2010). Their leadership has a very powerful effect on their employees and the business. The outcome is that owner/managers often draw on early formative experiences, most notably family, education and first jobs. Therefore it is the small business context that is the crucible where owner/managers learn to lead (Bennis and Thomas, 2002). There the relationship between the owner/manager and the business reinforces and arguably limits leadership learning (Kempster and Cope, 2010).

Cope (2003) noted that owner/managers learn from experience "on the job" and that practical learning takes place in reflecting on that experience, concluding that learning and reflective processes are inextricably linked. However, Kempster (2005, 2009a) identified that within the SME context leadership was of significantly low salience. Not that owner/managers were not leading – far from it: they were providing a very strong form of leadership, but there was a low recognition of the phenomenon of leadership and they had very little desire to study it, form the perspective of their experiences and be challenged in how they were leading. In major part this reflects a limited conscious desire in many owner/managers to aspire to becoming a leader.

Kempster and Cope (2010) showed that there was a striking contrast between employed managers and owner/managers in terms of the salience of leadership and aspirational desire to become a leader. For the employed manager, leadership was a highly valued concept and being seen by others (certainly those more senior who can promote!) as having potential to lead effectively significantly encouraged their attention to becoming better at leading. In contrast, for the owner/manager the everyday pressing demands were the focus of attention. Kempster and Cope showed that few owner/managers had mechanisms around them to stimulate attention and reflection to improving their leadership: they rarely had a superior to perform to, had few opportunities to observe others and fundamentally owner/managers were not switched on to a desire to review how they were leading, its impact, why they led as they did and how to revise their approach to leading.

It has been argued that the entrepreneur's vision, priorities and competencies influence the strategy planning processes and growth of the business (Majumdar, 2008). Although an entrepreneur is not synonymous with owner/manager, the leadership of a small organization undeniably affects its growth potential. The UK Government recognizes the relationship between management proficiency and performance. Bosworth et al. (2002, p. 8) state evidence which suggests that one of the fundamental problems holding back the growth of SMEs is a lack of leadership and management capability to drive performance and enable them to succeed. Successive government schemes have focused on SME growth through leadership development support but within the UK there is much to do in this arena as highlighted by Smallbone et al. (2015).

Leadership education programmes provide a significant opportunity to develop owner/managers if the designs focus on an understanding of how owner/managers have learned thus far to lead, the limitations of the SME context to enable learning and then put in place mechanisms that suit such learners. This is the fundamental thinking that shaped the development of LEAD. We sought to address two questions: how can we create a process for leadership learning that builds on the context of an owner/manager and delivers learning directly applicable to the circumstances of the owner/manager? How can we make sure that such an approach both develops the owner/manager and addresses the needs of the business? What we do know is there is a need to replicate social learning processes.

The latter question is linked to the relationship of leadership and SME growth. In a review of literature on the relationship between start-up, growth and leadership, Cope et al. (2011) showed that team-based start-ups were more successful in terms of growth than lone owner/managers. This is because team-based structures have a greater variety of talents and networks. Team-based SMEs adopt a broader form of leadership akin to distributed leadership (a useful review of which is in Bolden, 2011). There is a powerful irony in entrepreneurship. The commitments, skills, ambition and insight that drive the establishment of a start-up become a glass ceiling to business growth. The need for decisions, innovations and the exploitation of networks and opportunities to come out from the owner/manager leads to the lone owner/manager suppressing the distribution of leadership to others to exploit their networks, to be innovative and take local decisions. The necessary entrepreneurial qualities required at start-up do not reflect the leadership qualities for growth.

2. Induction: taking the LEAD – beginning the LEAD journey

In this chapter delegates make the decision to join LEAD and undertake the induction where they are introduced to the different elements of the programme in more detail and prepare for the Overnight Experiential.

It was the start of a new year. The economy was beginning to recover after a difficult few years of recession. Times were still tough and in the cold, snowy, wintry weather, new business just seemed harder to come by. Nevertheless, Freddie, Jane and Bill knew the time was right to take action. They wanted to improve their companies and change themselves.

All three had heard about a new ten-month long programme called LEAD aimed at owner/managers of growing businesses or companies with the potential to grow. LEAD encouraged delegates to "work *on* the business, not *in* the business" and to take a more rounded, strategic perspective rather than being pulled into all the daily activities. Clearly there was something in the wintry air suggesting that spring was perhaps around the corner – the notion that *learning with LEAD develops you and your business* was an offer Freddie, Bill and Jane could not refuse, so they agreed separately to meet with the LEAD provider.

Freddie was one year into the Managing Director role and felt he needed new skill-sets, new knowledge and role models as he was only exposed to and consequently had learned from "poor leadership". Leadership to Freddie was sitting around a Boardroom table twice a year focused on whatever the issue was at that time, with no agreed outputs at the end. The predominant mind-set was that directors were not needed and the business could run itself. Freddie wanted more exposure to business-related matters by rubbing shoulders with larger, more successful and more strategic thinking companies. He also wanted some insight into engaging staff better and how to build teams in the future. He knew that his company had had no business plan in over one hundred years of its existence.

He asked himself, "Is that a good thing or a bad thing?" The bank manager and external accountant thought the latter.

This very much led Freddie to focus on change management. It was clear to him that, as a company, if they did not implement widespread change at a continual pace with regard to employee engagement, communication and critical internal systems (including computer systems, accounting formats and administration streams) then the business would fall further into the gloom cast by the deep recession. It was now time to build on their perceived strong existing customer relationships and understand how the company could further tap into the great potential they had through referrals, new product groups and new markets to create sustainable margins.

LEAD seemed curiously right and the timing was ideal.

Jane loved the sound of LEAD with its blend of Masterclasses, peer-to-peer learning and one-to-one coaching. She relished the idea of coming on the programme and was excited by the opportunity to improve and go forward. She realized she needed guidance, to learn more skills and to feel that she had a sounding board who could provide clues on where to go and what to do next. She also looked forward to making some strong new contacts – and maybe new friends. She hoped that by becoming a stronger leader, everyone she worked with could get more out of their job, not just her.

Bill knew his decision to come on LEAD would be pivotal in achieving his goals. He believed that he was "inadequate" and that he needed to invest in himself, exposing himself to something he had not done before. Indeed, he reasoned that investing in time was more important than the monetary investment required to join the programme. He did not believe that he would have a "Eureka moment": he did hope, however, that he would find the very simple and possibly obvious thing that was missing in his leadership.

One month later, after discussing it with family and business partners, all had submitted their application to join the next LEAD cohort. The word "cohort" conjured up visions of a *legion* of directors and senior managers drawn from the local business community safeguarding the security of the community . . . indeed this was the case: safeguarding the security of the business and the related community the business draws from and serves.

Yet all three remained worried about the time commitment. How would they fit it in with all their daily duties? Normally, they did not have time to meet anyone, let alone spend time out of the business on a course. Practice was to keep their head down, comforting themselves with the thought that "one day things will ease up". If only!

* * * * *

1 March. The harsh winter was coming to an end and although the trees were still brown, the first buds of spring could be spotted and a few

hardy flowers had burst through the barren ground, giving the first hints of brighter colours.

The day of the LEAD induction had come around quickly. "Perhaps, too quickly," muttered Freddie to himself as he parked his sports car in the car park of the university grounds. Freddie had satisfied himself that LEAD was not an academic programme. It was not a conventional taught programme where students' heads were metaphorically cut open and knowledge poured in. No, the promises made by the facilitators from the LEAD provider were that the programme was practical, did not involve reading books and importantly had no homework. Freddie did not want to go "back to school". He had satisfied himself that LEAD would deliver on-the-job learning. This was not training from a text book. Learning about himself, his company and how to become more successful had a strong appeal.

As he walked the 800 metres towards the large, modern, metal and glass reception, Freddie was oblivious to the manicured sports fields on one side and the parkland with its lake and birdlife on the other. Full of trepidation, he was more apprehensive about who was going to be in the LEAD cohort. With every step, he realized he wasn't lacking in confidence – he had no confidence!

His nervousness was to the fore. Wrestling with all the thoughts speeding through his head, Freddie tried to reassure himself with the adage, "You don't know what you don't know". LEAD would take him out of his comfort zone. It had to, otherwise change could not happen. In his mind's eye he was being pushed to the end of the plank and was about to jump in. But into what? A sea full of tranquil fish or terrifying sharks?

"Will this work for me?"

The sound of the groundskeepers' lawnmowers, giving the first cut of the year, startled some of the birds. Freddie, though, didn't hear or see a thing, wholly absorbed by his own thoughts in his own world.

"What value can I bring? I have relatively little experience in leading and I am about to face a dozen or so *gladiators* for the first time who'll probably have 15–20 years of experience. Gladiators who already have the proverbial T-shirt and armour-plated at that!"

Thinking back to when he initially left home to go to university with its comfort blanket of a relatively short journey home, he thought, "There is no security for me now. Today, I'll be on show."

Freddie had tried to shake this overarching concern. "We all get worried meeting people for the first time. It's natural, isn't it?"

When they had met, the LEAD facilitator had shared some fellow LEAD delegates' names with him, people who would be on the cohort too.

Freddie knew some of the names and looked up others on the internet. "Wow, those are some businesses! Why are they on LEAD?"

Freddie puzzled over this, surmising that "they must need some support too". Strangely, that final thought helped Freddie as the reception's automatic doors opened with a whoosh in front of him.

The brightly coloured imperial purple LEAD sign immediately caught Freddie's eye pointing towards the meeting area for the LEAD delegates. Freddie liked being early to events, but not when it was the first time. Looking around, there were no familiar faces. Freddie wasn't being drawn to anyone.

David Chambers and Ann Devlin were the LEAD facilitators. Ann was looking after delegates as they came into the room. David was having a coffee with the early arrivers and already there were three small groups seemingly deep in discussion. Ann was first to spot Freddie.

"Hi, Freddie. Welcome to LEAD. Please sign the register."

At that, Ann motioned to David, who politely left the group he was with and, with his outstretched arm, shook Freddie's hand warmly. He then took him to the coffee area and introduced Freddie to Bill.

Unbeknown to Freddie, they both had much in common. Bill felt that coming on LEAD was like going back twenty years to school. He was unsure of what to expect. He too was filled with trepidation. He very much felt he was stepping out of his comfort zone. Heading a services firm, he had been trained to know all about his field of work. After all, his clients were paying for that knowledge. And that knowledge was gained over many years by reading and referring to books. Discussing *experiences* was not something Bill had ever done, let alone with strangers.

Having arrived a few minutes earlier, Bill was immediately captivated by the intoxicating atmosphere created by the presence of so many *successful* local business people. There was a genuine buzz, with relative strangers chatting away, creating a roomful of noise.

Bill was asking himself, "Why are they here? What have I let myself in for?"

Within minutes, Freddie and Bill were chuckling together as they realized that they shared many concerns.

Bill did not know what was going to happen today or during the LEAD programme beyond what he had read online and in the brochure. He was trying to keep an open mind, reminding himself that a mind is like a parachute; it works best when open!

Looking around the room, Bill was struck by the diversity of ages. There were people in their late twenties through to a couple in their late fifties / early sixties, though most seemed to be in their forties.

"What a cross-section!"

As Jane parked her family-sized estate car she saw a few others walking up the path towards the metal and glass building shimmering in the early morning, late winter sun. The splendid settings added to her heightened levels of anticipation and excitement. She was sure there'd be some highly regarded businesses and fantastic business people present.

"Who would be there? But hey, it'll be like the first day at college, meeting new people."

This was her way of building up her self-confidence. Privately she thought she'd be the odd one out as her company only employed ten people and would likely be the smallest. She also thought she would be the most needy and least able. She was convinced that she was about to walk into a room where she would be surrounded by larger, more successful businesses.

"How can they possibly have the same issues or the same need to learn as me?"

Within minutes she was sipping coffee with others. Although Jane was mindful that first impressions count, after introducing herself to Tom and finding out where he was from, what his business did and why he was on LEAD, she quickly found herself unburdening and sharing her business story with a complete stranger. It seemed natural.

Ann smiled to David and said, "It's amazing how cohort after cohort, delegates quickly strike up deep conversations. It looks like we'll have a great ten months together with them."

* * * * *

As the delegates took their seats for the induction half-day, it dawned on Jane that this was the start of LEAD and she was feeling very apprehensive. Like the others, she would be expected to contribute and reveal something about herself. She would need to open up and share details with people that she did not know. This would be nerve-racking, tricky and challenging. She would be on show. She was the performance, albeit for a few minutes at a time. Of course, everyone was in the same boat.

Looking around the room there was a variety of objects that the delegates had brought in to describe their business. And what a strange mix. There was a giant tin of food, a cactus, a brick, an engagement ring, a tax book, a model helicopter, a smartphone, engineered fittings, a teddy bear and a cardboard box, amongst other things.

"What an interesting and unobtrusive way to introduce each other, to get to know each other and remember each other by," they laughed.

On every desk there was a bright purple LEAD binder packed with details on all the elements of the programme and access codes to the online LEAD Forum.

As the delegates got to know each other, Bill repeated to himself, *what a cross-section*, as he found out that the diversity in ages applied equally to business types and backgrounds. His LEAD peers represented organizations from construction to marketing services, engineering to charities, manufacturing to retail, telecoms to food and drink, installation to distribution. The sectors described went on and on.

"What a range of personalities!"

The business people disclosed that they had much exposure to various functional backgrounds – sales, operations, supply chain, marketing, general management, IT, engineering, finance, research and development – before admitting that the role they were doing now, a leadership role, was thrust upon them for one reason or another.

"That's reassuring to hear," thought Bill as he recalled his introduction into the top seat.

Over the following few hours, the programme and timetable were explained briefly to help delegates understand what they could expect and in what order. Learning about the philosophy of LEAD confirmed to delegates that they were on LEAD to develop themselves and their businesses.

Freddie was not looking forward to the Exchange but satisfied himself that it was at least six months away. In the meantime there were Masterclasses and one-to-one coaching that held much appeal but he was wondering who would be in his Action Learning Set – *and what a strange name!*

All had a chance to log in to the LEAD Forum, post a message to their peers and understand what was expected from them. When they went back to their workplace, they were encouraged to learn "experientially" for themselves by engaging remotely with the LEAD Forum.

Throughout the morning, expectations were set, questions were answered and the delegates actively engaged in a series of fun but testing ice-breakers that allowed everyone to speak a number of times in short bursts in order to get to know each other. There was much revelation and a lot of laughter, not least when asked to draw.

"Gosh, when was the last time I held a colour pencil?!" exclaimed Jane.

The delegates were asked simple questions, things that their usual busy working days had robbed them of the time to think about. The questions centred on their complete lives, not just work but their families and personal ambitions. People's personalities were coming out as everyone began to share and open up to peers. There was no role-playing, eliminating Jane's greatest fear.

The bombardment of questions was making Bill think about what he was looking to achieve and where he wanted to go.

Tom disclosed that he did not enjoy speaking publicly, indeed, the paper he was holding was visibly shaking due to his nerves. Yet you could see his chest fill with pride as the others applauded him when he finished sharing details about where he was from, what he did, his interests and his hopes and dreams.

Jane privately noted, "We're all in this together," eliminating another one of her concerns. "The process of everyone doing every part of the induction together as a group, as a cohort, was forming a sense of trust. No one ducked out and it was fun."

Finally, on one post-it, delegates were invited to write one thing they were looking forward to on LEAD and a concern or issue they had on another post-it. All delegates came out to the front, read out both their post-its and stuck them on the flipchart paper.

"Thanks for that," said Ann. "This exercise acts as a celebration of the induction day and provides us, the LEAD team, with the opportunity to take away your concerns and questions, which we will address throughout LEAD. We will type these up and post them on the LEAD Forum.

"We will see you next week at the Overnight Experiential. Remember to look in your LEAD binder where you will find all the details to prepare for the two days and one night away. Any final questions?"

And with that it was off to lunch.

* * * * *

Having enjoyed a hot buffet lunch with her new peer group, Jane was ambling back to her car, digesting the morning's activities in her mind.

What do I want my future to be? What growth opportunities are there for people in my organization alongside myself? Why is leadership important to me?

"There are so many questions and I am short of answers. But I know one thing for sure – I would like my staff to benefit from LEAD too."

* * * * *

THEORY SANDWICH 2   WHY IS LEADERSHIP LEARNING PROBLEMATIC FOR SMALL BUSINESS?

Owner/managers of SMEs have severely restricted opportunities to learn leadership. We present a critique of how leadership is a situated practice that can be learned and we explain the structural dynamics that shape leadership learning and how the small business context inhibits leadership learning. This sets the scene for the next chapter.

So they are beginning their LEAD journey. In many ways it is but another part of the continual leadership learning journey; a journey that starts from very early days. Anecdotal research undertaken in the class by Kempster asks managers if they have young children or know parents with young children. Ask the question, "What do you think leadership is and how do you know this?" The youngest understanding is a three-year-old and she/he links this to their parents (usually their mother). At four, though, the answer is nearly always: "It's the person in front". The answer to "how do you know this" – again a very strikingly similar learning context, the playground – "The teacher comes to collect us to take us into class and we all stand in a line".

So we all know what leadership is from our own perspective. We have our own individual implicit theory of leadership, what it should look like, and if we meet people who match up to this, then we attribute leadership to their actions (Hall and Lord, 1995; Lord and Emrich, 2001; Lord et al., 2001). However, few of us deeply understand how we have learned this. It is perhaps unsurprising (although it seems to remain surprising to many academics) that there are almost as many definitions of leadership as there are people who have attempted to define the concept (Bass, 1990). We have our own journeys through life so why not different ways of understanding leadership if it is a learned phenomenon? So Bennis' wonderful quote exquisitely captures the essence: "Leadership is like beauty, it's hard to define but you know it when you see it" (Bennis, 1989, p. 2).

So with a sense of inevitability for no certainty of definition, leadership is omnipresent and prevalent in everyday usage. Alvesson and Sveningsson (2003) suggested that as they searched for leadership it disappeared; people were unable to point to it, yet most people accepted that it has significant influence in their lives.

When managers are asked the question *are leaders born or made* there is prominently a discussion that it must be both, but examples are often given of people they have experienced who are "natural leaders". In some way that is partially right. In fascinating research undertaken with thousands of twins, Arvey et al. (2006) identified that up to 30 per cent of leadership is genetically inherited. More important to the context of this book is that the remainder is learned through the multiplicity of everyday experience – that life journey. So the answer is, of course, both: leaders are both born and made. In fact it would be impossible to identify someone who is leading that hasn't been born (McCall, 2004). Individual attributes or traits that reflect certain characteristics that improve leadership effectiveness can thus be developed. However, the key is not so much the traits but rather the stimuli that shape the learning towards leadership.

The major point we wish to emphasize is that life course is dominant to leadership learning. Yet the learnings from life course are rarely recalled without careful prompting (Kempster, 2009a). A corollary as asserted by Kempster (2009a) is that leadership is a socially constructed process learnt through social interactions, not necessarily in a conscious manner.

This leads us to explore the social processes that shape leadership learning. There is a growing consensus that it is the following:

- *Observational learning from notable people throughout our lives.* At early years parents, teachers, elder brothers and sisters, uncles and aunts, family friends, our own friends (Cox and Cooper, 1989) create for us a formative model that reflects a romanticized notion of leadership (Meindl, 1995). As we proceed through our careers, notable people are senior managers, line managers, mentors and extended social networks (McCall et al., 1988; McCall, 2004; Janson, 2008). The observed learning refines people's understanding of leading in practice. The final stage is one of selective assessment to confirm what is learnt (Kempster and Parry, 2013). Observational learning is the dominant early stage learning process that we all experience (Kempster, 2009a; 2009b) – including our children in the playground.
- *Enacted learning from roles.* Often described as "assignments" (McCall, 1998), these are activities we take the lead in. They enable the observed learning to become applied, tested and refined. If the learning from such testing seems applicable we firm up our commitment to a way of leading – we shall return to the implications of this issue shortly. Clearly this draws on our trait dispositions (hence Arvey et al.'s (2006) work remains relevant here) but Bandura (1977, 1986) argues that it is the observed that is the dominant informant to the enacted approach. Research related to the roles performed focuses on the context in which these occur. The greater the variety, the greater the learning (Davies and Easterby-Smith, 1984). Similarly the context (or crucible; Bennis and Thomas, 2002) and the roles enacted often create hardships (McCall et al., 1988; McCall, 1998 and 2004) that influence leadership learning – captured by Avolio and Luthans (2006) as trigger moments that stimulate considerable reflection and introspection. This is a most important dynamic to the development of an individual in terms of practice of leading, sense of identity and purposes for which to lead (Kempster and Jackson, 2011).
- *Identification with and salience of leadership.* Recent discussions on leadership learning have begun to point to the relationship of

a desirable social identity and associated learning to become this valued identity (DeRue and Ashford, 2010). Such a desire stimulates a hunger to observe more people (people previously unobserved) and then test out such learning in roles. Yet much learning *to become* is obscured by the milieu of everyday life alongside limited stimulus to observe, enact and become a desired identity.

- *Situated learning and the development of practice.* Much learning occurs unnoticed. We probably have all experienced the process of joining a new group, company, club, partner's family and feeling an outsider – Freddie, Jane and Bill provide a clear example of this when they describe their experiences of the induction event. Given a few years of the flow of countless participative interactions we become a central part of the particular community, sharing in stories and engaging together in a comfortable way. We cannot recall what has happened but we have become connected – a form of unconscious development. This process of learning is what Lave and Wenger (1991) captured as legitimate peripheral participation that sits within a wider framework of social learning: situated learning. It enables the development of shared meanings, shared practices and understanding of interconnected identities: a sense of on-going becoming in terms of knowing, being and doing. Situated learning plays an important role in leadership learning and what manifests as the practice of leading (Kempster, 2009a; Kempster and Stewart, 2010). In the leadership field much attention is growing in this space associated with the notion of leadership as practice (see for example Carroll et al., 2008; and Raelin, 2011).

So what does this tell us for owner/managers?

Kempster and Cope (2010) sought to answer this question by suggesting that the owner/manager context structurally impedes the development of leadership learning. Their argument: the formative observed learning becomes translated into leadership practice.

The owner/managers often leave large organizational contexts early before travelling far up the career path where there are an abundance of people to observe, a plentiful variety of roles to enact (Davies and Easterby-Smith, 1984) and a variety of experiences to extend this learning. Furthermore, the valued career pathway leading to becoming the identity of a leader is foreshortened – the career pathway enables leader becoming.

The owner/manager context is one of having few people to observe, a limited variety of contexts to enact a varying approach to leading and a limited sense of salience of leadership as a desirable identity that they wish to invest in. This structural context then means that the practice of leading shaped by early formative models is not tested by alternative approaches. The practice of leading becomes relatively fixed to a style that appears to reflect that of a parent/family metaphor of leading, which becomes most dominant. In this metaphor it is hard to assimilate multiple parents as with the earlier described notion of distributed leadership. Control, rights and wrongs, instruction, nurturing and guidance are the aspects most prevalent in style.

Further, the practice of leading emerges alongside the development of the business as a Community of Practice (Wenger, 1998) as a consequence of the process of situated learning (see theory sandwich 5). To elaborate, the dominance of the owner/manager within the small business has the effect of shaping processes of interaction, participation and identity formation – the owner/manager is dominant in shaping the knowing, doing and being aspects of how the business functions. A relationship with relatively fixed practices within the leader–follower dyad is most common. In this way situated learning occurs for the leader and the follower so that everyone knows what to expect, yet it is so hard to shift the practices of both leading and following. Figure 2.1 captures this dynamic.

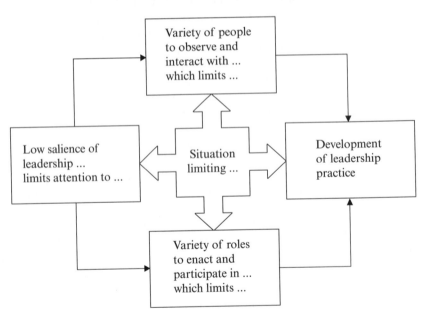

Source: Kempster and Cope (2010, p.25). Used by permission of the publishers, Emerald Group Publishing Limited.

Figure 2.1   Restricted leadership learning in the entrepreneurial context

It is this argument of a structural dynamic limiting leadership learning for owner/managers that needs to be addressed at the core of designs shaping leadership development. It is fundamental to the design of LEAD. Building on Figure 2.1, the design needs to reverse the "limiting" and replace with "enabling".

3.   LEAD journey: month 1 – March

This chapter introduces three LEAD elements – Overnight Experiential, Masterclasses and the online LEAD Forum. The Overnight Experiential gets the delegates to critically think about where they are now and illustrates the trust and bonding that quickly forms amongst the strangers. The chapter discusses the new insights that Masterclasses bring and the on-going discussions that are available through the LEAD Forum and how engagement is created.

OVERNIGHT EXPERIENTIAL

In the week leading up to the Overnight Experiential all the delegates went on the LEAD Forum, uploading a headshot photograph, their contact details and a brief summary of their business.

The LEAD Overnight Experiential is not the stereotypical outdoor experience where a group of businesses are taken into the wilderness and left to fend for themselves, tasked with building rafts, climbing rocks or surviving in some form of discomfort.

No, the LEAD Overnight Experiential element combines a healthy balance of discussion and debate about leadership within each of the delegates' businesses alongside some light physical project "experiential" work. It provides the opportunity for delegates to be physically away from their business and to engage in experiential activities designed to relate learning back to their real-life work situations.

The Overnight Experiential begins to develop the critical reflective thinking skills that will continue throughout LEAD and that will ultimately provide delegates with lifelong skills to become better leaders, address problems productively and have the confidence to make changes and be more strategic within their businesses.

More specifically, the objectives of the Overnight Experiential are to get the delegates to know each other and start to build trust; to prepare the ground for the rest of LEAD; to learn about their own leadership and to have some fun.

The Overnight Experiential is held in a country hotel a good 40 kilometres from the nearest town. It is not a typical corporate hotel, rather it is more relaxed and informal. With its main conference room, three adjacent break-out rooms, coffee lounge, restaurant, bar and en-suite bedrooms for each delegate, it provides the unique atmosphere that the LEAD team is keen to create for the new delegates. There are many access points to the rolling gardens, wide lawns and various enclosures where most of the experiential activities take place, all of which are hidden from sight.

For the Overnight Experiential, David and Ann are joined by Sammy, a specialist in outdoor training. All three arrived an hour early. The large conference room was laid out as per the brief. The hotel staff had done a good job. Seats are set in a small, tight, horseshoe shape, all angled slightly so that delegates will face each other. There are no tables and no projector as there are no PowerPoint slides. Four flipcharts are stationed around the room. Three other chairs are situated at the top of the horseshoe. To the side are half a dozen differently sized and shaped bags. The size of the room is deliberately juxtaposed against the size of the horseshoe.

Bill was anxious. He felt he would be exposed at the Overnight Experiential. He would be there for the "duration" – two whole days and one night. That was a long time. It was going to be intense, demanding. However, he was looking forward to meeting everyone again and being part of a "team".

After meeting everyone at the induction, Freddie was also looking forward to the Overnight Experiential and to the social side, which was common in his industry. As he peered out of his car window and looked up to the sky, three questions were tumbling through his mind: "Where is the rain that David and Ann were ribbing us about? Why have they told us to bring outdoor gear? What are we going to be doing?"

Just as the induction did, he knew that the Overnight Experiential was going to take him out of his comfort zone again.

Emotions were running high as Jane drove towards the hotel. The Overnight Experiential was "quite a big thing" to her as not being able to escape at the end of the day was weighing on her mind, although part of her was excited that her peers seemed to be a nice bunch and it would be fun to be around them again.

However, she was worried that people would be making judgements about her as inevitably she would be doing the same too. Later, in the bar, she would hear Tom say the same and conclude, "I couldn't have been further from the truth. No one makes judgements about each other. You can be yourself, listen and then join in the discussion. From the start, people are collegiate, learning together, sharing and building trust. It's marvellous."

Jane was wary about entering the room. *Who would be in the centre having to perform?* Shortly, she would find that was another fear created in her mind that did not play out in reality.

As usual, all delegates are met by Ann, they register and are issued with a name badge before joining their peers for a coffee and a catch up. Discussions naturally turn back to the induction, the objects that they had brought along to describe their companies as well as asking, "How is business going?"

Amidst the noise, the chatter and the laughter, David whispered to Sammy, "You wouldn't think that they only met a week ago for the first time!"

Half an hour later, after introducing Sammy and confirming that the LEAD team was there to facilitate and support conversations, David stated, "In order to work on your business, we have taken you out of your business. We understand that you have smartphones and need to check emails etc. in the breaks but we would encourage you to chat to each other as much as possible. This space is a learning space where in your conversations you will take much from the discussions. You will find that there will be less need to check in with your office as you go through LEAD.

"We, will get started immediately with you doing things and involved in activities. There will be many different activities over the two days and there is learning in every one. One phrase you will hear throughout LEAD is 'trust the process'. Some things may not make sense at the time but often the learning message will become clear at a later date when it is more relevant to you.

"First, I'd like to introduce you to the Johari Window, which is a useful model to help you improve your self-awareness and add to the mutual understanding between you and your peers. We will refer to the model during the next ten months. It has four parts: the *Arena* represents things that both you and your peers are aware of. The *Façade* or *Mask* represents information about you that your peers are unaware of and it is then up to you to disclose this information or not. The *Blind Spot* represents information that you are not aware of, but others are, and they can decide whether and how to inform you about these blind spots. Finally the *Acorn* represents your behaviours or motives that are not known to you or your peers that may provide potential or an opportunity for development."

David invited everyone to say their name and company again – helping people to identify with each other – then to share something that no one else would know about them. The metaphorical mask within the Johari Window model was being lowered as the peers disclosed some information about themselves. The tone and informality was being set.

Whilst you could detect the nervous energy, people were sparky and in good form. All manner of insights were shared. Wearing of striped socks, grass phobia, having poetry published, fear of touching door handles in public toilets, discarding clothes item by item on arrival home from the moment the door was closed en route to arriving in a "man cave". And so the descriptive disclosures continued. All joined in.

Jane thought, "What a leveller! Here we are, out of our comfortable environment, dressed casually, all sitting on chairs in close proximity, all exposed to the same, seeing everyone equally, revealing personal details that ordinarily we would probably not do, laughing yet not knowing what we are going to be doing outside."

Sammy clapped and rubbed her hands, cutting through the last of the laughter. "You have given yourself a tremendous gift for the next ten months – time out of your business to think about leadership and what it means to you and to your organization. You will consider what the components of leadership are and what they mean to you and your organization. You will be spending the next ten months with your cohort, this group of peers. So please look at them now for the next minute. Do it in silence. Look hard. They will not be the same people that you see in ten months. Indeed, tomorrow you will be looking at each other differently and you will know each other much more by then too.

"It's rare in business to have such close networks, such a trusted environment," Sammy continued. "LEAD is completely different from any other leadership programme. Firstly, it is ten months long, allowing you to develop over time and embed your learning in your business with on-going support. It is interactive between you, your peers and the LEAD team. It is experiential, with its focus on your personal experiences, your business experiences and your relationship with your business. So, be honest about yourself, be honest about your business and consider what you are trying to achieve. LEAD is about exposing yourself and discussing real world issues. We will explore the relationship between doing (activities) and thinking. Remember, the more you put in, the more you will get out.

"There will be lots of questions over the next two days but there will be no solutions. You have ten months to work matters out for yourself. You will learn from each other. There will be a lot of interaction between you and you will naturally respond to each other. We will have a lot of fun together too, which will help you make sense of key learning points.

"At this moment, you might be feeling that you are at the doctor's surgery, thinking, 'I wonder what is wrong with him or her?' If you are here then it is probably because you want something different for you and your business. You are with like-minded people. LEAD is quite a force in helping you to do something different."

Bill muses that Sammy's enthusiasm and confidence were there for all to see. She clearly had so much experience and was so relaxed. Perhaps this might be better than anticipated – perhaps even an enjoyable two days. Certainly, that message was coming across strongly from Sammy and the LEAD team. As this was the only part of LEAD that Sammy was involved in, could the delegates break free from general politeness and the appearance of fitting in to get the most from their time with her? That was their challenge.

Jane thought, "I can safely put myself in Sammy's hands. I can trust Sammy . . . well I hope so."

"Now, let's go outside!"

* * * * *

Fifteen minutes later the group were in a circle, with Sammy dressed in a blue woollen jersey, orange anorak, black washed-out jeans and walking boots. All were benefiting from the spring sun and discussing what had just happened. The activity went as planned. Chaos ensued as delegates focused on the exercise and their task-in-hand in particular.

Sammy led the discussion. "Lots of mistakes were being made. It's a natural behaviour to say, 'It is not my issue, there's nothing I can do about it'. Is that happening in your business? If I am a customer and I walk in, is that what I see? How many people think their business is like that?"

Issues of permission, control and power were to the fore. Sammy asked, "Why did you not say 'Stop'? Why did no one do anything about it?"

The full force of the meaning struck Freddie as if a brickbat had hit his head, momentarily dulling his thinking.

"At first I really didn't see the logic to this exercise but it soon became clear. This is so true; all that juggling is happening in my company. We are disorganized, chaos occurs regularly and we fire fight each and every day, and this has been the case for many years. The directors are not directing. They are not leading, they're just helping out. Do you know what? They are an expensive set of helpers!

"I can now see I need to get outside the circle, to direct and concentrate on making us work more efficiently and effectively rather than me doing the work. This means placing people in the right places at the right times, overseeing the work and not getting involved in the day-to-day issues. After spending ten years within the organization I do find it hard to let go of some of my former duties. I realize the importance of not getting involved in the gritty lower level issues which affect most businesses and instead focus my attention on building strategy and vision at a higher level.

"I came on LEAD hoping for a light bulb moment. I did not expect it to happen in the first hour!"

Although he did not have the courage to say it openly, Freddie was strangely pleased that no one else said "Stop" either. *They must be guilty too!*

Sammy continued, "You need to have a level of comfort to stop it. The bottom line is that it is your business, so consider how your staff perceive permission in your company to do things differently, to ask questions, to stop the show or the chaos when things are not going right. Things might not be right for a whole host of reasons, some of which may be due to the culture created in the organization. However, for the next ten months, the thing you can effectively influence the most is you and what you call your business."

Jane was pondering if this happened in her workplace. "Of course it does," she said to herself, not yet comfortable with dropping her mask to show vulnerability. "How should I manage workflows better? We seem to fall into processes and expectations."

Building on Freddie's observation, Bill said, "I agree. This happens in my company too but I have tried to set 5 per cent of my time aside to think about matters more and spend time with key individuals to support them. Previously, I left them to it. Five per cent doesn't sound a lot but if you think a normal working month is twenty days long then 5 per cent equates to one whole day."

"Wow! Setting one whole day aside to think, reflect and consider how you can improve your business. I am not sure what others think but I couldn't find the time to do that, as much as I would like to do it," exclaimed Jane.

Momentarily, the cohort fell silent, astounded by the 5 per cent admission, rationalizing in their own minds their reflective time commitments.

"Again, that was what I was like not so long ago but I had to find a different way of working," added Bill. "It sounds strange but I diarize what I call 'My walkabout'. At certain parts of the day/week, I walk around the company speaking to staff. I build my 5 per cent into every day as opposed to having a dedicated day.

"Another example is I diarize two hours every Friday to reflect upon my working week and organize the next week."

"I like the clarity and certainty that you have shown. I think to take that amount of time out is a bold and assertive thing to do, Bill," parried Jane. "You have taken control of your own environment and decided where you need to spend time. I wonder if I am constantly there for my team and clients to draw upon?"

David then spoke up. "I do not want us to get ahead of ourselves, but in the months to come you will hear from two Masterclass speakers who will share research confirming that a typical manager spends 5 per cent of their time on reflection and ideas and 95 per cent on doing. So what Bill is describing is not unusual for business leaders like you."

"Some of us are not even doing that! I am not sure how feasible it is to do either. Is there an appropriate balance?" asked Jane.

"Yes, I can empathize with you as it wasn't too many years ago I was like that as well," continued David. "You will hear from the Masterclass speakers that leaders involved in transformational change should be spending 60–70 per cent of their time on reflection, ideas and thinking and the remainder in action."

Jaws dropped as the cohort again fell silent, reflecting on this example of suggested practice.

"Seventy per cent! That feels like a different world," remarked Jane. "That might be possible in large corporations where the CEO has no operational responsibilities and sits with a clean desk, no piles of paper and a shining glass coffee table. It is hard to imagine how this translates into a small business. The nature of work in an SME squashes an organizational hierarchy flat and the flexibility required of a small team means managers have to help each other and step in."

The cohort was struggling to comprehend the 70 per cent. It felt like fiction, a million miles from their reality. It was possibly an example of best practice but the step from very little time reflecting to 70 per cent was a massive one, so much so that it was hard to visualize as a reality or to imagine a path of how to get there.

Breaking the speechlessness, a now quite bewildered Jane uttered, "If we are not spending 5 per cent reflecting on ideas to improve matters, how can we spend two-thirds of our time on such activities? How do I ring-fence my time for bigger picture thinking?"

Bill reassured everyone by saying, "Five per cent is a good starting point. Also, we are all taking time out to do LEAD. We have scheduled that in our diaries. That will help too."

"It does throw up the question," continued Jane, "What is our job?"

Sammy intervened. "This is a great discussion and you will have many more conversations over the next two days and throughout your ten months on LEAD. But remember at this stage, I want you to focus on asking questions rather than finding answers. There are other parts of LEAD better suited to discussing possible solutions. Let's go back inside."

*****

Sammy unveiled the LEAD version of the DO–REVIEW–PLAN–DO continuous learning cycle, drawing a corkscrew diagram on one of the flipcharts. Different coloured pens illustrated the learning cycle as it develops from doing, encouraging reviews to take place and the creation and implementation of new plans, which lead to the doing stage again and so on.

"Who has heard of the Kolb Learning Cycle?"

Sammy encouraged the delegates to think about their own impact on the organization.

Jane thought it was familiar as she and her colleagues adopted such a model when planning work for clients. Yet this was somehow different as the challenge was to adopt it for her own learning. Yes, she could understand it, digest it and grasp it but whether she would use it to develop herself and the overall organization, well, that was something else.

With those thoughts still tumbling around in her mind, Sammy asked everyone, "Why are you in business?" An avalanche of answers flowed from the mouths of the transfixed delegates, their gaze frozen on the iceberg Sammy was revealing.

"So what you really are saying is that you are in business for more than money?

"Who do you have in your business? Yes, people. So our conversations over the two days will not be about systems, procedures or tasks. It will be about you, behaviours and how your behaviour impacts on your people.

"LEAD is about you taking responsibility for the impact you have on the business. So, think back to the last activity. You said you were focused on the task that you had control over to the exclusion of people around you. Ask yourself, 'What is going on in your business right now?'"

Bill was still trying to reconcile Sammy's final point to himself. "Can I change my behaviours? Can I do it?

"I feel a bit of a phoney about this leadership thing. If I don't feel it, how can I act it?

"What do I value? That is quite difficult to know. Who am I as a person and what do I believe in? How do I tackle those questions?"

Freddie was preoccupied with the realization that his fellow directors' behaviours were impacting on others and how that was counterproductive for staff. "How true, I will need to address that."

With Sammy's rhetorical question hanging in the air, Ann leapt up and took the session in a different direction.

"I'd like you to establish the ground rules for the cohort. This is a learning contract that will bind you together in a trusted, confidential environment. We will display these in the Action Learning Sets, Learning and Reflection days and during the Shadowing and Exchanges."

After a few minutes' discussion, the delegates were pleased with what they had agreed. What was important was that they had agreed that while the discussions on LEAD were confidential, they could take any learning from the discussions back to their place of work as long as it was anonymized.

As they went off for a coffee break, Ann chuckled as all the delegates reached for their mobiles, turned them on and began reading messages, making calls and so on. As much as Freddie had heard them say that the breaks were important space to spend time with peers and take advantage of the valuable conversations with other delegates, all he wanted to do was check emails.

* * * * *

After the break, delegates were again outside, but this time split into small groups of five, each with its own "leader", one of whom was Freddie.

"Aagh! I've been thrust to the front," a rather nervous and worried Freddie thought. "I'll now need to show a sense and level of responsibility as I'll be leading a team of fellow business people and I don't want to let them down. Also, I am competitive; I want to win." Freddie satisfied himself that "all business people want to win".

Sammy briefed the leaders then let the exercise begin. Again, chaos ensued and the groups were unable to complete the task. Sammy changed the conditions, started the exercise again and removed the leaders. This time the task was completed.

Sammy pulled everyone together into a circle and joined it. "These tasks are designed to bring out certain behaviours and so the outcomes in the activity are no reflection on the 'leaders'. Indeed, please give the leaders a round of applause!"

Sammy began exploring the differences between the two parts to the activity. The delegates thought that initially the leaders did not explain the task well, wanted to retain control and were micro-managing on matters where the leaders had no technical skill. When the leaders were removed, the delegates believed they worked well together to successfully complete the task.

"What are you doing to encourage dependent behaviour?" asked Sammy.

"To what extent is this going on in your business?"

"Oh, no," sighed Jane. "You kinda know this and it is a good reminder but the reality is I jump in. I like being involved and I'm probably too prescriptive. I am also possibly doing it more often than I realize. The fact is, my team often have the answer if you give them the chance to know what to work towards and provide the tools to do it. They need to know the objective, strategy, vision. I need to lead by stepping back and not micro-managing."

"Thanks, Jane, for sharing that and this is maybe something to explore in other parts of LEAD such as Coaching, Action Learning or Shadowing," Sammy continued. "The analogy with work is that when the team fully understand what the task is, they need little direction or management and the leader's role is changed to one of indicating the sequence of work etc. That was the point Jane was helpfully making."

"I am not so sure if this is relevant," interrupted Bill. "I came on LEAD not expecting a 'Eureka moment' as I thought there was something simple that I was missing. I am not saying it is this, but it has just dawned on me that I assume everybody's strengths and weaknesses are exactly the same as mine. Tom was our leader in this activity and he just kept going and going in the same way in both activities with the same approach to all team members. It clearly didn't work. That is what I do every day in my workplace and it totally frustrates me that I do not get the responses that I want. I am doing daily what Tom was doing in that activity."

"That's a brilliant reflection, Bill, and you can directly apply that learning when you go back to your office," smiled Sammy.

"Let's build on that observation. Behaviours, attitudes and feelings all impact on the task. As your business grows, you may find yourself in a position of being called away from your business, which is akin to the second part of the activity. Be aware of situations when you, the leader, do not have the specific technical skill to do a task, but still try to micromanage it. Go back to the levels of the iceberg that we discussed this morning and consider how your behaviour impacts your people. In this activity, the leader was given the instructions, therefore felt they had to be in control. The impact is that the leader micro-manages the task and staff become disengaged. You are all on LEAD because you're growing your business, so how important is it that you are *in* your business as it grows?"

With that question hanging in the midday air, Sammy ushered the cohort back inside for lunch before meeting with Ann in the main room to introduce the next part, the learning logs.

* * * * *

"One of the aims of LEAD is to develop your reflective skills and critical thinking about what is going on," began Ann.

"On the Overnight Experiential, it is very easy to forget something you were thinking because the two days pass so quickly. The LEAD learning log is a private and confidential means for you to plan and keep an on-going record of your own personal development and the changes you will be implementing to your business while you are on LEAD. It demonstrates examples of how you are putting skills into practice and provides an insight into your preferred ways of learning and increasing subject knowledge. Your learning log will encourage a greater sense of confidence, self-awareness and identity as well as acting as a benchmark throughout LEAD on where you are in achieving your learning objectives.

"The learning logs are for you and you only. We don't ask to see them and you don't have to show anyone. Feedback from previous cohorts was that they found this hard. So please 'trust the process'."

And so began the recorded reflective learning journey of Freddie, Jane, Bill and their peers from the cohort. Little did they realize how their written observations would assist them in the months to come – and become central in this book!

* * * * *

Lifting their heads from their learning logs, the delegates were faced with a flipchart displaying paired names for the next activity.

"Please find your partner, grab a blindfold each and I'll see you outside," shouted Sammy, in what was now a common excited tone.

Outside, the ground was drying from a recent shower, it felt fresh and there was Sammy, waving her arms in a manner to gather people together. "In this activity, your partner's safety and security is paramount. I also want you to think about trust, leading and being led."

Sammy then explained the context, boundaries and encouraged delegates to take controlled risks with their unsighted partner and to push boundaries. With that, they were off.

Some blindfolded people clung to the arms of their partner, others linked arms or were guided by holding onto a shoulder. Others walked without any support. Almost everyone walked.

Freddie thought to himself, "Here I am, I can't see and I am putting my safety in the hands of a relative stranger. I'm not really sure about this."

Suddenly, Tom shouted, "Bill, let me go. Let me run." Bill had already been blindfolded and now it was his turn to be sighted and look after the safety of his partner. When blindfolded and with a sighted Tom leading, Bill had felt very nervous and assumed that his colleague would feel the same now that the roles had been reversed. Bill decided to be unambitious and led Tom very slowly, with lots of direction and much communication. Such was his desire to keep Tom safe, Bill spoke constantly.

Now he was being directly challenged. "What do I do?" thought Bill. "I can't let him run unsighted. What happens if he falls? No, I'll hold him tighter and walk a bit faster. That'll do!"

Sammy again gathered the delegates together and asked, "Which was easier – leading or being led?" Bill opened, "I had no fears about being led and I was too timid in pushing him when leading."

The sense of responsibility for their partner's safety clearly weighed on all the leaders and, when blindfolded, many complained of being held back.

Jane noted, "It was hard to judge what was safe, how hard to push and what the appropriate level of communication was. Nonetheless, I felt that there was complete trust when blindfolded and that there was no risk; just the perception of risk."

Bill continued, "This has taught me that I should not assume others feel the same way as I do. This has reinforced my learning from the activity before lunch where I thought everybody's strengths and weaknesses were exactly the same as mine. Perhaps, sometimes 'hands on' leadership with detailed direction, however well-meaning, can be counterproductive."

Tom agreed. "I asked Bill a few times to 'Let me go' and he didn't! It was really infuriating. I knew I could do more. So, the question I guess Sammy would want us to ask is, 'Is this happening in our business?'

"The message is clear: 'Do not shackle your employees'. When I was blindfolded I wanted to run. In other words, I wanted to be free to do the task, the role, drive the change, be creative etc. I would have gone further and faster than the leader could ever have imagined and done so safely. I was content to manage myself. I think all too often we as leaders suffocate empowerment, change, creativity, innovation and job satisfaction. My plea of 'Let me go' should be a salutatory reminder to all leaders that it's us, the leaders, who are the challenge limiters in our businesses. We all can run freely. Part of a leader's role is to give people the confidence to metaphorically run and the confidence to do more. By trying to make our staff safe and secure we are actually working against the progress that we are seeking. I would never have thought I'd hear myself saying that. Through our own behaviours, we are failing to challenge and stretch our people. We need to heed the 'iceberg principle' that Sammy shared earlier. We must be more aware of our behaviour and its impact on our staff."

"May I add something?" asked Bill. "Prior to LEAD, I could never coach anyone. I set my sights too low, meaning that I had to get involved in all manner of decisions and consequently I did not have the time to do the things I should be doing. I can now see that I need to look at the capability of the person then leave them to get on with the task and even to press them to achieve more than they ordinarily think they can achieve. Tom pushed me but I didn't reciprocate. I can see now I have a more cautious approach than Tom has and I projected that onto him. That was a mistake. Tom has shown himself to be far superior to me in this exercise.

This activity has shone the spotlight on my weaknesses and failings as a leader. That is quite humbling for me to disclose.

"Also, just thinking that through as I speak, if I had pushed Tom more and he wasn't ready to accept that pressure, then it could have gone the opposite way. There is a situational aspect to leadership."

"That's a great set of observations," remarked Sammy. "Thank you, Bill, for sharing your thoughts.

"Did any of you feel you were pushed outside your comfort zone in that last activity?

"The shaking of your heads suggests not. If we factor in that usually people do not want to go outside their comfort zone, how do we create conditions to encourage them to do so?

"The good news is that you have ten months together to consider that question and many more through listening to Masterclass speakers, discussions with your coach and Action Learning Set members as well as the opportunity that Shadowing and Exchange brings.

"Now let me explain what we will be doing next. . ."

* * * * *

The next debrief was underway after sighted delegates again led blindfolded partners but this time they were encouraged to release their charges and let them go. Initially they were passed to a sighted peer then they were left on their own to find their own way forward. Predictably, chaos and this time silliness ensued, with people walking into hedges and being left there. Some sighted leaders were walking fast, others were slower and more deliberate. A few were overtly "breaking the rules".

Jane reflected on this experience. "Again, it was not easy leading. I felt I had to drag people with me and use more energy in doing so. There was an inference from my unsighted partners that something was going on that created a tension and resistance."

"Great observations, Jane," noted Sammy. "If we bring that to the world of business, some of you may have staff in your company who are just there to work for a paycheque. It may feel that you are dragging them along."

Jane continued. "When I was being led it was very, very disorientating and I felt very isolated, so I slowed right down. That in itself is a powerful message. Are my people slowing down, awaiting leadership from me? I don't honestly know.

"Also, when I was leading and I let go, most people just stood still. So, if I just link those points together, are my people slowing down and actually stopping to wait for me, the leader?"

"That's fantastic, Jane. A question for everyone, 'Where in your business are people standing still?'" enquired Sammy. "And, what is this behaviour costing you in your business? Remember, I am not looking for answers today, I want to help you to think about the questions."

"Sammy, there is more," continued Jane. "During the activity, I experienced how things don't work without communication and a sense of connection. When blindfolded, it was amazing how in such a short time I went from moving confidently to feeling completely vulnerable. This can happen in an instant, which has proven to be very true of my experience of my confidence and the way it comes and goes when I have been exposed to poor leadership. There are literal and figurative touch points that can change the direction of confidence. It is we, the leaders, who have the power to use effectively or misuse. The impact of the misuse of that power on those around can paralyse or, in the example of this activity, bring people to a standstill."

Freddie's reflection to the group on the process was to think about how business links to this exercise. He commented, "Historically, in my company, there was a distinction between doing a good job and doing a good job 'my way'. Those dictatorial ways by my father and my predecessor caused tension and looking back I can now see people being dragged along. I am trying to lead in a more open way but do my staff really want to be led by me? I would hope so, but I have never asked them. We don't do employee surveys."

"Thanks for those insights. To wrap up now, remember, your business is not the same as the one that you created or joined. It should be all right to let go. During the next ten months, ask yourself, 'How do I limit my staff?' Who is available to do the stuff you are currently doing?" posed Sammy.

"Let's get back inside."

* * * * *

"For the next couple of hours you will begin to consider what leadership is, what it means to you and to your business," began Ann. "Shortly you will describe what good and bad leadership looks like and share with us examples of good and bad leaders. As owner/managers of small–medium sized companies, research shows that you do not feel that you are a leader. LEAD helps you identify yourself as a leader."

After asking, "What is leadership?," flipchart paper was quickly filled as delegates shouted out, "Setting the example, instilling confidence, creating and communicating the vision, motivating people, taking and judging risk, listening, problem solving, teaching, providing solutions, taking action, empowering." The list was endless.

Another long list was created with names of mainly politicians, histori-
cal military leaders, sports coaches and other notable people, all of whom
were thought to be examples of leaders who exhibited this leadership.

A battery of positive and negative attributes were then opined, many of
which were contradictory.

"So who can be all these things?" asked Ann before delivering the knock-
out punch, "Nobody. It's a myth that any one leader has all of these things.

"So, what is your leadership style? How have you learned leadership?
You have probably not given this much thought, I guess."

Ann continued. "The way you understand leadership has been shaped
by your own experiences. These will have been learnt in an unconscious
way, usually by observing others and subsequently experimenting with
styles. We now want you to create your own timeline of leadership experiences, which will help you uncover what has shaped the way you think
about leadership. When you have done that we want you to share that
with your partner, who will ask some questions and vice versa. Start your
timeline from around the age of eight."

Freddie and Bill were paired and went off to find a quiet corner each to
create their timelines. Freddie was unsure of what value this exercise was
going to bring.

Within an hour they were sharing their own personal history lessons.
The focus was on the critical incidents and significant experiences around
leadership that had happened in their lives, going back to their childhood
and involving their parents, friends, teachers and other notable figures.
They discussed how these experiences shaped their views about leadership
and what influence they had had on them as leaders today. They realized
that many of the experiences were not all good ones; indeed both had
encountered poor leadership and strong negative role models.

Freddie shared, "Ninety-five per cent of my learning is from poor leadership. Understanding where I have come from is a very powerful lesson
and I can see why I am what I am. I avoid disciplining others, which is the
polar opposite to the blame culture that I was brought up in where there
was always a consequence for an unfavourable outcome. Similarly, I do
not put my feelings on the line as that vulnerability is sensed as a weakness
and will be exploited by others.

"I have developed my own leadership credentials, creating my own style
through learning from the mistakes of other leaders I have worked with in
the past. This must be why I sometimes come across too placid and not as
authoritarian as I should be as a leader because I have seen very aggressive
styles of this kind of leadership not working.

"What I have realized from completing the timeline and what is also
quite startling is how little support I have received within my family

business over the ten years that I have been involved. The directors, and indeed my father, have never taken me to one side to coach, nurture, praise, or reprimand when required.

"Bill, this is the first time I have ever shared this with someone.

"Showing emotion is an eye-opener to me. It is amazing that you are interested in my experiences. Just talking my timeline through with you has given me a perspective that I had never had previously and I have understood a lot more about myself than ever before."

Freddie's poignant experiences brought the pair closer together. Bill asked some more questions and the pair became deeply drawn into the process.

Moreover, Freddie thought, "Bill is clearly a mature and experienced person. I now must listen attentively to his timeline. I need to ask some good questions in return. This is important to him and to me. It is important to his development and to mine."

From initially questioning the value of the activity, Freddie now felt responsibility for another, had a strong sense of camaraderie and fresh insights into his own leadership in the context of his business. The identification by delegates of the salience of leadership is a key underpinning of LEAD. This in itself would become a significant moment in Freddie's own LEAD learning journey.

When the pair switched roles Freddie found remarkable similarities in Bill's journey, even though his background was different and his company was in the service sector.

Here were two relative strangers exchanging experiences that had never been verbalized before and empathizing with each other.

Bill admitted that he added three influences to his timeline as a result of Freddie sharing his experiences. He had not thought of them, and one of the individuals he had not considered for over twenty years. But they were very important to him as they were good examples of people who were "clear leaders, mentors, who set and achieved high standards that had much self-discipline and were fair".

Bill had also learned from his father who he viewed as a role model but he disclosed to Freddie that his father was "understated, not essentially leading, he was an unwilling leader and lacked in self-confidence". This approach did not sit with Bill so he had consciously tried to act in an opposite manner in his working life.

* * * * *

Ann gathered everyone together again.

"For the final part of the day, you will work in your Action Learning

Sets. These are the small groups that you will work with over the next six months. You each have ten minutes to talk about a significant moment from your timeline to share with the group. If you do not fill ten minutes, the others can ask you questions on that moment until the ten minutes is up. The reason we do this is so that you're in a better position to support each other. When you are finished come back to the main room."

* * * * *

"The main part of the day is almost at an end," said Ann. "How are you feeling now? Lots has gone on this afternoon, so please take a few minutes to jot down some ideas that you want to take away from today before you forget.

"We encourage you to continue the conversations this evening. We'll meet in the bar at 7 pm for drinks before going for dinner at 7.30 pm. Breakfast tomorrow is at 8 am before we gather again in the main room at 9 am."

With that, the bunch of business people who eight hours ago had started their Overnight Experiential not knowing what they were going to be doing, left together as a cohort heading for the hotel check-in, chatting, laughing and joking about what they had experienced.

They had a better insight that LEAD was not a conventional, nurturing, taught leadership programme. Rather they could now see that LEAD is more of a guided discovery requiring delegates to be themselves, to understand who they are, and that the Overnight Experiential lays the foundation for the whole programme, providing an appreciation of how the programme works. They had experienced at first hand that there is no script. LEAD follows what comes up and as such each experiential can be different, which, with different delegates, will have different questions.

"We know that the Overnight Experiential is designed to make the delegates feel a little uncomfortable, which is necessary to make LEAD work. We have achieved that today," concluded Sammy. "Tomorrow, we'll pick up the pace."

* * * * *

Building relationships is a key part of LEAD and the overnight part of the Overnight Experiential is essential as it further builds the bonds of trust in a relaxed environment.

Freddie, Jane and Bill had all experienced the loneliness of leadership. Yet here they were in the bar before dinner, having a drink with a roomful of relative strangers who were laughing, joking and swapping stories from their day's experience together and having wider business conversations. Everything seemed so natural, enjoyable and fun.

* * * * *

The Ground Rules were prominently displayed as the cohort sat down in the horseshoe for the start of the second day.

"Good morning everyone," beamed Ann. "There was lots going on yesterday and many, many conversations over dinner. Don't lose those thoughts. You all have a successful company. How can you improve? I'd like you now to take ten minutes in silence to answer questions 4 and 5 of your learning log."

* * * * *

All the delegates had participated in a challenging exercise where selected leaders adopted two different styles of leading: laissez-faire and dictatorial. Sammy was now hosting a plenary session listening to the experiences of the two groups who had experienced being on the receiving end of a particular leadership style.

"Firstly, a round of applause to our 'leaders' who were asked to lead in a particular way, which is no reflection on them. We know it was really uncomfortable for them and not natural to do," said Sammy.

"You have correctly identified that there were two types of leadership displayed – extreme examples of autocratic and democratic to exaggerate the point."

"Sammy, I didn't find this comfortable at all as it actually felt like my workplace," piped up Freddie. "I was in the autocratic leader's group and he was strict and abrasive. We are a competitive bunch and we tried to beat the other group but after a short while we sensed they were better. The upshot was that the team didn't do well – there was lots of finger pointing, we were frustrated and became argumentative and yet again we failed to complete the task."

"That's illuminating," replied Bill. "I didn't find the exercise comfortable either and I was in the democratic leader's group. I thought the task was relatively straight-forward and could see what needed doing but I was frustrated by 'the leader'. In the beginning we helped, but towards the end we were completely disengaged. In fact, I didn't realize the leader was acting. I thought that must be his leadership style and I was beginning to have sympathy for his staff! In the end, my anger boiled over and Sammy made me sit on my hands and instructed me to be quiet!"

"My learning from this is that there needs to be a balance between the different styles," said Freddie. "Too much of one kind appears to be detrimental."

"Yes and no," retorted Bill. "Autocratic leaders make decisions without consulting their teams. I would suggest that this is considered appropriate when decisions genuinely need to be taken quickly, when there's no need for input, and when team agreement isn't necessary for a successful outcome. On the other hand, democratic leaders allow the team to provide input before making a decision, although the degree of input can vary from leader to leader. This type of style is important when team agreement matters, but it can be quite difficult to manage when there are lots of different perspectives and ideas."

Sammy commented, "One style is not necessarily better or worse than the other and you shared with us where each style could most appropriately be used.

"There is one other style to be aware of and wary of. *Laissez-faire leaders* don't interfere; they allow people within the team to make many of the decisions. This works well when the team is highly capable and motivated, and when it doesn't, there needs to be close monitoring or supervision. However, this style can arise because the leader is lazy or distracted, and here, this approach can fail.

"Think back to your business, what is happening there and how your behaviour has an impact on others. You have just *felt leadership being done to you*. What do your employees feel? What behaviour manifests as a result of your leadership style? What is the subsequent impact on their performance and the performance of the business? Think back to the Kolb Cycle we discussed yesterday. If you keep doing what you are doing, you will continue to get what you are getting. You need to undertake a review then plan again.

"I now want to introduce you to the 'Leadership Style Spectrum'," said Sammy. "At one end, represented by that wall, is the autocratic, highly directive style and at the other end of the spectrum, represented by this wall, is the democratic, highly participative style of leadership. Where on the spectrum would you put yourself?"

Bill went to stand by the autocratic wall.

"Hey, Bill," shouted Freddie from the opposite end of the spectrum, "with your views and manner, you should be on the other side of the wall!"

Bill joined in the laughter with the cohort but privately he knew his energy and natural drive propelled him towards his preferred highly autocratic behaviour so that goals were achieved. He also realized he quickly lost interest in tasks. He saw the limitations and dangers of being an autocrat. He knew that at this moment in time it was not right that he stood in the middle of the spectrum. He did want to involve staff more so he realized that he would need to change. From his vantage point, he could view the spectrum extending in front of him. Being able to see and appreciate the range of the spectrum was important to Bill. He realized that he would need to move along it depending on the situation, the task and the support that a direct report required. In stark contrast was his preferred leadership position. There was his challenge: how to move?

"Leadership styles do vary according to the situation and the people involved," said Sammy. "So, if it is necessary, the leader may need to become more autocratic."

"That's comforting to hear," thought Bill.

The questions poured out from Sammy, each one unleashing queries in each delegate's mind.

Without pausing, Sammy tellingly enquired, "Where will your staff put you on the line?"

All eyes were fixed on the diminutive, raven haired and fiery facilitator. Sammy paused, deliberately using silence to amplify the question and accentuate the moment of reflection.

"Who has moved?

"Whose perception of your leadership style matters most? Yours or your staff's? Of course, people's perception is more important because your business is not about the systems and procedures, it's about the people. Remember the message from the iceberg from yesterday.

"But how do you know what your people think? They won't tell you the truth. Their salary, mortgage, feeding their family depends on them retaining their job. Can they be honest? Truly honest?

"People want you to be who you are, the person that they know, the same person. So, if you move along the spectrum they will naturally become highly uncomfortable because you have changed, you are no longer the same.

"Now, where would you like to be by the end of LEAD?

"Who has moved?"

"I have, Sammy," said Jane. "I was towards the democratic end and have moved towards the middle. There are times where I need to be stricter, more autocratic. Am I sometimes a soft touch? Maybe, as I think my staff know it is easy to turn me from a no to a yes."

"I've moved too," announced Freddie. "I put myself at the democratic end as I actively try to be different from the highly autocratic style used by father. I believe my staff see that too. I realize that I need to move towards the centre. I cannot be fearful of saying what I think in personal reviews as doing so will lead to more constructive discussions."

"It's mid-morning and time for coffee. See you back in the main room in twenty minutes and we will brief you for the next activity," said Sammy.

* * * * *

Over coffee, Bill and Jane were reflecting on the activity. "That experience was good for me," said Bill. "I need a bit of humility. My anger and frustration boiled over and I can see that I am an 'in joke' but it was good joining in the laughter with everyone. It was chastening. I realize there is a side of me that is a caricature. Sometimes I am not in control. Instead of doing the right thing by not saying anything, I do the opposite and I am deliberately extreme. For example, at one stage in the last activity I refused to help, then I dived in. I am completely task driven."

"You can change your behaviour, Bill," assured Jane.

"Yes, I am beginning to understand that I can and that I need to, especially in certain circumstances," replied Bill.

* * * * *

An hour later, the delegates trooped back inside after the final activity of the morning.

Sammy began. "Thank you all for participating. To reiterate, the task is designed to elicit certain behaviours as a direct result of you experiencing a particular style in a certain set of circumstances. This allows issues to come out that everyone can learn from. This activity pulls everything together from the Overnight Experiential so far and addresses the very real problems around communication and the intent versus reality."

"That was amazing, despite there being chaos again, mutiny in the ranks and the failure to complete the task," started Freddie.

"I was a worker and at first, together with my colleagues, we were very jovial, appreciating the stress-free nature of our job. We wanted to succeed and felt part of a team. However, when we seemed to be going nowhere and colleagues were being lost to the competition, frustration started to occur. We questioned the manager's directions but he was only taking instruction from his director. We began guessing what to do and we worked out a way to win the game ourselves but the manager wasn't listening. We felt let down and totally powerless. We challenged the manager as we thought he didn't know the 'rules'. There was a lot of blame. We then started to argue amongst ourselves, with two of the guys wanting to walk off, and the other being a model employee. With both sides trying to influence me, I was undecided on whether to depart or remain in the game. The manager could not control the situation and morale and engagement were at a low. By the end, we were indifferent to the success of the task."

"And all that happened in such a short period of time," reflected Jane. "I was a director in a remote office. It was difficult at first to quickly comprehend what needed to be done. I was conscious people were waiting on my direction, my instructions, so I didn't want to let anyone down by giving the wrong ones. I didn't want to let myself down either. I felt a huge sense of responsibility. I actually thought I gave a clear message but when the manager checked back a few minutes later it was obvious something had been misunderstood somewhere. I didn't realize that the manager did not take notes and in the heat of the moment I did not check that he understood what to do. I knew there was a better way to do things but due to the pressure of time, being on the spot and caught in the moment I tried to direct the manager to direct the workers. I then made assumptions to fill the gaps. Under pressure, common sense goes out the window.

"Eventually, I gave control to the manager to manage things locally. For long periods there was silence, no communication. I had no idea of what was going on and I was unable to influence matters. My energy levels were dissipating. In my head I was flapping but outwardly I was trying to remain calm. Then the message came back that we lost three people. Lost three people! How did that happen? It was chaos, I had no idea what was going on. It was very frustrating."

"Same for me too," added Bill. "As the manager I didn't receive clear goals from the director. I was just trying to do my job and pass on the message. I was so consumed in trying to fulfil the task that I didn't even realize how disgruntled the workers were. I felt squeezed between the director and the workers and it was not a pleasant experience. I had no support from the director. I was given a task and expected to do it. The director hugely overestimated that she had communicated the task well to me. Communication was one-way: downwards.

"Yet this has been one of what seems to be a series of light-bulb moments during the two days. I have just appointed a new manager in a role similar to the one I have just enacted. I have given her direction and left her to manage the people in her area as I thought that was the right thing to do. I've not given her any support as I thought she'd benefit from the free rein. Does she feel how I now feel? I need to find out.

"This activity translates to communicating with staff further down the organization," continued Bill. "There will be people who will be doing things without understanding why they are doing them and what the purpose is. I want to know 'why' and I believe staff should understand that too."

"Sammy, this whole activity has shown me that I am on a very steep learning curve," said Freddie. Throughout the two days together you have been challenging us to think *what is happening back in our businesses?* I don't think any of this is happening in my business. The truth is, I don't know, but I am going to find out. I must get out of my remote director's office. How do my shop floor workers and staff feel in my organization? Do we keep them in the dark? Do our 'rules' restrict? Are our people left to their own devices? I am not sure if we ask them for their ideas. Is the communication one-way or two-way? I need to find out if we communicate with them effectively, or indeed at all.

"I wonder if they are bitter towards management due to a negative perspective to the questions posed above. This activity has made me realize that our behaviours have a major impact on our people. It is their perception that matters as the situation is real to them."

Sammy spoke. "The behaviour and style of a leader and the impact of that on your business, profits, investment, employees etc. is enormous. Think about where your blind spots are as a leader. You need to be able to move, see, feel different perceptions of workers within your business to make sure your employees are on-board, with you, wanting to succeed.

"Ask yourself, 'What am I doing that makes communication one-way?' You know this leads to blame and results in people being less likely to succeed. On the first day we spoke about micro-managing but still the directors and managers in this activity tried to do exactly that. As you grow and develop your business, you will be spending less and less time in your company, that is, you will be more remote and absent from your business.

"You will have a great, great year ahead of you to address issues like this and so much more," concluded Sammy.

* * * * *

Jane was busy scribbling down Sammy's words as she shared a coaching model that can be used throughout LEAD.

She was struck by how small the words looked on the paper but how big the questions were. They were not radical questions either, yet she knew they were questions she was not asking.

What is my current reality? What is my vision?

"Or put it another way," she thought, "what is it that I want to chase? Working out that vision will be an important step forward. Whose vision is it?" Supplementary questions began sparking in her mind.

What are the barriers, perceived or real?

The final question made Jane pause, analyse and reflect. "This is a process in itself," she realized. "It is not the tool that will benefit me, it is actually stopping, critically thinking and reflecting that will do much good. It will hopefully propel me beyond relying on gut feel and hunches."

Looking around the room at her peers, Jane had a sense they had a clear vision, both at a business level and at a personal level. She was not clear what the future would look like other than she wanted things to be better. "I want to lead a company that I want to be running and be part of. This is an ambition that had sense," she thought.

"Often perceived barriers are greater than real ones," commented Sammy. "Similarly the internal barriers we artificially create are larger than external ones. You started to unwrap these on our first day together and you should now be beginning to develop a better sense of your relationship with your business. In your Action Learning Sets you will be discussing really difficult situations. Think about using this model – real versus perceived and vision versus current reality and the barriers between them. You can do something about internal barriers; they are workable."

Jane looked at Sammy and thought, "This is the first bit of real thinking I have done on where I am and what is actually real."

* * * * *

"We are coming towards the end of the Overnight Experiential and I'd like you to spend ten minutes in silence completing questions 6, 7 and 8 in your learning log."

* * * * *

"Thanks for that," continued Ann. "Using the post-its, please write down your significant learning moment, come to the front, say what it is and place it on the flip chart. We will then type these up and upload them to the online LEAD Forum."

One by one, members of the cohort came up and offered up their comments. These included:

> The power of experiential learning. . .putting myself in the role and mind-set of staff and the frustrations they may have. . .the influence of significant people from my past on my leadership style today. . .don't hold people back, let them go. . .avoid micro-managing, brief the team and let them create a workable solution. . .how changing your leadership style affects your staff. . .how a leader sometimes hinders progress. . .realization that my perfectly clear communication has not been understood.

"This has been the most fun two days in work that I have had in ages," said Freddie.

"Best fun in two business days ever," observed Jane.

"Thank you for that feedback," replied David. "This is just the beginning of your ten-month learning journey together. We have created a topic on the online LEAD Forum called 'What I have learned from the Overnight Experiential'. In the next few days, we would like you all to go onto the Forum and share your top three learning points and what you will do differently in your business as a result of that learning. Writing your thoughts down will be a good record of your journey. They will also be read by your peers who may learn from your learning points."

"I have a meeting on Monday where an issue has been stuck for a year. I am going to try a different approach to my leadership and see if that helps. I'll let you all know how I progress," said Tom.

"David, if I may," said Freddie. "A few of us last night at dinner thought it would be a good idea to meet up in a couple of weeks' time for a drink and to swap notes. I'll formally invite everyone through the Forum."

"Excellent. We believe that the social space that you share is an important learning area for you so we thoroughly encourage you to meet.

"All that is left for me to do is to thank you all for all your inputs during the last two days and making it so enjoyable and thought-provoking. A big thank you too to Sammy and Ann for their facilitation and before you go let's go outside once again for a cohort photograph. See you at the end of the month for your first Masterclass," ended David.

* * * * *

LEAD FORUM

Tom is all excited. His day went really well and the outcomes exceeded his expectations. He chuckled, "Who'd have thought by changing my leadership style so much would be achieved in so little time.

"Now I promised that I'd share the experience with my LEAD delegates so I had better keep to my word. After all, that's good leadership, isn't it?

"I know that the online LEAD Forum is a virtual environment that provides a confidential space for us, the delegates, to access the cohort and the LEAD team / facilitators, when we are not physically together, to ask questions, share learning points, download LEAD resources and extra course material as appropriate. We can also use the LEAD Forum for posting messages, materials and discussions. I can see Freddie has arranged a get-together for next week. I'd like to go to that too. Well, here goes, my first posting."

Evening all!

As you know, I had a prearranged managers' meeting this morning, scheduled to discuss possible changes to our accounts production process.

We made changes twelve months ago which haven't worked as planned. At that stage, we told staff what we were going to do rather than discussing it with them and listening to them as they were doing the work.

I knew what I wanted to be done but following on from my learning on the Overnight Experiential, I thought I would try a democratic rather than autocratic leadership style.

I only expected to get part way to my preferred outcome, which would have been a result. After fifteen minutes, there were some minor changes but not what I wanted. After coaxing them a couple of times that this was their chance to put in place what they thought would work best, they finally opened up.

It took another ninety minutes to completely redesign the process and rearrange some rooms but I ended up getting much more than I wanted, with their complete buy in.

I made the mistake of not telling them to keep it to themselves until I had spoken to those it affected though, and I now have two accounts production staff telling me they will leave if the new system is brought in! The plus side to that is that they are two people we could do without as they are holding back others and stopping new blood coming in.

So the new system will be in by the end of the week!

Moral of the story – it does pay to listen, the hard part is to get them talking. Be prepared for the unexpected and to take some hits.

Tom

Within a day, Jane replied and shared her thoughts.

Hi Tom

That sounds like great progress in a short space of time, very inspiring!

I find getting people to open up in a staff meeting can be quite difficult too – people will happily talk to me at their desk and then clam up as soon as we all get together. I like the fact that by repeatedly asking the question and showing that they could design the system, they opened up – when it would have been easy to stop after the 'tinkering'.

Hope the new system all goes to plan!

Best wishes, Jane

Freddie was online, looking at the string of comments. He had also read his peers' key learning from the Overnight Experiential. Now it was his turn to give some feedback.

The final activity on the morning of day 2 at the Overnight Experiential really got me thinking last week and the reality of it really hit me in the face yesterday!

A customer service course was undertaken in two separate sessions by a group of workers on Monday.

The course tutor had outlined in his review notes to me that many employees had muttered the following:

- Their managers do not keep them in touch with major company decisions or indeed listen to their opinions/ideas
- Senior managers and directors don't seem to 'chat' to them when walking around the business
- There is very much a 'them and us' mentality

Interestingly, I wasn't included in their rant.

As a result of this feedback, I will be holding a meeting with my senior management in the coming weeks to discuss these points and to suggest the following recommendations:

1. A monthly or quarterly meeting to include an employee (worker/staff) from each department (non-managerial) who will represent their team to discuss any ideas/issues/problems they may have
2. Senior managers/directors to be more interactive with staff on a daily basis

I clearly remember the question Sammy posed last week, "How much of this is going on in your business?" I didn't think very much, but I stand corrected!

Regards,

Freddie

Jane was again first to comment.

Hi Freddie

That sounds like good timing to have had the feedback via the trainer, so that you can address the perceived 'divide'.

I think we have a really 'flat' structure within our company, partly because we are small in number and there are often times when we need to muck in and help each other, despite our different roles and levels of experience.

But despite being based in one open plan office and talking together frequently, I think we've let the casual conversation swamp the structured communication. One of our team will be going on maternity leave in the summer and we let her share the news with everyone herself, because she's quite quiet and didn't want lots of fuss. Everyone's delighted and we talk about it openly within the office.

In appraisals last week, however, two or three people asked about what was happening about maternity cover and were anxious about taking on her workload as well as their own. We were able to reassure them that we'd be getting cover, but it showed a real gap in our structured communications. I was doing that thing again where I assumed everyone would know what I know, or that they'd simply ask me if they weren't sure. I must stop making assumptions.

So I'm reinstating a regular full team meeting as of next week!

Jane

* * * * *

MASTERCLASS 1

Ann had finished uploading a message to all delegates on the LEAD Forum about next week's Masterclass together with a copy of the slides that were to be used.

Subject: Winning Strategies to Maximize Sales and Profits – Professor Malcolm McDonald

Malcolm is widely recognized as a world authority on marketing planning. The Masterclass discusses a framework that enables you and your company to realize the true potential of your market and embed into your businesses the marketing skills and processes which deliver sustainable improvements in value. Malcolm will challenge you to unlock the marketing potential of your business.

* * * * *

It has been almost three weeks since the Overnight Experiential and less than a month since the delegates first met, which belied the cacophony of noise emanating from the ante-room where everyone met before attending the morning-long Masterclass.

Freddie was one of the first to turn up in the morning. He wanted to catch up and have a chat with his peers prior to the Masterclass. He also wanted to make sure he was not sitting in the front row of the Masterclass. "I'll sit a few rows back," he thought, "I'll take a few notes and *hide* if I need to. When I go to events, I consciously am *not* the person who puts up their hand and asks a question. I always leave that to someone else. If most of the others ask questions, I wonder if they will notice if I don't?"

Freddie reminded himself, "I am not a good listener so I must try to listen intently."

The delegates understood that the purpose of the Masterclasses was to give them access to inspirational and informative speakers who are, or have been, recognized leaders or business management experts with an active interest in SMEs. There are two types of Masterclass: business-related, focusing on the business itself, and leadership-related. Of the ten monthly Masterclasses, five are on business and five focus on leadership. To varying degrees, the Business Masterclasses are interactive, pragmatic and engage with some theory or business model which delegates are encouraged to consider and if appropriate apply to their business. The Leadership Masterclasses explore different aspects of leadership and leadership styles, reflecting the broad spectrum of leadership approaches.

Today was their first Business Masterclass.

The LEAD facilitators, David and Ann, sat at the back of the

Masterclass, observing the dynamics of the room. The speaker was truly a master in his subject, providing insights, sharing anecdotes and creating a two-way dialogue with the delegates where questions ignited discussion between the peers. Experience suggests that delegates will take different things from a Masterclass depending on the circumstances surrounding their own personal development and that of their organization. The theme of a Masterclass may or may not have personal or business relevance at that moment in time but may make more sense later. Context was important to fully understand the meaning.

At the end of the Masterclass, Ann thanked the speaker and invited everyone to continue discussions over lunch and address more specific issues with the speaker then.

"I will open up a topic on the Forum where we would like you to share your top three learning points from today's Masterclass and what you will do differently in your business as a result of that learning.

"Thank you all for sharing your reflections after the Overnight Experiential and we are pleased that you have found it really interesting reading the reflections of others. As you are now finding out for yourselves, setting aside a few minutes to pause, reflect and record your thoughts and outcomes is really important and has considerable value.

"Next month, we will introduce you to two new elements of LEAD. Firstly, there is one-to-one coaching with David and then there is Action Learning Sets in your small groups facilitated by myself. Dates and times are in your timetable and electronic diaries. Later in the month there will be a Leadership Masterclass. Enjoy lunch and see you next month."

Over lunch, Freddie was sharing his thoughts with Bill. "Since I started on LEAD, I've used the word 'amazing' a few times and I'll do it again now. There was a lot to take in but the Masterclass seemed more real than any business planning course I have been on before. I am going to take the slides back to the office, I'll highlight the key points, circulate them and commence a more effective business planning process.

"We have never had a business plan in over a hundred years of trading. If I involve my managers in the creation of this plan, it may begin to change, for the positive, the working atmosphere of the firm.

"There were a couple of things which were maybe too advanced or aren't relevant to our business at this moment in time. Certainly, there were some key learning points around market segmentation and the SWOT analysis.[4] These were huge eye openers for me.

---

[4] McDonald, M. and Wilson, H. (2011), *Marketing Plans: How to Prepare Them, How to Use Them*, 7th edn, Chichester: Wiley.

"I am guilty of drawing the old SWOT cross and populating it with general and sometimes contradictory points. Looking back now, you wonder, '*What were we doing that for? What were we actually going to learn from that?*' Nothing! I now know to put a big cross through the cross because it's completely pointless.

"When you suddenly start thinking about it you realize you're challenging your learning from university. I had just accepted models and blindly used them many times since. I have never actually questioned, '*Why are we doing that?*' I can now see that it's not relevant to anything. Breaking it down into the format of market segments and applying a SWOT analysis to the segments is a real insight for me.

"When you actually put yourself in a room with other local businesses and with people who have been there and got the tee-shirt, including Masterclass speakers, it makes you think that you don't know anything. It's not that I don't know anything. . . I realize I need to learn, I need to actually listen intently and acquire new skills.

"You could go through your business career, probably like my predecessors have, and not really learn anything and just fight daily in the company for twenty to thirty years. Or, you can actually go out and learn some new skill sets and really drive the business forward with a new focus where you'll be out of your comfort zone and where you make a difference. That's what I want to do. I want to make a difference and I can't do that on my own.

"You could talk all day about going to a decent school or university and going on a good graduate management course but *how does that mean you know how to lead and develop your organization?* Gaining experience leading in business is vital as is being able to stand back, consider and reflect on how you can do things better."

"That's quite an insight, Freddie," said Bill. "I was looking forward to the first Masterclass and I wasn't disappointed. I had sensed in my mind how I was going to approach this part of LEAD. I am a good studier, I learn by listening and I take notes. Today, I worked hard in the Masterclass. I plan to set aside thirty minutes or so after each Masterclass to go through key words, review the concepts that have been discussed and then make further notes so I can come back to these in the future."

Bill paused and smiled, "I do like structuring and making meaning. However, I know that I think linearly, which has its advantages but also its disadvantages. I always try to structure things before I have all the facts and I end up in a straitjacket having only touched the surface and often jumping to conclusions. I have become a slave to structure. I need to critically think more and assimilate information in order to take better, more rounded decisions. This does not come naturally to me. I would like it to be a natural part of how I work."

The two peers laughed together as they realized one was too structured and the other was not, but both were guilty of favouring methods and models that fitted their taken-for-granted ways of working.

"So when I get back to the office," said Freddie, "I am going to ask my financial controller, '*where does the company make most money and what is the profit mix? What are our key market segments in order of priority and profitability?*' Finally, I need to ask, '*why do our customers buy from us in the key market segments that we have chosen to operate in?*'

"Sadly, Bill, I think I already know that we don't have the answers to any of those questions."

* * * * *

LEAD FORUM – MASTERCLASS REFLECTION

Jane was the first of the Freddie, Jane and Bill trio to reflect on the Masterclass.

The Masterclass was really strong and has had a powerful effect on me in lots of ways. I found I had a real thirst for what was being said. We covered much ground, it was enormously practical and the introduction to new tools and techniques provided a quasi "how-to" guide. No one has shown me how to do business planning before and as I sat and observed I thought, "This is how really successful businesses must do it".

I'm still digesting yesterday's immense feast of information, wisdom and practical advice, but the overriding revelation for me is how UN-strategic we have been as a business.

We've started from the point of "we're really good at doing marketing" (which I now realize was not strategic marketing as per Malcolm's definition). We also looked at "who can we sell it to?" (sectors we're experienced in) rather than analysing the needs of the customer segment or even asking ourselves, "of all the customer segments that we could satisfy, which ones have the greatest commercial opportunity?". No, that's not quite true. We have taken a "finger in the wind" gauge of which are the most promising sectors to go after, but then got distracted with the urgency of just getting on with it, getting on the phone and selling our wares.

Now that I say that out loud, I'm a little embarrassed.

Although we've always tailored our services to each client, we have neverthe-less treated everyone (clients and segments) as equal. We measure profitability of each client in terms of service levels but that's pretty superficial. We're going to take a more detailed look at profitability per client, and make some decisions about how we service them.

So, we'll be working our way through pretty much every exercise in the slides. . . .

I started with a small step today, declining a new business meeting that may have generated some revenue but didn't have a hope of being profitable.

Last year, the Board's focus shifted from fire-fighting and "survival" to preparation for growth. My participation in LEAD has been a significant part of that strategy.

Early this year, I began developing our business plan. Each year a business plan is produced, and for the past couple of years I have written it in conjunction with the Chairman (who also acts as Finance Director). This has tended to be centred on financial targets, supported by some strategic goals – but LEAD has revealed the inadequacies and lack of rigour in the previous plans.

There is a clear imperative for developing a more robust business plan: our ambitions for growth are not yet being achieved.

Sitting in the lecture room yesterday felt a bit like being back at school with the teacher at the front but within minutes I knew that this was different. I felt as if I was being equipped with tried and trusted techniques. It felt incredibly powerful.

This is the secret. . .this is the thing. . .

The speaker equipped me with a vocabulary, a language for business. For so long I have been unable to express what I truly mean to my other shareholders. Now I can say, "See, that's what I mean?"

It is clear no one in our senior management team knows how to construct a market-based business plan which demonstrates and delivers where we make profits.

This Masterclass has introduced me to tools and concepts for market segmentation for the first time, demonstrating the value to be gained by analysing our customers (and their motivations for purchase or critical success factors) and closer examination of our productivity and profitability.

THEORY SANDWICH 3   LEADERSHIP LEARNING

Description of the theory behind the Overnight Experiential including leadership timelines, the purpose of the "taught" element of the programme as part of the LEADership Learning Cycle in relation to Masterclasses and the reflective learning process of the LEAD Forum.

Underpinning the development of a delegate on their LEAD Journey is the LEADership Learning Cycle through Lived Experience. Seven main elements of LEAD: Overnight Experiential, LEAD Forum, Masterclasses, Action Learning Sets, Coaching, Shadowing and Exchanges are unveiled in the first four months of the programme. The delegates experience the first three elements in the first month on LEAD, which are constituent parts of three of the five dimensions of the LEADership Learning Cycle in Figure 3.1. In effect, each delegate constructs their own LEADership Learning Cycle based on their own history, their own experiences of leadership in their business and their own experiences and reflections during LEAD.

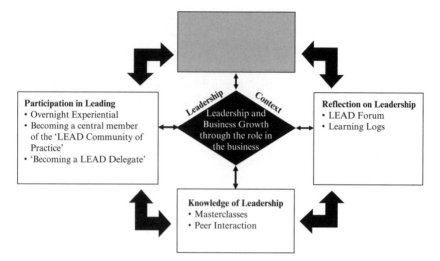

*Figure 3.1   LEAD journey, month 1: construction of the "LEADership
            Learning Cycle" in the context of a LEAD delegate's
            development from their lived experience*

For owner/managers to translate and integrate learning from leadership education to their everyday practice there is often a significant gap (Kempster and Smith, 2014). In Figure 3.1, the delegates' everyday social setting, their workplace, is situated at the centre of the LEADership Learning Cycle – Lived Experience. This *leadership situation* (Figure P.1) is the crucible of leadership learning (Bennis and Thomas, 2002) where their sense of identity of "owner/manager as leader" has been formed and where it unconsciously continues to develop in the everyday happenings of business (outlined in theory sandwich 2).

Before coming on LEAD, each delegate is effectively interviewed to ascertain if they have the desire to develop themselves, their organizations and their business, that is, expand the central diamond of leadership and business growth through their role in the business. They must be able to verbalize that a change is required and that they are prepared to change as part of the process. At the beginning of their LEAD journey, Freddie, Jane and Bill expressed their unease about coming out of their comfort zones, which essentially is going beyond what they know in their own respective workplaces – the central diamond – and engaging in the four outer dimensions of the LEADership Learning Cycle.

The LEAD programme seeks to connect "becoming a delegate" with "becoming a leader" (represented by the large arrows in Figures P.1

and 3.1) and we contend that a delegate needs to do both during their LEAD journey, as we discuss in theory sandwich 5 in Chapter 5. As LEAD is not a taught programme, delegates need to learn to become a LEAD delegate. By utilizing Situated Learning Theory (Lave and Wenger, 1991), a Community of Practice (Wenger, 1998) is co-constructed between delegates and the LEAD facilitators, which we expand in theory sandwich 5.

LEAD draws on the delegates' language and meaning from their own world into a shared world – the LEAD Community of Practice – which has a major impact on delegates in terms of leader becoming embracing leadership practice and leadership identity. We have recently written a chapter making sense of how Communities of Practice can be developed inside a leadership development programme, and we explain why this is so important for the development of leadership learning for owner/managers (Kempster et al., in press).

Communities of Practice (CoP) is a term associated with groups of people engaging in a common activity and through which shared meanings become developed related to this activity. Further, such shared meanings also develop shared identities and practices interlinked with the pursuance of activity in a particular setting (Wenger, 1998). The notion of CoPs has much insight to give to understanding the complex pattern of meanings, identities and practices that make up the complex ecosystems within small businesses. It also speaks to the difficulties of engaging in developing such businesses interwoven in complex relationships with the pivotal leader, the owner/manager.

Yet it is more complex still if effective leadership development is to occur. The development of the individual is a focus on human capital development – the owner/manager. However, the development of the individual should not be separated from the development of the business; the relationships embedded in common meanings, practices and identities can be seen as part of social capital (it also encompasses networks that reach out beyond the relationships of the business).

Leitch et al. (2013) have persuasively argued that entrepreneurial leadership development needs to be considered as the development of both social and human capital; but additionally they add a further capital – that of institutional capital (Anderson, 2010). Leitch et al. draw on empirical research taken from a similar programme to LEAD (leadership development of owner/managers) to show how the activities within the programme "constituted an institution in terms of being governed by a set of rules and norms that are accepted by all the members". Additionally, they showed the emergence of strong organizational structures – such as agendas and procedures – and the beginnings of governance approaches to handle sharing, collaboration and learning: "In other words, the emergence of a strong resilient institution that can provide space and support for its members" (2013, p. 360).

The resonance with the design of LEAD provides a powerful sense of triangulation with our research. That is, leadership development of owner/managers requires careful attention to human, social and institutional capital. How institutional capital occurs and can be developed to be integrated effectively for the benefit of the owner/manager and their colleagues in the business is the central focus of this book. It is an examination of social learning oriented to developing the leader (human capital) with the practices, meanings and identities of the business (social capital) through the asset of institutional capital – the LEAD programme as a Community of Practice.

The nature of a programme CoP suggests that a shared set of meanings, practices and identities are developed. The meanings draw from the respective owner/manager businesses and thus the meanings mixed through collective communication and participation generate understandings of leading that are interconnected with the businesses – yet are meanings understood inside collectively in the cohort.

As part of the establishment of a CoP, members share identities. So this is the case here – owner/managers become LEAD delegates and have a sense of what this means. Finally, connected with shared meanings and shared identities is the emergence of shared practices within the programme. We shall show how this occurs. Importantly, though, the value of this CoP is the creation of institutional capital – something that the LEAD delegates draw on to support the development of the social and human capital developments. The first and most important stage of building the CoP is through the Overnight Experiential.

In the first month of LEAD, the delegates are exposed to three LEAD elements: Overnight Experiential including learning logs, LEAD Forum and the first Masterclass. Each of these elements promotes different types of learning: Participation in Leading, Reflection on Leadership and Knowledge of Leadership (see Figure 3.1).

The delegates' first act of *participation in leading* is on the Overnight Experiential.

The Overnight Experiential is a two-day event including an overnight stay that builds the foundations of trust and confidentiality between the delegates and facilitators necessary for the effective running of LEAD. It incorporates a healthy balance of discussion and debate about leadership alongside some light physical project work and activities. It provides the opportunity for the delegates to be physically away from their business and to engage in experiential activities which are designed to relate the learning back to their real-life work situations. The *participation in leading* activities allow delegates to experience short, sharp, simulated situations of leadership in practice, which, through plenary discussions, begins a process of reflection where the delegates consider what the key messages are, how they apply to their leadership and to their company. *Reflection on leadership* is made explicit during the Overnight Experiential with questions in a learning log that delegates complete and retain in their LEAD binders.

Reflection provides the necessary conversion of experience from uncoded data into thoughtful and productive knowledge (Usher, 1985). This is consistent with Cope (2003), who found that owner/managers learn from experience and that learning takes place in reflecting on that experience and their own practice, noting that learning and reflective processes are inextricably linked.

Delegates are encouraged to critically reflect and question their own taken-for-granted assumptions. After completing the Overnight Experiential, they write on the online LEAD Forum their three key learning points from the Overnight Experiential and what changes they may make to their leadership and/or in the business as a result of this learning (these changes may not be immediate). Learning can be seen as the transformation of experience into knowledge, skills and attributes (Jarvis, 1987) where learning is the potential or capacity to take action (Kim, 1993).

The DO–REVIEW–PLAN–DO learning cycle revealed on the first morning of the Overnight Experiential is a variant of the Kolb Learning Cycle where knowledge is created through the transformation of experience (Kolb, 1984).

The Overnight Experiential is vital in breaking down barriers through learning and social activities to enable peer-to-peer working activities throughout LEAD. The social setting allows the delegates to eat and drink together and the social interactions begin to address the loneliness of leadership, the power of a support network of like-minded individuals and appreciation that delegates' problems and issues are common, irrespective of the size of their companies or the sectors that they operate within (see Thorpe et al., 2009 and Pittaway et al., 2009).

The Overnight Experiential provides the opportunity for the LEAD facilitators to interact with the delegates and understand their business and personal development needs. The LEAD Community of Practice begins to be established, and after two days, strong bonds are formed between delegates and between delegates and facilitators, respectively.

The Masterclasses have a fundamental twofold role: first as an important synthesized insight on a particular theme offered as a set of ideas to provoke both thinking and reflection (and at times guidance on key questions to consider for initiating change) and secondly as a dynamic to bring the cohort together as part of building "institutional capital". The cohort becomes a valuable asset for gaining insight and challenges for the development of their own leadership – human capital – and the development of their business – social capital.

The pedagogy underpinning the Masterclasses works by speakers sharing their experiences, enabling delegates to reflect on their own leadership style and management skills: the human capital aspect. The Masterclasses also allow for the cohort to come together and discuss their learning and interpretation of the subject matter with fellow delegates: the institutional capital.

The style of the Masterclass is such that, rather than teaching delegates the answers, the speakers instead stimulate awareness of key issues, encouraging delegates to reflect on such issues within their own business context. Delegates are invited to share three key learning points from each Masterclass on the online LEAD Forum, recording what changes they may make to their leadership and/or in the business as a result of this learning: social capital.

Delegates' contribution to the Masterclasses is welcomed and encouraged; however, delegates are asked to respect their fellow cohort members and the Masterclass speaker by not dominating the session with issues specific to their company. Delegates are given plenty of opportunity to discuss their thoughts after the session.

Delegates are encouraged to bring a colleague from their business to each Masterclass where relevant. This can be extremely beneficial if the delegate has a member of staff who works within the specific area that the Business Masterclass is focusing on. Delegates often find that Masterclasses stimulate ideas to change areas within the business. By bringing guests along to the sessions this will enable the delegate to better explain any proposed changes to their business and will encourage support and understanding from staff within the organization – a mechanism to stimulate social capital.

All the elements of LEAD represent triggers for reflection and Masterclasses should be viewed as part of an overall programme of activity linking to Coaching, Action Learning and the Business Exchange process.

A fundamental assumption in the design of the programme is that an important source of *knowledge of leadership* is peer interaction and learning from peers. LEAD provides the opportunity for the delegates to learn from one another, largely through dialogue. Their experiences resonate with one another, which addresses the often noted feelings of isolation as owner/managers (Kempster and Watts, 2002). The learning is social – with and from one another. The small business context of the delegates provides a shared context that draws upon their individual histories. In addition to their experiences it is often their tacit knowledge of running their own companies that contributes to the circulation of ideas and exchange of knowledge through peer-to-peer learning. Often a problem that a delegate has, which they believe is unique to them and the context of their business, is occurring or has occurred with another delegate or in their business. This allows one delegate to share their knowledge and experiences with another, enabling a learning opportunity to occur.

In the first month on LEAD, discussions for such peer interactions occur during the Overnight Experiential, at dinner, in the bar and before, during and after Masterclasses. A valuable learning space is created (Wenger, 2000). The salience of the experience and conversations within a Community of Practice contribute to their leadership learning and affirmation of their identity as leaders of their businesses.

Tacit knowledge as conceptualized originally by Polanyi (1966) envisages it as a way to know more than we can tell. Wenger (1998) acknowledges that tacit knowledge includes what is said and what is left unsaid and, because it is often what we take for granted, it tends to fade into the background. Similarly, Nonaka and Takeuchi (1995) argue that more attention should be paid to tacit knowledge held by individuals.

We outlined in theory sandwich 2 how leadership learning is overwhelmingly naturalistic, often occurring through daily interactions that go unnoticed. Thus the difficult issue is how to reveal the everyday routines and events that make up the milieu of our lives. A narrative approach is argued to be most appropriate for exploring tacit knowledge (Kempster, 2009a), and a narrative methodology, through the drawing of a timeline of leadership experiences, is deployed on the Overnight Experiential to uncover what has shaped the way delegates think about and practise leadership.

The timeline exercise was developed in Kempster's (2009a, p. 115) research on "how managers have learnt to lead". We have taken an extract from this work to illustrate the method employed on LEAD:

What I would like you to do is concentrate only on leadership and address these three questions:

- What do you think leadership is?
- How do you approach leading?
- What has shaped your thinking and approach to leadership?

To address these questions please do the following:
Think about how you would define leadership and write this down. Draw a line and create a timeline which you will populate with memories on leadership.

These could go far back as childhood and probably would incorporate organizational experiences. As you recall these memories try to capture them onto the timeline and then go back and work your way through the details and clarify what these memories mean to you. Don't rush this – you have 90 minutes. Conclude with listing how your thinking shapes your approach to leading. The list might reflect advice you would give about leading in your organization or another context. For example, "be in control and be seen to be in control". Look at the list and see if you can determine whether the points can be connected to your memories.

The personalized timeline allows delegates to examine the leadership influences on their own lives and provides a base for each delegate to explore the development of their leadership style with their coach during LEAD.

4. LEAD journey: month 2 – April

In the second month, delegates are introduced to two new LEAD elements which are two different types of coaching using two different coaching models and techniques: one-to-one Coaching (using Solutions Focus[5] and OSKAR model) and peer group coaching in Action Learning Sets (using the GROW model[6]). There is a Masterclass and delegates are encouraged to use the LEAD Forum.

(FACE-TO-FACE) COACHING

It was a typical, showery, April day. The rain had eased to a drizzle but everywhere was wet. The grey clouds hung low overhead. Deep in thought, Freddie was hopping along, trying to avoid the puddles.

"OK. Coaching is the next stage of my leadership development, isn't it?" Freddie said to himself.

He was trying to reassure himself as he made his way along the tree-lined pathway towards meeting his LEAD coach. He was attempting to shake off the feeling that this first face-to-face coaching session was just like going to the doctor.

"I don't know what he's going to tell me."

Freddie stopped and shook his head, trying to make sense of the situation.

"No, he's going to tell me that something might be *wrong* with me."

Wrong? The word chimed in Freddie's mind. "What am I going to be told?" The words whirled through his head as he struggled to rein in his imagination, which was beginning to run away with itself.

"I've always liked to look at the positive rather than the negative but I have a picture of being placed in a cupboard with a lot of skeletons. Someone else has placed them in there but I need to open the cupboard doors and go in.

[5] Jackson, P.Z. and McKergow, M. (2007), *The Solutions Focus: The SIMPLE Way to Positive Change*, 2nd edn, London: Nicholas Brealey.
[6] Whitmore, J. (2002), *Coaching for Performance: GROWing People, Performance and Purpose*, London: Nicholas Brealey.

"Wow, where am I going to start on this?"

As he approached the meeting room in the neutral venue where the session was to take place, Freddie came to his senses. He reminded himself that one of the reasons he signed up for the LEAD programme in the first place was to work with the LEAD coaches. He'd heard from a friend that coaching was useful but he expected it to be painful, particularly if he was going to exorcise his demons.

* * * * *

"The purpose of coaching is to provide delegates with an opportunity to personally grow and explore issues in confidence. It is undertaken with a trained business coach who has much experience of working with leaders in small and medium sized companies," said David, who was the LEAD coach for all of the delegates. "Coaches help LEAD delegates to work out their own strategy for improving their performance rather than telling them what to do; to learn from their own experiences rather than teaching them; and to find their own solutions to the challenges they face rather than dispensing advice. My primary role is to help you to develop ways of learning for yourself.

"Coaching is offered to all LEAD delegates on a one-to-one, coach-to-delegate basis. While some of the description of coaching is superficially similar to that used to describe action learning, the important distinction between the two is that where Action Learning Sets are a group-based activity, coaching is done on a one-to-one basis. Like action learning, the coaching conversation is a confidential one between you and me. Coaching consists of an initial face-to-face meeting between you (coachee) and me (coach) to establish rapport and introduce the concept of coaching, followed by four one-hour long telephone coaching sessions to demonstrate how coaching can work using that medium and then a final face-to-face coaching session.

"Coaching provides you with the opportunity to stop and reflect, and to focus on real-life issues in a structured, confidential manner where you will find solutions to real-life issues. You will understand the benefit of coaching skills and techniques and begin to adopt these in your own working and personal life.

"I will quickly take you through the Solutions Focus approach and how to use the OSKAR coaching tool, then we can agree what you would like to achieve from our coaching conversation today.

"Solutions Focus is a powerful, practical approach to positive change within people, teams and organizations that focuses on solutions. OSKAR is a framework for solutions-focused coaching and is an acronym standing for:

- **O**utcome – Where the coaching outcome is jointly defined and comprises a Platform and a Future Perfect.
- Scaling – On a scale from 1 to 10 where are you?
- Know-how – Relevant know-how, resources, skills and attributes.
- Affirm – Complement skills and resources.
- Action – Note the know-how, decide next small steps.
- Review – What's better? What's helped? What next?"

* * * * *

"David, initially I wondered how we were going to fill the time. An hour and a half is a long time but once you are actually in the session, the time flies by and before you know it, I was looking at my watch thinking *we've got to close up here*. Once again, I built a wrong first impression of what a LEAD element was going to be like. Coaching is far from what I expected and the coaching process seems a natural one for me. After an initial five minutes of social interaction, you go beyond your own insecurities and it becomes beneficial. As you now know, I was increasingly becoming bogged down in the day-to-day minutiae and as a result I was not doing the more strategic aspects of my role. Talking that through with you today has allowed me to think back to the discussions about micro-management and communication that I was exposed to on the Overnight Experiential. I'm now able to apply that learning to my current situation. I'm beginning to consciously work 'on' the business, rather than 'in' the business. It'll be good not being dragged into the daily fire-fighting!

"Defining a 'Future Perfect' [an ideal state where current problems have vanished[7]] as part of the outcome from the coaching session is very powerful. The focus of taking small steps to get to the overall goal is very helpful, as was defining what we are doing well and identifying where certain improvements can be made. Rather than becoming a specialist in the problem, this approach allows me to create and focus on a practical solution."

With a little reminder from David, Freddie dutifully offers to complete his coaching reflection log. "One thing I already realize is that I must prepare better for the next coaching session. I will think more deeply about what I want to discuss next time and send you the preparation form in advance."

* * * * *

---

[7] Jackson and McKergow (2007, p.3).

True to character, Bill had spent an hour or so the previous night pulling all his notes together. He was looking forward to coaching, which, together with his penchant for structure, had made this task an even more pleasant one than normal. As he looked down at his summary sheets, he could see that he had lots to talk about but no one thing stood out.

Bill recognized that his leadership style was too crude, too one-dimensional and too directive. This had been humorously but brutally exposed at the Overnight Experiential. Control was important to him, which drove his need to become involved in all sorts of tasks. Yet he got bored quickly and consequently became distracted from day-to-day activities, no matter how important they were.

He smiled to himself, recalling the fierce discussions on the Overnight Experiential when he revealed he spent 5 per cent of his time on strategic matters. Here was an area that Bill felt he was ahead of his fellow peers but he knew he had to find more time focusing on strategic issues. But how?

So in discussions with David, that became the "Platform" for the solution that was going to emerge from Bill's coaching session.

"Now imagine the Future Perfect where your issue is resolved and you are spending the time you want to spend on strategic matters. Describe what you see," said David.

Bill paused, looked up to the ceiling, gathered his thoughts and said, "In my Future Perfect I am spending half-a-day a week being available to meet staff and engage with them. I am also spending half-a-day a week on strategic matters. I am also putting time aside at the end of the week to plan the following week's activities. I have delegated key administration tasks to others and I have employed an assistant to act as my number two on technical matters."

For the next twenty minutes Bill continued, richly describing his Future Perfect. David asked questions every now and then, seeking clarification of meaning to obtain more clarity as well as querying points to further improve Bill's understanding of his desired state.

David was conscious of Bill's leadership development needs. Bill had spoken with David about them when he first discussed coming on LEAD. He then reiterated this in his LEAD Application Form and of course they were the subject of conversations on the Overnight Experiential.

During coaching, David was keen to use the 'Affirm' element of the OSKAR model to help build Bill's confidence when progress was being made on his developmental needs.

"That's a fabulous description of your Future Perfect, Bill. On a Scale of one to ten, where your Future Perfect is a ten, where are you now?" asked David.

"I am at a three. The reason I say that is because I am in better control than a year ago. I'm monitoring who is doing things and I feel more on top of work."

"So what is working for you at position three on the scale?"

Bill then described the few things that he believed were working for him now. As he spoke, David was listening attentively, searching for counters that could be used to build upon. As he was fairly low on the Scale (S), Bill quickly exhausted the contributing factors. Building on what is working and being mindful of the Future Perfect, David then invited Bill to discuss what relevant Know-how (K), whether it be resources, skills and attributes inside or outside his organization, could assist Bill to move one step up the scale.

Bill was not short of thoughts or ideas and quickly identified a number of sources of support.

"Well done, so what actions will you now take?" enquired David.

Within five minutes, Bill was smiling, looking down at his notepad with four Actions (A) that he committed to do before the next session in a month's time.

"I really enjoyed that, David," said Bill. "I admit that I struggled with the OSKAR model. My mind is more linear, more cause and effect but I realize that has its limitations. I really like the 'Where do you want to be?' question that sits behind the notion of the 'Future Perfect'. I can already see that will be a powerful concept, especially if I bring coaching into the workplace. I'd like to but it's too early yet.

"By talking matters through with you, I have confirmed the actions I need to undertake and build into my normal working day and week. I believe that will change my behaviour and in turn will result in different outcomes. In the past, I did not have the discipline to do these things regularly, which was why things had become stuck. I look forward to reviewing progress with you next month."

* * * * *

Jane had never been coached before and was looking forward to the session, the process of coaching and being asked questions rather than being given advice. Jane saw this was a new way to learn. She was determined to embrace coaching and to explore thoughts, even unformed ones. She realized she relied on her gut instinct, possibly too much.

By way of preparation, she had reflected on what she had learned about her own leadership style from the Overnight Experiential. She had begun to explore in her own mind what aspects of her leadership style she wanted to adjust and strengthen. She had considered which aspects of her business were doing well and what could be improved. However, she was unsure of what she wanted to talk through in the coaching session.

"Don't worry about that," said David, "that is quite usual. Part of what we will do is to explore your problem or problems before agreeing a 'Platform' to build."

"My confidence as a leader fluctuates wildly, but is mostly under par," Jane responded. "I lack assertiveness, and don't always follow my instinct and then regret it. I lose myself in the day-to-day tasks and deadlines and then feel on the back foot when I realize I haven't progressed our business. So thinking that through as I am speaking, I'd like us to discuss my confidence as a leader."

And so began Jane's coaching journey. She was very open; the Solutions Focused process and the OSKAR model worked very well. She identified that she was good at building up the confidence of her team and shared many examples in different situations of where she remained calm and unflustered, encouraging of others, relaxed and dedicated. By focusing on the positives she pulled out aspects of her past that had worked for her previously, which had been obscured by more recent pressures. This allowed her to agree a simple, straightforward 'Action'. She agreed to complete both the reflective notes for that day's session and the preparation form for the next coaching session – the first telephone coaching session.

* * * * *

ACTION LEARNING SET 1

The following week, the weather hadn't improved. It was still mainly dull and overcast with the odd moments of sun and blue sky.

Freddie, Jane and Bill had arrived and were to meet together with Tom for their first Action Learning Set. Ann was their coach for the six half-day long Action Learning Sets that would run over the next six months.

Coffees and teas were available on a station outside the room where all the members were chatting and swapping stories. Freddie, Jane and Bill were laughing at the fact that they had all struggled to bring a problem, issue or challenge into their respective LEAD Coaching sessions but they each had left with meaningful actions to improve their situation.

Ann had already set the room up for the Action Learning Set members. There was no table, to avoid adversely affecting group dynamics; there were just chairs in a circle facing each other. To the side were two flip charts: one with a copy of the Cohort's Ground Rules that were created on the morning of the Overnight Experiential; on the other was a cartoon drawing of a tree complete with many, varied characters in different poses.

Tom arrived, completing the small group.

"Come on in everyone," said Ann, "and welcome to Action Learning. Grab a seat and place your LEAD binders on the floor under your seats.

"The purpose of Action Learning Sets is to enable delegates in small groups to raise pertinent business issues in a confidential, non-competitive, trusting environment, and in cooperation with like-minded people, to identify solutions through questions and dialogue.

"We run Action Learning Sets in such a way that enables you to ask open, insightful questions and understand why these are so important in effective problem solving. You will learn to develop and use active listening skills and understand the importance of 'self-management'. You will become more aware of your own agendas and assumptions and how to manage these. You will learn how to give and receive feedback through working with fellow set members in an environment that is appropriately supportive, yet challenging. Note: Action Learning Sets are not about giving or receiving advice. There are other parts of LEAD where you can gain advice, for example on the LEAD Forum or during breaks.

"Action Learning Sets are made up of two types of activity: 'air time' and 'process review'. During the air time the issue holder presents their issue to the group, who then ask questions which enables the issue holder to move towards actions. The group therefore enables and facilitates each member to complete the learning tasks he or she sets for himself or herself. In this respect, sharing and learning from experience is a very important part of this process. The process review allows each member to discuss how the process of questioning helped their own learning as well as helping the issue holder move towards some actions.

"The value of Action Learning Sets stems from the interaction among the group. For an Action Learning Set to function well, members must conform to Ground Rules established by the group during the first session. These may include attending every session, being punctual, respecting confidentiality and each other, and trusting the Action Learning process. These rules will not be imposed on you, rather you will decide on what is right for you as a group. I have brought along the Ground Rules for the overall cohort, which may assist you in agreeing your own for the set.

"A major advantage of Action Learning Sets is that you can bring your own concerns and problems to the table and have them discussed in a supportive and confidential environment by interested peers. Action Learning Sets provide a way of focusing on the real problems that concern you, rather than concentrating on hypothetical ones. In this way there is maximum choice and flexibility because you personally will be responsible for the selection of your own topics / problems to be discussed. In addition, an Action Learning Set provides the ideal opportunity to learn from the experience of your group members and engage in shared learning. It is also a means of developing reflective thinking and of making commitments to action."

Over the next hour, Ann introduced the set members to the Jelly Baby tree – an icebreaker to get them to share how they're feeling at that moment in time and explain why. The group then participated in an exercise asking closed and open questions. Finally, Ann introduced the GROW coaching model and handed out laminated sheets containing a set of open questions that could be used at the different stages of the GROW model.

"Who would like to go first and share their issue?"

During the morning all set members stated their problem and their peers then asked them questions. Ann guided them through the GROW model, suggesting when to move onto the next stage.

At the first process review, Freddie was the first to speak. "This is difficult. I have never been to anything like this. When I first sat down it felt like I was in a rehabilitation session similar to those you see on television. I have really struggled asking open questions. I don't think it is just me, we have all struggled. You don't realize your natural style is to ask so many closed questions."

"I agree," said Jane. "The process is difficult at first. It is not instinctive. I think it will take quite a few goes before it becomes natural to ask open questions. I do like being in the small group though, it feels comfortable."

By the second process review, Bill observed, "Ann has had to interject a number of times and say, 'No, you can't ask that. That's a closed question. Please reframe it'. It is necessary but quite frustrating when that happens. Also, I have wanted to give others the answer and say, 'Look, you know you need to do this, it is obvious. Why can't you see it?' It is really difficult not giving your opinion.

"I know I can't give my opinion here. The real question is, *what do I do back in the workplace?* That is a question I almost don't want to think about," groaned Bill as he lowered his head into his hands.

Everyone laughed, including Bill.

Recovering from his embarrassment, Bill remarked, "I think two things are at play here. By volunteering a problem to discuss, in effect you are asking, *what do you think I should do about it?* Something is not working, we are all showing some sort of vulnerability, so it is almost natural to have some level of discomfort. Also, open questions make people feel more uncomfortable as they invite or demand an explanation. There is a requirement by the 'presenter' to provide more information. Maybe Action Learning is beginning to take us out of our comfort zones?"

Little did Bill know how prophetic his last comment was going to be.

Next to share an issue was Jane. All eyes were focused on her. Ann sensed Jane's apprehension, smiled and asked, "What would you like to talk about?"

"I have thought long and hard about what I want to discuss today. It is the single biggest issue in my life. It is one that I have only discussed with my husband. It is one that physically keeps me awake at nights."

Jane's hands were trembling. Her eyes were welling up. Freddie and Bill awkwardly fidgeted in their seats, unsure of what was coming next. Both diverted their eyes away from Jane, playing their part in reducing the tension level in the room.

"One of our ground rules is confidentiality," said Jane. "I know it is the first time that we are together and we are finding our way with each other. I am sure I can trust you all but I need to clarify that what I am going to say stays in this room."

All nodded.

Jane's body language displayed a sense of relief but immediately she tensed up again.

"I spoke with David in coaching about my wavering confidence levels as a leader. To be honest that really wasn't the issue. It is a symptom of something else that I have never addressed or ever discussed in a business environment. What I would like to talk about is my relationship with the majority shareholders who are part-time Board directors. I doubt my capability to provide leadership. I do not know what I should or should not be leading on. I feel I can never do enough to satisfy them. There are too many disagreements and rows, which I then take home and my poor husband bears the brunt of my frustrations from work."

Jane's voice was trembling. She paused, reached for her handbag and pulled out a tissue and dabbed away tears that were rolling down her cheek.

Freddie audibly gulped.

"I am sorry for my tears," apologized Jane. Ann immediately reassured her, asking her if she needed a few moments. She didn't.

"I don't know what to do," Jane concluded despairingly. "I am sorry it is such an emotionally charged problem for our first session but I really would appreciate some direction."

The subject, its sensitivity and the will to assist energized Jane's peers and over the next half an hour Jane started to find a path forward as she consciously began wrestling with the concept of power.

At the end of her process review, Jane opened up some more. "During my air time, as I was answering your questions, I thought that some of the things I said just sounded foolish. Oddly, by speaking it through and hearing my own voice, I began to identify where I am going wrong and I started to come up with my own answers.

"As we got to the heart of the issue, it did feel a bit uncomfortable though. Not in an aggressive or confrontational manner. If I am honest, I'm not used to having these deep discussions as I tend to avoid the more difficult conversations."

Conscious of time, Ann reminded everyone, "It's important when using the GROW model in Action Learning not to jump to solutions too quickly. It's your turn now, Freddie."

"It's funny, it's difficult to pick out a problem as I have so many to choose from! However, two that have already been raised are similar to ones I have got, so I won't repeat either of those but I've already got a few ideas to take back to the office to help me deal with them. That's a bonus. Thank you.

"I welcome being challenged as no one questions me at work other than my autocratic father. Consequently, I may have a tendency to coast rather than constructively look for the best solutions."

"It's payback time," salivated a grinning Bill, whilst rubbing his hands.

Another round of laughter consumed the tightly grouped set in the seemingly cavernous surroundings.

* * * * *

"How much listening have you actually been doing in that first session?" asked Ann at the end of the final process review.

"I've always been a bad listener and that is something I want to improve during LEAD," replied Freddie. "I have tried to actively listen to what all the presenters said and to my peers' questions. However, I do wonder how much actual listening I was doing as I was consciously thinking about what I was going to ask next. I need to work on eliminating that behaviour from my make-up if I want a different and better outcome."

"I think being a listener and a speaker is a skill we will develop over the months to come," noted Jane. "I can see a process, a learning technique, of being able to listen, then ask open insightful and relevant questions that guide others through an exploration of their problem to agree some actionable steps."

"Well put, Jane," observed Ann, sensing that things may be coming together.

Jane continued. "I found it is so much easier taking an outsider's per-spective. I could see others' challenges and options even before they said it. However, when it is your problem, it is different. I often cannot see the wood for the trees.

"I did find it therapeutic sharing my problem. I felt the others listened. With the very nature of what I wanted to discuss, it was emotionally packed; sorry again about my tears but I have got practical actions to take away."

The set members smiled reassuringly at Jane.

"Thank you everyone for your contributions today," said Ann. "It was interesting to hear at the coffee break how quickly you realized and commented on how similar your problems are and that you were able to swap experiences. It is a testament to you all and the process that you were able to break down seemingly huge problems in such short periods of time into small, practical actionable steps which you have all agreed will be completed before we meet in a month's time for the next Action Learning Set session.

"Before then I'd like you to do two things. Firstly, send me your reflection log on your experiences today. There is a template in your LEAD binder and in the Resource section of the LEAD Forum. Also, a couple of days before the next session, please send me your preparation form.

"Please do continue your conversations on the Forum where you will find a confidential area that only your Action Learning Set and the LEAD Team can access."

* * * * *

MASTERCLASS 2

Ann smiled to herself as she pressed the "post reply" button on her computer. Next week's speaker would stretch the delegates' thinking on leadership performance. The short PowerPoint presentation belied some of the interaction that she knew the speaker had planned.

Subject: Leadership Performance – Professor Steve Kempster

> The Masterclass outlines the growing shift from management to leadership. The changing emphasis of leader as hero and expert, to leader of meaning making, challenge, consideration and learning. The session will explore changing expectations of employees and their desire for meaning to work and a desire for greater involvement and responsibility. These broad themes will be placed into the SME context and illustrate how the growth of small businesses is often curtailed by the phenomenon of the crisis of leadership and the self-imposed glass ceiling.

* * * * *

"These folks sure know how to grab your attention," muttered Bill under his breath to Freddie as they queued for the buffet lunch before the session.

It was a week later and they had just attended the second LEAD Masterclass, but this was the first Leadership Masterclass, with its focus on exploring different aspects of leadership.

The link between leadership and followership was in focus. The romantic myth of the charismatic leader was being challenged. The "hero complex" was also under scrutiny. The inspirational speaker had announced that by the end of the morning the delegates would be giving their "Martin Luther King" speech – one they can make around a water cooler or to a small group of people as well as to a larger audience or to construct more effective email communications.

Three hours later, three different reactions were in evidence from Bill, Jane and Freddie.

"The 'hero complex' is a eureka moment for me," admitted Bill. "It has connected dozens of things in my life. For example, I perceived a lack of contribution from my colleagues and I resented them for it. Therefore, I would constantly undertake more tasks personally to fill the gap. This had two negative effects. Firstly, and obviously, it meant I was under time pressure as my workload continually increased. Secondly, and more importantly, by undertaking tasks that others had previously done, I disempowered them so they retreated into their narrow job roles. I crowded out initiative, created over-reliance on myself and a vicious circle was created whereby my responsibilities expanded as others' shrank.

"I am in danger of turning everyone into sheep, unthinking followers. It is not their fault. It is my fault. My leadership style is unsustainable. What I can now see is that my heroic style is imprisoning others and imposing impossible pressures on me. I am being overwhelmed. I cannot do everything nor can I be the best at everything, something I have been driven to continually display.

"I have been disempowering people. I can almost hear them say, 'I can never do what you do'. It is almost as if they have been waiting for *my words of wisdom*. They wait, they check in, which consumes time, something that time-poor leaders do not have in abundance.

"Good people want to help. Not so good people. . .well, they left it to me to do whatever was needed to be done. And, I foolishly did!

"I am a poor delegator. Even worse, I see-saw between over-prescription because I want to retain control and a laissez-faire approach where I allow people to get on and do it themselves without any direction or support.

"I know all that sounds negative but strangely I see it as positive because the failings of the firm are, at least in part, due to failings in my leadership.

This should mean that the solutions to those failings are within my power as the leader. This is why I believe this is another light bulb moment for me."

"That is a great breakthrough for you," smiled Jane, who was quietly reflecting on the concept of leadership and followership. She posed to herself the question, "There are ten people in my company – four directors/shareholders including myself, and six further employees. How many of them do I lead effectively? How many of them do I lead at all? What are the consequences of my answers to these questions?"

Freddie came into the discussion. "I didn't want to stand up and speak in front of everyone and give my Martin Luther King speech. I think my confidence is growing, but I am not quite ready to do that yet. Hats off to the three that volunteered and gave their message though."

"I agree. I don't like public speaking either," observed Bill, "but I am going to give the water cooler speech a go when I get back. Communication is poor in our firm. I don't spend enough time with staff and I do not interact with them enough. This sounds like an easy thing to implement that will also increase my visibility in the firm but I will need to build in the discipline to do it regularly.

"When I am speaking, communicating, I am influencing others. I now appreciate that I am shaping how others see the world. At the same time, my message is being interpreted. In effect, as a leader, I am sense-giving, whereas the follower is sense-making. The follower is dealing with all the data coming at them, working through what they have to work through – solving, refining, delivering etc. In essence, they are making sense of all the messages."

Bill rubbed his face in a thoughtful manner and cradled his chin. "It is an interesting idea that the main perception of a leader is 'off stage' and that followers look for integrity and consistency in leadership. If they don't believe in the leader, then they won't. Personal values are important and the Masterclass speaker said that study after study has shown that integrity was the number one value.

"I find the concept of the off-stage leader very, very challenging because with my logical mind I tend to look at set pieces. I see staff meetings as a set piece where I take a leadership role. Similarly, financial reporting is where I would take the lead. You are expected by followers to take the lead in those situations, whereas the Masterclass speaker said it is when you're off duty that you really get tested, summed up, judged and appreciated.

"It is off stage where a leader must perform.

"When he said that, I thought, 'Well, that's not me, I can't do that'. But it is clearly important, so I need to do something. Perhaps my version of the water cooler speech could be that thing?"

"You have your eureka moments, Bill, and I have my eye openers," chuckled Freddie. "I'd never heard of the notion of in-groups and out-groups and they are a real eye opener for me as again they exist in my business.

"I now appreciate that a leader has a preference for people in their in-group over outsiders and that they blame the situation when things do not work. The leader does not blame the followers because they could not have seen it. Similarly, the followers do not blame the leader. The situation is the issue.

"The opposite is the case in out-groups. There, the leader blames the followers, not the situation and the followers blame the leader, not the situation.

"It's a fascinating insight," laughed Freddie. "My firm must be a text book company!

"I have two senior managers who regularly clash about the performance in their respective areas. One has an in-group and the other an out-group. Manager A rasps at Manager B disbelievingly at how he often chastises people in his out-group, whereas Manager B regularly complains that Manager A continually blames events rather than taking responsibility for what is going on in her area and managing the performance of her in-group better.

"I have struggled to understand how to manage them and support them better in their daily duties. It's amazing when you apply a theory to certain events that occur each and every day that you can actually comprehend what's happening. I can now go back to the office and have a discussion with these managers about the pluses and minuses of both approaches to improve the performance of their areas and their dealings with staff. You never know, they may even start to get along!"

"You may not remember," stated Bill, "but on the first morning of the Overnight Experiential I asked, '*In terms of time spent on reflection, thinking, conceptualizing and on action/doing what should the appropriate balance of leadership style be in my business now and in the future?*'"

"I do and it prompted a big discussion."

"I wonder, *how my managers and my staff – my followers – would describe my leadership style?*"

"Yes," added Freddie. "And, *how does that differ from your view of your leadership style?*"

Freddie paused and rubbed the stubble on his chin. "There is something else to consider, Bill?"

"Yeah? What's that?

"*What will you do as a result of this increased self-awareness?*"

* * * * *

LEAD FORUM – MASTERCLASS REFLECTION

Jane was the first again to reflect on the Masterclass.

1. Success is achieved by your 'followers' – our role as leaders is to be clear about the purpose and allow others to be 'heroic'. But how often do we, as leaders, clearly express the purpose?
2. I'm going to try to stop swinging wildly from one end of the spectrum (thinking I have to have all the answers in order to be a good leader) to the other (where I think nurturing and supporting my team is enough). Clarity of purpose will be my mantra.
3. The power I possess as leader is attributed to me by others as a consequence of my behaviour; we might as well call it 'trust' rather than 'power'. Recognizing that you possess it is humbling, it is precious and, upon first realizing this, it is surprising.
4. Our Board has become an 'in-group' which blames the situation, not the leader or followers, and this has been the case for as long as I've been a director. (Prior to that the Board all blamed each other, it was divisive and reached self-destruct.) LEAD is helping me to take responsibility by questioning every part of our business, so that we can figure out how our actions can overcome 'the situation' rather than be a slave/victim to it.
5. How easy is it in the whole pursuit of team spirit to become an in-group that blames external forces rather than ourselves? I often hear us say, 'We lost that order because they changed the rules, it is not us, it is everyone else'.

Freddie responded:

Bringing the 'Martin Luther King' speech back into a business context, if I gave a big speech in front of my staff, I'd probably get tomatoes thrown at me. There isn't the same level of respect for me as him . . . but that is due to history.

Prior to me coming on to LEAD, the previous directors provided poor leadership; they were highly autocratic and the business largely was left to run itself. So that was the prevailing culture. Why would anyone want to listen to a leader?

The speaker has thrown questions out there which has started to get me to think about leadership in the context of my business. I know my firm is not ready for me to stand on a soap box and belt out a corporate message. I need to find out what they are looking for from the leaders, from me. I also realize I need to create a purpose in staff's everyday lives.

Perhaps there is a clue in the fact that integrity is the top value in repeated academic studies where followers are looking for consistency in behaviours and values?

Bill was still silent on the Forum. . .

THEORY SANDWICH 4   COACHING FOR GROWTH

Discussion on Solutions Focused Coaching and Reg Revans' observations on Action Learning. The power of open questions. Exploring the implications of coaching associated with growth within the SME context.

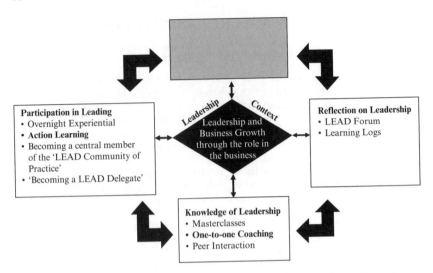

*Figure 4.1   LEAD journey, month 2: construction of the "LEADership
              Learning Cycle" in the context of a LEAD delegate's
              development from their lived experience*

Two new LEAD elements are introduced in the second month – Action
Learning Sets and Coaching – further constructing the LEADership
Learning Cycle (Figure 4.1). Action Learning provides delegates with the
opportunity to *participate in leading*, whereas the one-to-one nature of
Coaching allows delegates to obtain *knowledge of leadership*. Each element
has its own distinct pedagogy thus providing the delegate the experience
of two different ways of learning with associated techniques that can be
used back in their businesses. By the end of the six-month period delegates
will be comfortable with using the techniques they have learnt within their
own companies.

ACTION LEARNING

Although there is no universal definition of action learning per se, there
is a general consensus that it is a social form of learning whereby participants come together to work on issues and share learning. Action Learning
Sets can act as spaces to try out new or challenge existing identities (see
Anderson and Gold, 2009). The acquisition of new knowledge and the
practice of reflection are social processes achieved through participation
and peer exchange (see Gibb, 2009, p. 223).

Pittaway et al. (2009, p. 269) argue that action learning can enable entrepreneurs to engage in a social network of peers in which to become involved in a discursive process leading to reflection. The approach of action learning as connecting practice and theory through reflection, learning by doing and generating a social rather than individual cognition would appear to have immediate connections with the challenges of managing small businesses (Rae, 2009, p. 290). In this sense, action learning for the entrepreneur is more than creating a peer network as it allows real-life problems to be worked through with others who understand and can empathize.

The Action Learning Sets (ALS)[8] on LEAD are made up of small groups (between four and seven delegates) with a facilitator, meeting six times over the ten months. They are designed to provide the opportunity to address real issues through open questions, dialogue and reflection and, crucially, not giving one another advice (Smith, 2009). The facilitator follows the approach of Revans (1983) and matches the criteria set out by Pedler et al. (2005) whereby questioning is the main way to help participants proceed with their problems, and learning is from reflection on actions taken.

Action Learning is a powerful process used in a group setting to tackle problems where there are no clear-cut or simple solutions. It draws upon the principle that we learn most effectively when we address problems within a small group which provides a supportive yet challenging environment. The process of action learning encourages set members to reflect on how they learn, thus increasing their capacity to respond to new situations.

Action Learning was originally developed as a concept in the 1940s by Reg Revans who believed that the most effective learning arose from combining the existing knowledge held by the problem holder with insightful questioning of this knowledge by others (Revans, 1982). It rests on the premise that no one person's issue is unique to him or her (Revans, 1983).

Revans (1983) claimed there is no learning without action and no (sober and deliberate) action without learning. Adaptation, he argues, is achieved through learning, that is, being able to do tomorrow that which might have been unnecessary today, or to be able to do today what was unnecessary last week (Revans, 2011, p. 1). He summarizes this approach through the learning equation:

$$L = P + Q \text{ (learning = programmed knowledge plus questioning insight)}$$

---

[8] ALS is used to refer to both the singular and plural of action learning set/s.

Programmed knowledge, such as formal instruction, has its place but is not sufficient in itself. Revans argues that problems require insightful questions and action learning deals with the resolution of problems about which no single course of action is to be justified by any code of programmed knowledge (2011, p.3). In this way, different managers (for example) might treat problems in different ways: the exploratory insight (Q) with the help of set members helps to explore the problem and opportunities.

In other words, Action Learning is based on the principle that we have all the knowledge and resources inside us to solve our own problems; it requires someone to ask those questions to help unearth these resources from within us. When exploring a problem, the set is expected to report, analyse and plan real-time action, which is continually being taken by the participants in their operational backgrounds (Revans, 2011). The issue holder is expected to "take action" as a key component of the process and is held accountable to the group for achieving this action.

The process of reflection plays a large part in aiding the learning process with space for the issue holder to reflect on their issue. The learning is social and set members benefit from the exploration of problems even when the problems aren't explicitly theirs. Quite often the set members comment that while one person is working through his/her issues they are sitting reflecting on a similar issue or are thinking about how they might deal with that situation, just as Freddie reflected in his first Action Learning Set. Fundamentally, Action Learning Sets provide a space to allow real-life problems to be worked through with others who understand and can empathize.

So, in effect action learning is similar to the model of coaching used, but carried out in the mutually supportive environment of a group where all members bring issues to the group whilst all other members play the role of coach. Their experiences resonate with one another, which addresses the often noted feelings of isolation as owner/managers (Smith and Peters, 2006).

It differs from other group problem-solving interventions in that in its purest form it is about the set members asking coaching questions of the issue holder (the "presenter") to help them reflect on their issue and identify their own solutions for moving forward and not about advice giving.

By properly developing questioning, listening and reflective skills, set members are equipping themselves with the ability to solve problems themselves in the future when there are no set members to ask the questions.

There are a set of underlying learning principles that underpin the process and the facilitator plays a key role in managing the group process and ensuring that the principles are adhered to. In addition to this the set members may also create their own ground rules for working together and again the facilitator will play a role in ensuring these are met.

COACHING

The growth of coaching within organizations has been exponential over the past ten years. The underlying assumption is that the development of the individual will contribute to the development of the organization. It has been identified that an increasing number of SMEs are using coaching (CIPD, 2008), but identifying the impact of coaching on any size of business is embryonic, although some studies are available (see, for example, Peel, 2004; Graya et al., 2011). Such studies show a positive correlation between business growth and coaching intervention. Interestingly, Peel (2004) argues that the organization and the culture within it need to be ready for coaching to be effective, in other words, the organizational culture can be a barrier to the effectiveness of coaching. As discussed, the companies on LEAD are recruited based partly on their openness to the learning interventions they will encounter on the programme. In this sense, they have the absorptive capacity (Cohen and Levinthal, 1990) for the learning interventions to have an impact.

The UK Government has, in the past, recognized the positive impact coaching can have on SMEs, which is evident in a number of funded business interventions that focus on or include coaching, for example the Department for Business, Innovation and Skills' coaching for growth programme and the North West Development Agency High Growth Programme.[9]

The quality of the relationship between the coach and coachee (i.e. the person being coached) is seen as fundamental in a successful outcome and is a prerequisite in creating the conditions for transformative learning (du Toit and Reissner, 2012).

LEAD deploys a Solutions Focus approach to coaching, with its focus on seeking practical, pragmatic solutions that the coachee wants rather than overly examining the problem (Jackson and McKergow, 2007). Every coaching situation will be different so the coach must assist the coachee to generate the right actions.

Coaching of owner/managers is concerned with the creation of new meaning or a different understanding of existing knowledge gained through critical reflection. In a coaching context, knowledge is the product

---

[9] North West Development Agency (2010), 'High growth programme,' available at: http://www.edocr.com/doc/63/nwda-high-growth-programme-criteria.

of co-construction between the facilitator of learning (i.e. the coach) and the leadership learner (i.e. the LEAD delegate). Co-constructed coaching is a new method for leadership development involving the coach and coachee acting as highly informed active partners in the leadership learning process (Kempster and Iszatt-White, 2012).

Co-constructed coaching allows reflexive dialogue within leadership development. It is a departure from mainstream coaching as it asks of the coach to pursue aspects of the coachee's situation through applying relevant theories to help dig deeper into a reflexive perspective. Reflexivity is reflecting on the consequences of reflection, action or inaction, it seeks to explore the taken-for-granted assumptions, norms and values that impact on everyday activity. Reflection is learning from experience, that is, "thinking about" something after the event (Cope, 2003). Reflexivity, in contrast, involves a more immediate, dynamic and continuing self-awareness, for example a coach needs to consider how their reflections and interactions with the coachee impact on how the coachee communicates and interacts with the coach – and thus how this affects the content/style of the coaching conversation.

The LEAD pedagogy provides the opportunity for workplace learning through a process of development, movement and change in knowledge and practices. Key is what the coachee (learner) is able to do as a result of that knowledge. Work-based adult learning encompasses more than the mere acquisition of skills; it includes the ability to reflect on experience, thereby identifying alternative ways of being and behaving.

On the LEAD programme, the role of the coach is to respond to the individual needs of the coachee and the process of releasing potential. Thus, the coach assumes the role of:

1. "Facilitator" of learning – providing support and encouragement.
2. "Empathetic provocateur" – encouraging critical thinking, challenging assumptions and norms and stimulating thinking.

The coach is both the facilitator and partner in the learning journey and in the co-construction of knowledge with the coachee (Kempster and Iszatt-White, 2012). Therefore, the coach facilitates the learning of the coachee and co-constructs either new knowledge or a different perspective of existing knowledge with the coachee.

For personal change to occur, it is necessary for the individual to engage in exploration of self, achieved through the use of critical self-reflection. However, reflection needs a companion to share it with, someone who can act as a mirror to reflect their thoughts back to them, that is, the coach and the wider LEAD cohort, all of whom provide interaction and debate and expose the learner to alternative views. Garvey et al. (2009) consider the non-linear coaching conversation to result in deep-seated transformation, while Neale et al. (2009) suggest that coaching is one of the most powerful ways of communicating, arguing that, when used effectively, it raises self-awareness.

The ability for deep reflection is attributed to the power of the coaching conversation and underpinned by an assumption that it is most difficult for the individual to achieve this in isolation. The coaching conversation enables the coachee to become aware of their values, beliefs and attitude that drive their actions and behaviours. Furthermore, it encourages the coachee to question and reflect on their identity and thus think critically. The greater the self-awareness an individual has, the greater the chance that they will be able to make more informed choices (Rogers, 1980).

It is through the power of dialogue that attitudes and performance are changed and shaped. For dialogue to occur it is necessary for participants to suspend their assumptions, requiring a sense of a shared quest for deeper insight and clarity. The coach is required to suspend their own assumptions for the purpose of gaining a deeper understanding of the world of the coachee (du Toit and Reissner, 2012). Furthermore, the coach challenges the coachee to do the same in order to gain a deeper insight into a particular situation or circumstance. Coaching deliberately provides specific time out from daily activities for guided thinking and reflection, which is facilitated by the coach.

The fundamental cornerstone of transformative learning is to understand how individuals construct meaning and in turn how such meaning will influence expectations of future events (Mezirow, 1991). It is through the process of creating meaning and changing of existing assumptions that transformative learning takes place, giving a different meaning to previous (or new) experiences. It is this process which develops autonomous thinking and the ability to learn within the coachee.

The outcome of such critical reflection and meaning making is a sense of freedom from perceived limited options that may have acted as a constraining force on the coachee, the result of which is often perceived in changes of behaviours. The depth of such learning is only achieved through critical self-reflection rather than through the acquisition of technical knowledge (drawing on the philosophical ideas of Habermas elaborated in Mezirow, 1991).

The way in which the coach "shows up" in the coaching relationship will determine the perceived value of coaching. Presence is a key requirement in the ability of the coach to cultivate real and lasting change for the coachee. Coaching directs attention to learning over time and the iterative process provides opportunities for practice and reflection. The equal status of the coachee and coach engaged in the co-construction of meaning further challenges the perceived role of superiority by either the coachee as learner or the coach as creator of knowledge. Instead, it is an equal partnership in which the one is incapable of creating meaning without the other and this co-constructive relationship is perceived as one of the key aspects of transformation on the part of the coachee.

A traditional coach is not seen as an expert of the content and does not offer solutions. In co-constructed coaching, the coach has to be or becomes an informed active partner. Both the coach and coachee are responsible for managing the coaching process, identifying what is relevant at a given moment in time so that the coachee takes ownership for their own development.

Coaching is thus essentially self-directed learning where there is a movement from conventional conversation (talking nice) to debate (talking tough) through to reflective enquiry (reflective dialogue) where the coachee is able to explore in safety the assumptions they hold, becoming aware of the possibilities of new knowledge unfolding. The coachee assumes responsibility for their own learning.

The use of coaching in leadership development has grown extensively. It is presently the zeitgeist within the leadership development industry. Setting aside the fashion influence shaping leadership development practitioners and customers (Guthey, 2005, 2013), the pedagogy of coaching within leadership development resonates with how managers learn to lead. That is, coaching allows the milieu of lived experience and the complexity of situated practice to be blended with thoughtful and structured reflection. It allows for the mechanisms shaping leadership learning to be brought to the fore and from which the manager can assimilate the learning into situated action. In this way the efficacy of learning is much more attuned to the immediate demands on the manager.

Explorations of theories on the best practices of leadership are helpful to stimulate questioning and reflection on practice, but applying prescriptions of the "best ten ways to lead" is fundamentally dangerous, despite its attractive and beguiling romanticism. In essence leadership is a complex practice developed in mutual relationship with others over time – intervening for enhanced effectiveness requires pedagogies that can be situated sensitively. Both coaching and action learning reflect such approaches.

5.   LEAD journey: month 3 – May

This chapter focuses on the layering of LEAD with another month of Masterclasses, Action Learning and the first telephone coaching session with the first signs of delegates connecting the various parts of LEAD becoming apparent.

(TELEPHONE) COACHING

Freddie called at exactly 9 am, his name and number illuminated on David's phone.

"Good morning. How are you Freddie?" enquired David.

Freddie didn't think he could share how he truly felt. He had been in work since half-past six, overseeing the loading of wagons with today's deliveries. He also had an avalanche of paperwork to sort and complete. Although Freddie had emailed David his reflection log a few days after the first coaching session and his preparation form 48 hours ago, he felt under-prepared and rushed. Only minutes before, people were knocking at his door and his mobile had been ringing whilst he was speaking to others.

Today was the first of four telephone coaching sessions Freddie had diarized with David. At the first face-to-face coaching session, David had explained the format of coaching and how the hour-long telephone coaching had been purposely designed to demonstrate that coaching could work just as well over the telephone as it could in person. Indeed, over the telephone, people's mannerisms and body language could not be observed, thus allowing the coach and the coachee to concentrate more on the spoken word, developing listening skills further and enhancing good conversational behaviour, allowing one person to finish speaking before the other spoke.

Freddie was now sitting at his work desk, his door was closed and he had his preparation form to hand. He was proud that he kept a clean and tidy desk. Everything had its place in his small but basic office. Files were organized, documents could be found when he needed them. His office window looked over the yard. The fully laden vehicles had left for the day. Outside, the sky was grey, overcast and rain was falling. Inside, the coaching session had begun. A Review, the 'R' of OSKAR, was under-way and Freddie was conveying the progress he had made on the agreed Actions (A) from the previous coaching session.

Freddie was smiling to himself as he confidently ticked his notes. He had instigated a monthly Board meeting; he had rolled out a bi-monthly newsletter to all staff to increase communications and a review of commu-nications across the company was underway. Moreover, he had an off-site meeting with his Commercial Director regarding creating a better business plan and he had also taken him through his 'Future Perfect'.

"I am now more driven and focused in important meetings," said Freddie. "I have already had a very productive 3½ hour long Board meeting."

"Well done, Freddie. That's excellent progress within the last month and I am impressed that you shared your Future Perfect with your Commercial Director. The review has worked well and is a good bridge to this session." Although this sounded a little "teacher–pupil", David was keen to affirm and praise the progress Freddie has made to build his confidence.

David continued. "What do you want to achieve from the coaching conversation today?"

David had deliberately used this form of words. He empathized with Freddie as he knew how difficult it was to understand what coaching truly is about even though delegates had all the materials and had a face-to-face session behind them. David was signalling to Freddie to think of an Outcome (O) rather than being preoccupied by a problem or an issue. Too often in business, managers focus on the problem, becoming an expert in what is not working rather than discussing what is going well or where the solution is already happening.

Like most delegates, Freddie was very vague about what he wanted to discuss. He didn't have a burning issue as such. He began by outlining various "problems". David was listening attentively, alert for useful ele-ments appearing that could be used to build the platform – the beginning in a Solutions Focused coaching approach in the quest for what works.[10] Subtly, David was turning talk about a problem into talk that, though not yet about a solution, was gently leading that way.

Like others at this stage, Freddie was drawn back into discussing what was not working. So when the Platform was constructed, David asked Freddie to write it down to ensure Freddie remained focused on the agreed Outcome (O), which in turn would help him imagine an appropriate

[10] Jackson and McKergow (2007, p. 227).

Future Perfect – the situation without the problem, the way Freddie wanted things to be.

In this first telephone coaching session, as Freddie began to describe the Know-how (K) – resources, skills and expertise that were counting towards the solution – David consciously affirmed, offering compliments to draw attention to what was counting. This appeared to give Freddie confidence that he was making progress. David invited Freddie to confirm what small actionable steps (A) he would do next.

"That was extremely useful and practical," said Freddie. "I cannot believe that I have gone from talking aimlessly to having a set of focused actions in such a short period of time. It was really helpful in talking through my problem. Effectively, I have just practised the coaching conversation I will have with my managers tomorrow.

"If I may, I can tell you now that I have been in work since half-past six this morning worrying about how we would fill the session. I know I have said this before but an hour is a long time to speak, yet our time on the phone has flown by. I guess it comes back to what was said at the induction – trust the process."

"You have made great progress," replied David in a reassuring tone (yet still trying not to sound too much like a parent or teacher). "What I would like you to do now is to reflect on this coaching conversation, complete your reflection log and email it to me within the next few days. Also, I would like you to complete the preparation form and send that to me a couple of days before our next session. Please do think about what you want from our next session as that will enrich our discussions. Have a good day."

"And you too," smiled Freddie as he clicked off his phone.

He sat back in his seat, swivelling towards the window. The rain had stopped, the clouds were lifting and beyond the rooftops of the sprawling town, he could see the large masts atop the rolling green hills. He thought about tomorrow and the first off-site meeting for his management team. Freddie was keen for them to input into the business plan and to create meaningful actions that they would take responsibility for that would drive change and improvements in their parts of the company.

"Yes, that's part of my Future Perfect," thought Freddie.

In over a hundred years of trading, the firm had never had a business plan so this was a big change. Never before had any managers been invited to get involved in a strategic matter. Freddie laughed to himself thinking, "They'll probably think they are going to get a telling off, especially since we are going out of the office. That's what they've experienced previously. Mmmmm, well, I need to get them on-side quickly so I had better spend the first five minutes tomorrow reassuring them that is not the case. I'll also make sure I use plenty of open questions. If they work in an Action Learning Set meeting perhaps they will also work here."

* * * * *

David was reflecting on his notes from his last session with Jane, who had shared her lack of confidence and her fluctuating confidence as a leader. In her role, she received little praise or recognition from her Board, which she acknowledged only added to her self-doubts. David assured her that was common amongst senior leaders. Jane also had disclosed that she lacked assertiveness, often regretting that she didn't follow her natural instincts, which led her to wallow in minutiae rather than taking a more strategic perspective.

"The Review (R) will be important today," thought David. "Her action to advance from last month's session would directly address her variable confidence levels, so hearing how she has progressed matters will be essential."

* * * * *

Jane called on time. She had prepared well for the session and was able to articulate what she had done better and what had helped since the last session.

Just like Freddie's session, the hour flew by.

"The reflection and preparation forms are a great help but I still found it difficult to focus on one issue," confided Jane.

"That's quite illuminating as you brought a new issue into the session today which we explored using the OSKAR model and you agreed a clear action. We spoke for a few minutes about what you wanted to discuss and granulated that down to form the Platform. So the issue was there. What we did together was to bring clarity to what exactly you wanted to discuss. So, I felt the coaching model and Solutions Focus approach worked really well and that you embraced it," replied David.

"Really? Thanks for the feedback. The Future Perfect is a new method of expressing what I want the world to look like – an outcome that I am satisfied with. I can visualize it but I find it difficult to describe the ideal scenario.

"As you know, my confidence wavers so that combined with my uncertainty on what I want to achieve, undermines what little belief I have in myself.

"What I found encouraging, that I didn't appreciate, was that aspects of my Future Perfect are occurring now, albeit fleetingly. What is more,

I don't have to change or do much to make improvements. That boosts confidence.

"So, if I can construct a Platform and articulate a clear Future Perfect then the whole process should flow much easier.

"If I may," continued Jane, "before I called you, I was disappointed that this was a telephone coaching session as I would have preferred a face-to-face session. I thought I would miss the engagement of eye contact and reading the body language, which I believe creates rapport."

"We deliberately expose you to the two different media," explained David, "so that you can experience that coaching can work just as well over the telephone as it does face-to-face. We believe that the 'leader as a coach' is an important leadership style to experience, understand and practise. Back in your organization, you will coach people both face-to-face and by telephone. By the end of your six months of LEAD Coaching you will be quite adept at coaching using Solutions Focus approach in both media."

"Actually it was not difficult, it was fine," observed Jane. "It was another mental barrier I had unnecessarily constructed. The absence of seeing each other focuses you on the words – the content of what we are talking about. Clearly I need to think about what I want to address but that only improves the quality of the discussion."

* * * * *

"I have been busy this month not only completing my actions from our last session but also implementing some of my learning from LEAD so far," said Bill.

It had only been two months since LEAD had begun but David was listening to a changed Bill. Gone was the frustrated manager who was thrashing out at his peers on the Overnight Experiential. Here was a more measured Bill, someone who wanted to improve himself. Bill was learning to become a delegate. He was also learning to become a leader.

"I have begun reflecting at home. I have never done that before. Every evening I now sit and speak about my business day with my partner. And do you know what? She is genuinely interested. Not only that, she is a very good listener and she also naturally asks open, insightful questions."

Bill laughed, "Ann knows from Action Learning that I am not very good at asking open questions or listening particularly well! I have found another good coach at home.

"We are only spending thirty minutes or so reflecting and chatting each evening but I feel it is bringing us closer together. It is also helping me to put into perspective my day and what I need to do next. I am also beginning to actively listen to what has gone on in her day too.

"I have also met privately with a couple of LEAD delegates to share our learning.

"Specifically, I have written down six key learning points from LEAD so far. I have observed that there is a pattern to them. Me. I am holding back the development of the company.

"The heroic–disempowered dynamic is a significant insight.

"I have woven more time into my diary to work on strategic matters rather than be weighed down totally by the minutiae of day-to-day activities.

"My weekly walk-about, which is my water cooler moment from the Leadership Masterclass, has been well received. I am trying to convey a more natural me, to let the staff see the 'off stage' leader. This will sound strange but every Wednesday I take what I call 'My Tour'. It is a diarized tour. Before I leave the office I grab the telephone list and plan where I am going, who I will see and what I will say to whom. Every week I see my staff and during the month I meet everyone. That may appear calculating. It is not. I need to do the planning to ensure it gets done.

"I've also begun to increase my self-awareness. I have met every one of my business partners for a one-to-one in the last month as I said I would," continued Bill, "and I have asked them how they perceive me and what they want from me as their leader. This has been illuminating. They want to do more; they want to take some of the work burden from me; they want to help me. It is incredible as this is exactly what I wanted them to do. The way I was acting and behaving stopped it from happening. I was disempowering them.

"We all know how easy it is to give a discount to win an order from a client or to appease a regular customer. From the first Business Masterclass, what I did not appreciate was how much more you had to sell to make up the margin you gave away in a discount. I went back into the company and found that we were discounting when we didn't need to; we were throwing away margin unnecessarily. So, with the agreement of the partners, I have changed our pricing strategy. We might lose an order or two but our overall profitability should increase."

"Well done, Bill. You have made giant strides both at a personal level and within your company. It is really interesting to hear how you are already weaving together your learning from different parts of LEAD to accelerate your overall development."

With the review complete, Bill and David began the coaching conversation.

* * * * *

ACTION LEARNING SET 2

A week later, Freddie, Jane and Bill met for their second Action Learning Set.

They were now familiar with the format – sitting in a closed circle, facing each other, laminated prompt sheets to hand together with their preparatory notes from which they would shortly disclose the issue they wanted to discuss and ask open, insightful questions of each other. All this was after the 'check in' from Ann with everyone sharing their position on the Jelly Baby tree.

"I cannot wait to hear how everyone has progressed their actions since the last meeting," thought Freddie as he locked his car and set off to the meeting room. "It's almost like a soap opera. Did Jane go into work and sort her issue out with her shareholders? If not, why not? I feel like I am being sucked into the next episode. We are a lot closer to each other now so I wonder if we will go beyond the politeness stage and start to ask more searching and more direct questions? It will be uncomfortable but I look forward to being challenged."

Four hours later, a mentally tired Freddie had his answer. Exhausted from the intensity of asking open, relevant questions and being asked searching questions of himself. He felt good as he walked back to the car park with Ann, reflecting on the morning's work.

"Do the other sets perform as well as us?" laughed Freddie, revealing his highly competitive nature again.

Ann side-stepped the question, letting Freddie continue.

"Everyone in our set had implemented their actions from the first session and had prepared for this one. There was a genuine sense of achievement and purpose amongst us as we recognized the progress each had made and acknowledged the importance of the issues we each wanted to address today."

"I always think that humour is a telling manifestation that a set is binding together and when you disclosed that you had three issues that you could discuss brought about some gentle ribbing," replied Ann.

Freddie winked. "Yes, I have to keep them on their toes. That'll get them thinking ahead of next month's session.

"I was impressed at the final review where my peers spoke of increased clarity as a result of the session, of being positive and feeling energized, and understanding the importance of preparation and doing what they said they would.

"In effect, we were embracing the adage, 'Say what you do, do what you say'. This is the basis of integrity which is a key leadership value. That was one of the messages from the last Masterclass speaker.

"I was impressed that such is the level of commitment to each other that we stayed back for 45 minutes to share our experiences of employee engagement in our firms. There is a genuine willingness to learn from each other.

"None of us can believe how so many problems are common to each other's business. This builds confidence. It certainly builds mine. I do enjoy listening to others' problems. I consider some peers to be ahead of me in terms of their leadership and business development. So they are giving me insights by discussing their problems and working out potential solutions.

"You can also learn from the question that is being asked. Bill enquired about the use of external facilitation to assist in dealing with key strategic matters that are often not progressed. When he asked that, I thought if someone as experienced as Bill is posing that question, perhaps I should consider it. We'll all benefit from external input during Shadowing and Exchanges."

As Freddie spoke, Ann was making mental notes. As a LEAD Facilitator, she was very interested in how the delegates were progressing as Action Learning Set members. During the session she would look for signs of bonding as a peer group, episodes of set members sharing experiences and learning, asking open questions, listening actively, reflecting on others' experiences, learning from actions taken and giving good feedback. In a sense, searching for the development of the important cohort institutional capital that all the cohort invest in and get the big dividend from. She had witnessed much of that today.

The set members still needed to form their questions better and improve the clarity when describing the 'G' of the GROW coaching model where G is the *goal*. Also, getting them to reflect on their actual learning in the process reviews was again quite difficult as they tended to reflect on the problem/issue from their air time. Still, that would come in time.

She was very satisfied with their progress to date as she bid *good day* to Freddie.

* * * * *

MASTERCLASS 3

Ann uploaded the handful of PowerPoint slides the next speaker was going to use, shared a short personal profile and sent the link to the delegates.

Subject: Growing Your Own Heroes – Professor John Oliver OBE

John is the former CEO of Leyland Truck, Europe's largest truck manufacturer. He was a prominent member of the buy-out team that rescued Leyland from receivership. John transformed the company from an unprofitable, declining truck-maker into the most cost-efficient operation of its kind in Europe through employee engagement, which John suggests is the safest, quickest and cheapest way of transforming your organization, delivering step-changes in efficiency, quality, employee morale and profitability. The principles can be applied in both large and small companies, across all sectors – private, public and voluntary.

* * * * *

The delegates knew the drill now. Pitch up thirty minutes or so before the Masterclass, sign in, grab a coffee, catch up with your peers and swap stories, whether it be a reprise of what is happening in their business, a LEAD experience or sharing a piece of learning.

A palpable sense of anticipation could be felt in the air. Today the group of business people were going to hear from a fellow business person, one of their own. Someone who was going to share his battle stories, the triumphs and disclose pointers that led to business success.

"I really look forward to the Masterclasses," said Jane. "I always take a few things back to the company to implement. When they say 'Masterclass', they mean it. It really is delivered by a Master in a subject area. Today we have a CEO who has led major transformative change in his business. I can't wait to hear what he has to say."

* * * * *

"My company will benefit from much of that session," Freddie announced. "There were so many good, practical points. It is what we need to do most – engage our staff more."

"I agree," said Jane, "but the session went so much further. Here was another business leader, like so many more we have heard from on LEAD so far saying that change starts with us, the leaders.

"John presented one of those crystallizing moments when he spoke of 'the shadow of influence' that we cast as leaders, both in our conscious and unconscious behaviour. The concept of the shadow of influence is easy to grasp but it is something I hadn't stopped to think about before and particularly how I am unknowingly impacting on people around me. I'm going to conduct a peer review within my firm and brace myself for feedback on the unconscious bits.

"For me, the overall resounding lesson from today's session was: *it is all my fault*, but in a good way. The only behaviour I have control over is my own, so it's lucky that by understanding my leadership style more, becoming more self-aware and making the necessary corrections, that will make me a better leader and my business more successful.

"Even before hearing the results of a peer review I can envisage the most obvious starting point is the very necessity of creating a personal development plan. I have realized that 'this is all about me'.

"I now understand that our role as leaders is to motivate others. It was liberating to hear that it's not about having all the answers just because you are more experienced or sit at the top of the tree. No, it's all about drawing out performance from people around you.

"I also really liked the simplicity of starting a staff meeting with 'what's troubling you today?' so that the staff set the agenda. That's something I'm going to adapt and try at our next full team meeting. Asking and listening to staff – I need to do more of that."

"Would you really put staff engagement as the first point on the Board agenda as John suggested?" asked Freddie. "That question stopped me in my tracks. Yes, staff make money in a business. Interestingly, when you bring money, employee engagement and the Board meeting together it does throw up an interesting conundrum. It clearly worked in his company.

"Certainly the employee attitude classifications within the 20–60–20 rule[11] and the paradox of leadership attention were insightful. The discussions lit the room up and it looks as if we are all like most business leaders who spend too much time with the bottom 20 per cent of our workforce rather than channelling our energies and focus onto the top 20 per cent who are the most positive and proactively wish to be involved in change. The key part that I did not appreciate was that by doing that, the mid-60 per cent then follow the top 20 per cent, meaning that 80 per cent of the organization is with you. Moreover, the bottom 20 per cent do not want to be left behind either and even they start following. So, you end up with the whole organization changing and moving in the direction that you wish with far less effort. The normal resistance to change is more effectively managed. That is a significant insight and something that I can start doing immediately."

"I hadn't thought about obstacles such as the 20–60–20 rule before," declared Jane. "I struggled to think about who is in the bottom 20 per cent. *I don't have them*. Then, I flipped my thinking as it may take a different form. Rather than poor performing, the bottom 20 per cent may be less

---

[11] Oliver, J.J. (2001), *The Team Enterprise Solution: A Step-by-Step Guide to Business Transformation*, Cork: Oak Tree Press, p. 227.

committed, more challenging to work with. They may not be always obvious, even hidden. What on the surface may appear as a positive contribution then something happens and it is not."

"I must say," continued Freddie, "John was personable, raw, practical and real. He was instantly likeable and I listened attentively to him as he shared his experiences, which I really appreciated. My ears pricked up further when he said that this common sense approach does not cost money as it can be driven by us, the leaders.[12]

"So you are right, Jane when you say 'It is all about me!' I need to ask, *what does my leadership shadow looks like? What does it say about me before I walk in the room?*"

"And following on from Steve's Masterclass last month where we now appreciate the importance of the leader–follower dynamic, *what is it that we actually say to our staff and how do we say it?*" noted Jane.

* * * * *

LEAD FORUM – MASTERCLASS REFLECTION

Bill (to everyone's surprise!) was one of the first to contribute online.

> The shadow concept is another eureka moment for me. It provides an additional layer of understanding to last month's hero-complex but it is more powerful and frightening.
>
> I believe that my shadow is the reason why I am so overwhelmed and not challenged. People (colleagues and friends) around me behave like sheep, following me, uncritically. My behaviour has caused this, I have made them like so. I cast a long shadow over the firm which I must address.
>
> The Masterclass speaker spoke about a 'no blame' culture. I agree but I am to blame for creating what I have created. The revelation is: if I have made it wrong then I can make it right. I feel hugely empowered by this realization. I can change what I do, how I behave and therefore the impact on others around me.
>
> The 'quick wins' achievable through simple improvements to communication and recognition were very enlightening too. I now better appreciate the power of communication and the need for it to be constant, at every level and two-way.
> Bill.

Two days later, Bill wrote again.

---

[12] Oliver, J.J. and Memmott, C. (2006), *Growing Your Own Heroes: The Common Sense Way to Improve Business Performance*, Cork: Oak Tree Press.

I have been feeling overwhelmed lately and I wanted to share my insight with you all as it may help you.

Reflection has just kicked in for me.

I have lots and lots of ideas and I do not know what to do with them. It is like having a bag of LEGO with ten different sets all mixed together. I have learned that my default learning method is linear and I have the need to break down all information into 'bite-size' pieces . . . into the ten different LEGO sets.

So, I have learned to overcome this limitation and embrace a lot of, apparently disconnected, data at the same time and resist trying to make sense of it immediately.

I now build whatever I want from this knowledge, bringing it all together. It is just like creating whatever you want from LEGO. I don't need to stick to following the picture on the front of the box. I do not need to be constrained by my old thought patterns. I can connect ideas from wherever in whatever manner to help me and my business.

This has allowed me to develop an understanding of far more complex concepts such as the relationships amongst my firm's stakeholders.

This has gone against a lifetime of learning methodology and is a breakthrough in how I act and behave.

Bill.

Jane shared her observations.

Hi Everyone

I have deliberately left it a few weeks before writing this post as I wanted to implement some of my takeaways from the Masterclass back in the workplace then see what I can learn from them before sharing them with you.

Firstly, I surveyed all staff using the Leadership and Management Style questionnaire.[13] Staff feedback included a desire for me to be more demanding and 'tougher' on people and to be more explicit in my expectations from staff. Someone commented it is 'easy to turn a no into a yes' from me! I listen to people's explanations, excuses, justifications and perhaps I'm too ready to empathize with their point of view. I think I'm being pragmatic and focusing on the solution rather than the problem, but perhaps this is giving out the wrong signals – that the problem isn't a problem!

So the team's ready for a more rigorous and demanding stance from me. In effect, they want me to move up the leadership spectrum towards the directive end from where I naturally stand – at the participative, empowering end. You may recall that was what we discussed at the Overnight Experiential and that I wanted to make that movement during LEAD. Well, the staff have just given me their blessing for me to move. Sammy will be proud!

The feedback also confirms that I have loyalty and respect from the staff. I have underestimated this and I have not made the most of it. I am not confident that I have the loyalty and respect of my two Board directors/shareholders and I plan to discuss what to do about that in my next Action Learning Set and my Coaching session too.

---

13 Oliver and Memmott (2006, p. 129).

It is my power, my problem, my opportunity, my responsibility to engender change and that begins with myself and it begins with insights from my LEAD learning. 'It is all about me'.
Jane

Freddie was the last of the three to comment:

The Masterclass alongside my learning from my very own role-play on the final activity at the Overnight Experiential has helped build a new communication structure within our business.

An employee newsletter is now completed bi-monthly and sent to the employees' homes (for reasons that may curtail negativity amongst partners where the employee could describe an inaccurate image and description of the work place).

The Leadership and Management Style questionnaire has helped to anonymously allow the employees to have their say on their manager's performance, particularly on how we do not manage poor performance well. They also want to see more of me!

The newly formed employee committee has let the 'voice' of the workforce be heard and provided some very valid points, issues and ideas for the company.

Directors have encouraged managers to relay essential information back to their teams after the Key Decision Makers meeting. This wasn't happening before as information channels were blocked.

These action plans have all been brought on by the realization that communication wasn't happening at all in our organization – in any format. The company endured a strict hierarchy with major barriers to cross-organizational communication with former long-standing directors struggling to communicate amongst each other, thereby meaning any interaction and exchange with staff at any level was minimal.

Employees have since been shocked at the pace of change, with the majority being content with the implementation of the improved communication channels. I realize that this is only the beginning of newly formed communication channelling and that as a business we must continue this through and add further value in our company message.

In the past at our company, under a virtual dictator regime, employees struggled to communicate with directors. My policy since becoming the Managing Director is having an open door and being approachable to all.

I have learnt throughout my LEAD experience that without the backing of the workforce the future vision and company targets are not achievable.

I find it hard to praise employees probably because it has never really happened to me – I can now hear Bill shouting, "Probably because you haven't done anything to be praised about".

In a sales meeting the other day I thanked each and every one of our external representatives. Two out of the six of them actually made a point of coming to my office afterwards and saying that my comments were gratefully appreciated.

Employee motivation will definitely rank much higher (sorry, I mean will actually be on the agenda) in my next Board meeting and in our Key Decision Makers meeting.

The Masterclass really opened my eyes to embrace a cost-effective, safe and quick route to far-reaching employee engagement. My learning and action points are:

- 20–60–20 rule – Realization that not all of the senior management team were in the top 20 per cent.
- Change my greeting reply – from 'not bad' to 'fantastic, great or really good!'
- The 'walk around' – daily chats with all staff, asking how their family is and using names. No discussion with bottom 20 per cent, only a 'Hello'.
- The thank you – email and face to face.
- Leadership shadow – communicated to fellow directors at Board level and through one-to-one coaching about the effects of your own shadow.
- Employee engagement now first agenda point on Board meetings – previously not even an afterthought.

I very much believe this 'simple' approach to employee engagement is the way forward and feel as leaders we must resist overcomplicating matters.
Freddie

THEORY SANDWICH 5   BECOMING A LEAD DELEGATE AND IDENTITY DEVELOPMENT

Discussion of "becoming" a LEAD delegate as participants learn to be a LEAD delegate by linking and combining learning from different elements of LEAD that bring the first insights into identifying with and "becoming" a leader in the context of their business. The importance of situated learning and Communities of Practice are advanced.

As introduced in theory sandwich 3, learning to become a LEAD delegate and identity development are key aspects of the LEADership Learning Cycle (Figure 5.1) and a delegate's learning journey.

The significance of context to individual learning is central to the role of engagement and interaction in a business setting, shaping what is learnt through an emphasis on what is considered important and salient to an individual within a community (Kempster, 2009a).

This is manifested by Bill who, after only two months on LEAD, has realized that the leadership outcomes he sees in his organization of disempowerment and his resultant feeling of being overwhelmed are due to his long-held desire to control, which has created and reinforced his heroic leader approach to running his company. Bill has reflected on his leadership learning from the first Leadership Masterclass (Chapter 4, Month 2) and the Employee Engagement Masterclass (Chapter 5, Month 3) with its focus on effective communication, engagement and a more participative

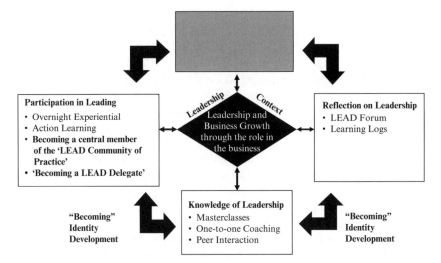

Figure 5.1   LEAD journey, month 3: construction of the "LEADership Learning Cycle" in the context of a LEAD delegate's development from their lived experience

leadership style. He has then connected the new knowledge with his experiences from the Overnight Experiential (Chapter 3, Month 1) – namely, the influences from his leadership timeline, his aim to move along the Leadership Style Spectrum and the experience of being made to sit on his hands to allow peers to speak. He used his new active listening and open question skills from Action Learning (Chapter 4, Month 2) to obtain insights from his staff and was surprised to hear that they were aligned to his own wishes. He has then further reflected and contextualized all that with what is happening in his business, which led to a "eureka" moment. This learning has directly led to a change in his own behaviour and his approach to leading.

Bill is beginning to learn the craft of being a LEAD delegate (see Smith, 2011) and is enacting the non-sequential LEADership Learning Cycle. He is becoming an independent learner, learning by experimenting through a learning cycle of experience. He is reflecting on each LEAD session, considering what the key messages are and what they mean to him and his company. He is contextualizing what he has heard, read and observed and he is contextualizing his own acts of leadership. He is then applying his new knowledge and experiences to the business context and changing his behaviour.

When talking about "studying leadership", Jackson and Parry (2011) state there are five activities: doing, seeing, talking, reading and writing. They argue "what we read influences what we see about leadership, what we talk about helps us to write about leadership, which, in turn, helps us to do better leadership" (2011, p. 5). LEAD uses all these activities within its various elements. Bill is beginning to learn how to better link and integrate these activities, though he is yet to bring them into a cohesive philosophical whole. All these activities manifest in changes in identity associated with leadership. This is one of the most significant aspects associated with the programme.

Bill is demonstrating that through the lens of identity development (Kempster, 2006) leadership as an identity can be seen as a fluid, dynamic process that connects an individual's past (lived experience) with both their present identity and future aspirational identity. Identity is argued to be an on-going activity (Kempster, 2006, 2009a).

Importantly though, an identity is not simply a claim alone. It requires a granting. In the context of the leadership relationship the person(s) following reacts to the person leading and allows this person to feel they are leading. In this way identity construction occurs as a malleable interaction between claimer and granter. Yet such claiming and granting cannot be separated from having impact on each other. For example, in the leadership relationship both leader and follower(s) shape the identity of follower becoming, alongside shaping the identity of leader becoming.

Very little has been explored in the literature to the development of identities – on the processes of becoming (save for the work of Tsoukas and Chia, 2002). Gergen (1971) first established the notion of aspirational identity – a desire to become. This was explored in a related way by Markus and Nurius (1986) as a process of socialization where they offered up the idea that people construct their desires of becoming related to "possible-selves" that reflect those they observe. Ibarra (1999) most helpfully drew a series of strands together to suggest identity construction as drawing on past lived experience that is applied to the current situation but importantly has an eye on the future anticipation of what the person wishes to become. Ezzy (1998) offered up the powerful idea that individuals have a sense of a narrative identity. They generate a plot and, like Ibarra, draw from their past and look to the future to describe a story in which they see themselves "emplotted" alongside others (1998, p. 245). The notion of a narrative identity has much resonance with mechanisms in LEAD – such as telling the story of the timeline of leadership learning in the Overnight Experiential or the process of coaching associated with the GROW model as an emerging narrative that becomes enacted in everyday activity.

Why is this important? In no small way it is because the sense of identity someone claims and is granted greatly shapes the way they behave. The notion of how behaviour and identity are linked has been influentially examined by Mischel (2004). Mischel argues that the personality of an individual is represented as a set of "behavioural signatories" that have tendencies to shape behaviour to suit recognized environmental situations. These "signatories" are representations of the self as an identity, drawn from memory recall of feelings, expectations, beliefs associated with people and past events. The behaviour associated with identity is a closely coupled process. Hill (2003), for example, looked at the development of junior managers. She suggested that as the junior managers moved towards a revised identity of a middle manager they "changed their perception of themselves and the world around them. They began to act like a manager; they began to become a manager" (2003, p. 84). The research undertaken to evaluate the LEAD programme reflects this assertion – there is identity change associated with leadership. Identity is closely aligned to behaviour. If an aspirational identity can be stimulated, so behaviours become modified associated with the (re)constructed identity. Importantly this is a sustainable change due to the association linked to the person's sense of identity.

When we speak of behaviours in the context of the leadership development approach that underpins LEAD we are speaking of practice – leadership behaviour anchored in activity that is situated in a business. And when we speak of a situated practice then we are making the commensurate link of identity shaping practices and vice versa. In this way identity is "being" and practice is "knowing and doing". These are the three focuses of all the LEAD activities and the focus of the outputs. It is this that Freddie, Jane and Bill are telling their stories of – the shift in their senses of becoming in terms of their identity – being; and their practice – their knowing and doing. Yet, as we say, this occurs malleably in interaction with their colleagues in their businesses. In this way the (re) construction of practice and identity of all are in a process of on-going becoming as the social capital develops.

A theory of social learning that very much connects together the aspects of the LEADership Learning Cycle model was introduced in theory sandwich 2 and is that of situated learning and the creation of communities of practice. It connects observational learning, enacted experience through participation with identity construction and the development of practice; but it also allows for the development of the three capitals we introduced: those of human, social and institutional.

Situated learning (Lave and Wenger, 1991) is learning that takes place in the same context in which it is applied. Situated learning is a model of learning that is socially constructed in a Community of Practice (CoP).

A CoP is defined as groups of people who share a concern, a set of problems, or a passion about a topic, and who deepen their knowledge and expertise in this area by interacting on an on-going basis (Wenger et al., 2002). A CoP is a joint enterprise brought together by mutual engagement as a source of coherence for the members (Wenger, 1998). On LEAD, this joint enterprise revolves around the delegates being owner/managers, with the mutual engagement being the becoming of leaders and engagement with the programme.

The notion of engagement in the "lived world" is extended by the concept of Community of Practice (Lave and Wenger, 1991; Kempster and Smith, 2014) whereby following a path of peripheral legitimate participation, individuals acquire knowledge by becoming full and active participants in a particular community. The degree of legitimacy accorded to individuals through their legitimate participation affects the range of learning opportunities and knowledge-in-action (Schön, 1983) offered to them. It is through the process of sharing information and experiences with the group, and by exploring real-life situations to find answers or to solve problems, that the members learn from each other and develop themselves personally and professionally (Lave and Wenger, 1991) as they share a common language around running an SME.

Kempster and Smith (2014) discuss that a CoP develops within LEAD through the notion of "enablers" who are the programme facilitators as they enable the delegates to become fuller members of the CoP. The LEAD facilitators provide the environment for learning.

By conceptualizing LEAD as a CoP the delegates become co-learners in learning how to be better leaders. They all have a valid contribution to make to the community. It is through this participation that the delegates progress towards fuller participation in terms of shared meanings and identities: an on-going knowing, doing and being that is shared and owned by the community (Kempster and Smith, 2014).

Smith (2011) and Kempster and Smith (2014) argue that the "enablers" engage with the delegates in a form of a co-constructed situated curriculum. There is an order of activities that all delegates participate in; however, the delegates bring a language and meanings from their own businesses and blend these together with the other delegates through the activities to form a unique CoP. Thus knowledge is co-constructed between the delegates and facilitators. The output is a CoP, with individuals becoming full participants with a central focus on learning about themselves and their businesses through a shared repertoire of meanings and identities of a LEAD delegate.

Typically, a delegate's identity and behaviour change with increased participation. Joining the programme as SME owner/managers, they often comment that at the beginning they do not feel like leaders, rather, they feel they are impostors. With little or no management team or hier-archical structure and sitting at the head of the company in the "leader" role, the owner/manager has nobody around them to share thoughts with (Smith and Peters, 2006). As they engage through the situated cur-riculum the delegates learn from one another. Through their "legitimate" participation they learn how to become a LEAD delegate, which, in turn, develops their own situated sense of being able to lead and results in an increased identification with being a leader. Remarks such as, "*I know that I am a leader*" or "*I have the confidence now to be a leader*" are common.

Increased identification with leadership can be seen as a by-product of learning to become a LEAD delegate. Legitimate peripheral participation is linked with learning to become a delegate (rather than explicitly becom-ing a leader). It seems curious that the end goal of leadership development occurs indirectly and covertly. Yet Kempster and Smith (2014) suggest this perhaps more adequately reflects naturalistic leadership learning – a sense that the co-constructed situated curriculum fuses together delegates' "business" language and experiences into being a full participant of a CoP that is about learning to lead. In turn, this becoming has an impact on their sense of identity outside of LEAD – there is a shift from owner/manager to leader.

6. LEAD journey: month 4 – June

This chapter describes the delegates' introduction to Shadowing where the delegates choose their partners. The chapter addresses their concerns of going into another business to observe a peer's leadership and introduces feedback models to provide constructive feedback. Delegates also reflect on their progress to date. Delegates continue with a further Masterclass, a telephone coaching session and meet in their Action Learning Sets again.

SHADOWING

It was a beautiful warm and sunny morning. The sky was blue and the sun was glinting on the lake. The stillness of the day was in stark contrast to the racing pulses that Jane and Bill were fighting to control as they got closer and closer to the next element in LEAD: Shadowing.

"This is the biggest challenge for most of us," said a worried Bill to a nervous Jane as they took a shortcut across the grass towards the meeting room where the pair had spotted the open plate-glass doors.

"Yes," replied Jane, "I am apprehensive again not only because it is new but also because I will be exposed both by going into someone else's business to observe them and then when they come into my company. Also, it will be the first time my team back at the office will directly encounter LEAD.

"However, it is really intriguing and I suppose there is a lot resting on it too."

They both caught up with a slow-moving Freddie.

"Hi guys. Before you ask, I am not looking forward to this. Four months ago when I came on LEAD I was really worried about Shadowing and Exchanges but I satisfied myself with the fact it was four months away. Well, that day has now arrived."

"I know how you feel," Bill said in an attempt to reassure his friend. Yes, friend. They had gone beyond just being peers. They had met up a couple of times outside of LEAD and work for a drink, for a catch up and to swap a joke or two. They had come a long way from sharing their timelines on the first day of the Overnight Experiential. They were confidants now on selected business matters, offering an insight or piece of advice when it was needed. In some instances, when it was much needed.

"I was just about to say to Jane it is a universal fear of being intrusive with others," continued Bill. "What right have I got to shove my nose into someone else's business? What on earth have I got to tell them that could possibly be of interest to them?"

"I am pleased with what I have achieved so far. It is as if I have climbed to the top of the first mountain," puffed Freddie, "then, gosh, there is another mountain behind it, but this time it is larger and steeper."

Bill smiled. "We can all take strength that we know each other a lot better now, some more than others, which will help in this part of the journey. I am not sure who we will get as partners."

"I do wonder who I am going to be with. Can I add value, and will they be good for me?" remarked Freddie, a touch selfishly.

Pausing for a few seconds, he continued. "I wonder how much I will benefit from the Shadowing and Exchanges. David and Ann said, 'trust the process' and I believe in what they say."

Ahead of today's Introduction to Shadowing Day, Ann had posted a new topic on the LEAD Forum inviting all delegates to share one thing they were looking forward to and one concern they had. Ann recognized that this pulse check was useful at many levels. It encourages the delegates to begin to think about the Shadowing and Exchange experience; it allows delegates to read each other's comments reinforcing that they are not alone; and, it provides Ann and David with an insight into how the delegates are feeling.

LEAD FORUM – INTRODUCTION TO SHADOWING DAY: PREPARATION

Freddie shared his comments:

> I believe Shadowing and Exchange will add an extra layer and level to the networking and Action Learning Sets we have encountered to date within LEAD. It offers a valuable insight to explore another company from the inside, to potentially learn new systems and to exchange ideas between each other.
>
> As always I am sure that there will be some 'open' and honest questions raised about our businesses from Shadowing, which will benefit both parties moving forward.
>
> My concerns centre around what schedule to work to during the day at my business and which areas of the company and ultimately employees to get involved as this is a trip into the unknown for me! I'm very good at guided tours but they normally last twenty minutes, not a full day!

All the best and look forward to this new challenge.

Jane had mixed emotions:

I imagine that shadowing someone in another business will reveal lots of interesting approaches to management that I'll want to pinch. It will probably reflect back at me some of the things that work well within my own business (without me previously noticing or thinking about them) and some of those that don't work very well within my own business but that I haven't done anything about until now. . . .

My concern is the fear of the unknown, as always. Fear of someone shadowing me and thinking, 'Oh my, you do what?!' Fear of not being able to offer anything really useful back to the business I'm exchanging with. All the usual gremlins are at play. No doubt I'll be reassured when we meet!

A cautious Bill wrote:

Frankly I am a bit apprehensive because I don't know what this is going to entail so there is fear of the unknown. I think we will all have a much better idea and be more confident after the Introduction to Shadowing Day.

* * * * *

"The purpose of the Shadowing and Exchange is to provide an opportunity to learn from each other's organizations, learn about your own behaviour and learn about your own organization through a fresh pair of eyes," said David to the full cohort.

"Shortly you will be choosing a partner or partners to work with in pairs or triples. Shadowing and Exchanges enable you to look at your peer's leadership style and business and compare these with your own. It provides an opportunity for self-reflection about your own leadership style and the culture within your business. You will also learn about the ways another business operates and see if the different perspectives and practices can be beneficial to your own business.

"The Shadowing and Exchange process provides a valuable opportunity to give and receive feedback. We will share with you tips on how to observe leadership and to give and receive constructive feedback as you will be doing this during Shadowing."

David went on to explain that the process is made up of two elements – shadowing and exchanging – and that these involve pairs of delegates or triples, either drawn from Action Learning Sets or the wider cohort, taking part in reciprocal visits to each other's businesses.

"You will also receive a Shadowing and Exchange workbook which will guide you through the process. In today's session we will help you understand how to do the Shadowing. You will work with your partner or partners to agree on the objectives of what you want to get from the process. You will then conduct the Shadowing and in a couple of months' time there will be a feedback session to share your experiences and learning with your peers in the wider cohort. At that stage we will introduce you to the Exchange part of the process."

Ann joined in. "On LEAD, we encourage you to reflect on your learning as you progress. You are now beginning your fourth month on LEAD so by using the learning logs, we want you to reflect on what you have learnt and what changes you have made to you and your business as a result. When you have completed the learning logs please turn to your neighbour and share your LEAD success stories."

The silence of the delegates diligently filling in their learning logs was in stark contrast to the noise and excitement that followed as they swapped stories with great gusto, much arm waving, genuine interest and delight.

It was then time for the business of the day, the moment most had been dreading ... choosing their partner. Thankfully, this was not a beauty parade or sprint across the floor to get to the person you most wanted to be with. Nor was it a return to the haunting memories of the school yard where no one wanted to be the last in line when being picked for the sports team. *Who would want me?*

Ann explained the one-minute elevator pitch that each delegate was to make. She encouraged the delegates to think deeply about what they wanted from Shadowing and what they could offer in return. She asked them to consider what kind of organization they might benefit from pairing up with. She advised them to choose someone different from them and not the same type of organization. The partner could come from the wider cohort and not necessarily from the Action Learning Set that they are members of. Finally, Ann reminded everyone that their Shadowing role was as an observer, as a *fresh pair of eyes* and that they were not acting in their professional role.

By choosing their own partners, David and Ann knew, from experience, that the delegates were more likely to be happy with their pairing. This emphasized that it is the delegates' responsibility to undertake the Shadowing with the support and guidance from the facilitators.

Within an hour, everyone had prepared their individual pitches, stood up and spoken, which again gave them the opportunity to practise and improve their skill of speaking in front of others. This process of choosing a partner engendered a confidence. The bonds that had developed between them and the trusted environment they had created reassured all.

It was now time to choose.

* * * * *

"It never ceases to surprise me how quickly they choose their partners," remarked David to Ann.

It had only taken ten minutes. Whatever slight awkwardness the delegates faced, they quickly got over it without coming across as overly keen and grabbing a partner.

Jane and Freddie had paired off as had Bill with James, one of two brothers from a long-established family business.

"The elevator pitch is in effect a sales pitch, 'Pick me because I can really help you and you can help me'," said Freddie. "I enjoyed that, Jane. It was nothing like I imagined it to be. Then LEAD never is – that seems to be a repeating pattern. I was one of the first ones to speak, which helped as it then allowed me to concentrate on what the others said. I wrote three or four names down that I would have been happy to go with.

"I also benefited from our very brief chat of a minute or two. It wasn't the case of, *well do you want to go with me?* It was very much, *do you think you can add something and vice versa?* We quickly discovered that we could and I know I made the best decision. I believe we can certainly work together and make a difference to each other's company."

Jane knew she could work with anyone and made sure she chatted to a number of peers. Freddie's business was of a different magnitude but was in an industry that piqued her interest and Freddie genuinely seemed interested in her and her company.

Bill wanted to partner with someone from a substantial business as he wanted a challenging experience. He wanted to be stretched. He'd heard that James's company was a successful business. Bill liked James and recognized that he was a very different personality from him, which he thought would bring a very different response. Bill also felt that James would be very honest and would not pussyfoot around. He felt James would tell him how he saw it. Bill relished critical feedback on his leadership and his business. So although James approached Bill first, Bill was quite selfish as the pairing was about what he would get out of the experience rather than what James would get out of it.

"We are going to spend the next couple of hours preparing you for Shadowing," said Ann. "Firstly, we are going to coach you on observing and then on giving and receiving constructive feedback."

* * * * *

"You often hear people say two heads are better than one, well two pairs of eyes are better than one as they see more," laughed Jane.

"Yes, it's amazing what you see and what you miss," remarked Freddie.

It was lunchtime now and the pair were reflecting on the observation activities.

"I had not considered how much each of us remember and how we all filter things differently," continued Freddie. "Every individual notices different things and interprets things differently too. We have biases, which I know I have never stopped to think about. These biases mean we interpret things that we see in a certain way. They also block what can be seen too."

Freddie pondered. "I guess that is why we see what we want to see."

Jane nodded. "The filters are interesting. As leaders, we can't and won't be everywhere or see everything, therefore an organizational filter is applied by our followers, our managers. The more layers of managers, the more filtering that will be applied."

"We have a few layers in our place, Jane. I am sure your fresh pair of eyes will see different things. I am hoping that you'll be able to ascertain culturally what is going on in my business. It will be good to receive your perspective on how things are done in my company."

"The message was strongly made by the LEAD facilitators that in the context of Shadowing we can't assume," noted Jane. "We have to listen intently. We must allow our eyes to be opened to things that we have become blind to, things that we would ordinarily filter out."

"Understanding how to give and receive constructive feedback will be very useful, both in Shadowing and back in the workplace. As a senior leader I have the power of position in my business that I can use, if I want, to get my message across. That'll not work when I am feeding back to you, Jane, a fellow managing director, in your own company."

"Like everything on LEAD, it is the practical simplicity of the tools and techniques and the personal and business relevance that appeals to me," said Jane. "We all have to provide feedback. But how often do we stop and think about it? Do you have a process for providing feedback that brings consistency to your approach to leadership? I know I don't but I have one now.

"We all laughed watching the video of poor feedback during The Performance Appraisal. Poorly delivered feedback can have an adverse effect," continued Jane.

"By reframing and summarizing a situation, feedback becomes a vital part of learning. Feedback is like holding up a mirror – it provides someone with information about their strengths and gives them clear areas for change.

"I realize I need to *own* the feedback and take responsibility by using 'I'. It is better saying, 'I felt unclear about your company's marketing strategy' rather than declaring that 'Your marketing strategy is poor'.

"I appreciated the pointers on giving positive feedback. I know I jump in too quickly and start with negative feedback focusing on what is going wrong. I recognize that it cannot just be all positive, I need to address the areas of concern without falling into poor practice of sandwiching negative comments between two positives. I noted the suggested two-to-one ratio of two pieces of positive feedback to one concern but crucially they should be made in that order. The aim is always to provide learning points to improve rather than barbed criticisms."

"I agree, Jane. Those are all good insights. Feedback is something I do without critically thinking about how best to do it. I found by focusing on the person's specific behaviour rather than generalizing about them as a person the most revealing. I don't like conflict, preferring to talk around a subject. However, as leaders, we must take responsibility and be accountable for the specifics. If we don't, who will? No one!

"The BOFF feedback tool should be useful to help bring responsibility and accountability alive. Again it is memorable, simple and thus more likely to be used in practice."

Freddie tries to recall it without success and reaches for the hand-out:

Behaviour – describe the behaviour you wish to provide feedback on.
Outcome – describe the result of the behaviour in question.
Feeling – how the behaviour / result made you feel.
Future – what you expect in the future.

"Being able to practise that a few times with you in the last session was useful so be prepared to be BOFFed in Shadowing," chortled Freddie. "I'll also try it out in work when I get back tomorrow."

Freddie continued. "As you know, my listening skills are not the best so I wrote down the three things to do when receiving feedback. Firstly, listen to the feedback, don't interrupt or justify things. Secondly, clarify if necessary and ask a question, don't jump to conclusions. And thirdly, you can ask for feedback on certain areas.

"I think that last point is important as during Shadowing you cannot feedback on everything so we will need to consider, 'What is it that we want feedback on?' There must be absolute clarity on what we each want from Shadowing so we both understand what we need to observe."

"The other thing I learned this morning that I will use for my own self-reflection," noted Jane, "is asking myself three questions. What went well? What would I do differently next time? What have I learned from this experience? I can apply this to Shadowing but actually I can use the questions in any aspect of my life. I can also modify it and use it as a reflective structure when working with my teams back in the office."

Jane looked at her watch. "It's time to go back in."

"You know what?" observed Freddie, "We have chatted all the way through lunch and we have not once turned our phones on to check for messages. I scoffed at David and Ann when they said by the end of LEAD we would not need to check in. Well they were wrong. It only took us until we were a third of the way through LEAD."

The pair laughed and went into the afternoon session.

* * * * *

The delegates began the afternoon agreeing dates to undertake the Shadowing and establishing some "ground rules" for Shadowing reflecting the code of conduct each partner wished to have observed in each other's organization. The LEAD facilitators handed out the Shadowing and Exchange Workbook to the delegates and guided the pairs on how to use the workbook and in particular what parts had to be completed today.

Importantly, each partner agreed the objectives both for shadowing their partner and for their partner shadowing them. Guidance was given on what delegates may want the observer to see and developing the internal space that is receptive to feedback. Delegates then began to work together, noting the strengths they could offer to their partner and the strengths their partner could offer to their own business.

David and Ann then focused the delegates' thinking on what information they needed for Shadowing. What did they need to know about the person they were going to visit? What didn't they know and thus what did they need to find out? The delegates were challenged to consider what it is they would hope Shadowing would accomplish and what they needed to do in order to prepare themselves to shadow their partner. The delegates then considered what they needed to do in order to prepare themselves and their organization for Shadowing.

Finally, the 'Shadowing Brief' was agreed, highlighting the three areas that each partner wanted to be observed and receive feedback on. A title was given for each, with supporting details.

"This is very thorough," remarked Bill, "but then it needs to be as after all we can't be let loose in someone else's company."

Bill turned to James and said, "It is really important that we get the most out of the experience. Earlier when we were doing the observation activities together it felt like you and I were a team. We were looking at everyday ordinary things together and we observed lots of behaviour that you take for granted that you don't even notice normally but I think it engendered a position of trust between us. I am looking forward to working with you."

* * * * *

(TELEPHONE) COACHING

Freddie was pleased with himself. By his own assessment, he had opened today's coaching session with an excellent Review (R). He shared with David how he had progressed many actions and dealt with them by applying some of his LEAD learning.

This was the second of the four diarized telephone coaching sessions. Freddie had shared his reflection form and his preparation form in advance. He was better prepared than he was last time. Familiarity with the process had given him more confidence.

On the phone, Freddie sounded enthusiastic and was keen to learn and improve. He had become a great advocate of all aspects of LEAD. He was involving his senior management team in his LEAD learning and introduced concepts such as business planning, segmentation, employee engagement, Future Perfect and open questions. He was discussing matters with them and listening to their views.

"I feel that my reflection skills are far more enhanced. I observed my Commercial Manager in our recent senior management meeting and I heard him using closed questions. Three months ago, I would have done the same. I have changed. Before I speak, I now reflect on how I will ask a question. I also let silence continue. I no longer jump in. I leave the space for others to fill."

Freddie shared the headlines from the successful off-site business planning day he'd had with his management team, though it did throw up some concerns about the weakness of the management team he had inherited. Nevertheless the managers had bought into Freddie's vision, understood the financial targets and had agreed to create their own departmental action plans playing their individual parts in meeting the collective targets. There was a groundswell of energy and a growing sense of optimism for a brighter future but this was in danger of being undone by a critical matter, a burning issue that was the subject of today's coaching conversation and that would require sensitive handling. Freddie wanted to address the volcanic behaviour of his father and the adverse effect that it had on the day-to-day running of the business. The shadow of his father was omnipresent.

Freddie was able to verbalize the Platform quickly and richly describe his picture of his Future Perfect. The Outcome, the 'O' of OSKAR, was clear. Freddie had clarity, arguably for the first time in his short tenure as a business leader. Scaling (S) was next and it very much had its place in the coaching conversation as it enabled Freddie to appreciate where his father's contributions were of value and where there were instances of the Future Perfect occurring now, albeit briefly.

"There is hope," observed Freddie.

David then explored what Know-how (K) was available inside and outside the firm. Freddie was pleased to discover there was much assistance available through the external advisors such as the company accountant and solicitor as well as from LEAD peers from family businesses who had dealt with similar matters previously. As a skilled Solutions Focused coach, David used his judgement to share with Freddie his expert knowledge in the field of succession in family businesses to improve his understanding of what LEAD resources were available. Freddie agreed three Actions (A) that he committed to complete before the next coaching session in a month's time.

"Thank you for listening, David. It has given me the opportunity to discuss a very sensitive matter and I now have some direction. This is exactly the support I need at this moment in time."

* * * * *

David was making his own notes following the coaching conversation with Jane.

"In many ways, Jane is the perfect coachee," noted David. "She prepares well and acts upon the agreed actions. In the Review (R) she was able to give several examples of positive outcomes since our last session. She had carried out the agreed *next step* and that had gone better than she could have hoped for. That has boosted her confidence.

"There were lots of opportunities for affirmations. We spent some time on the preparation form and the Platform that she wanted to build came to the fore. Lots of Know-How (K) counters were identified and an Action (A) agreed.

"The session started and finished on time.

"Jane still lacks confidence in her ability to lead. However, this is improving month by month."

* * * * *

"That was really helpful, David. This is the first time I have ever spoken to anyone about this issue. It's important to bounce ideas off someone who understands me, my business and the process of leading change."

"That's quite an accolade from Bill," thought David.

"Bill still wants answers, a mentor. He is more than capable of working things out for himself and reflecting. He is still very directive and impatient but he is aware of those traits. I do believe he is more measured in his discussions with me than before but I sense he is straining at the leash with others. As long as he manages that and gives people the space to step forward then that will be progress."

To deal with his growing sense of being overwhelmed, Bill had identified that he needed to recruit a number two, someone who could take on some of the technical aspects of his professional role. Bill reasoned that would free up his diary, enabling him to spend more time on developing the clarity and consistency of the necessary inputs to be an effective leader in order to improve the process of leading to ensure that the overall leadership of the firm achieves what it sets out to achieve.

Change was underway and, by his own admission, Bill's staff were on a steep learning curve. An explanation of what to do, how to do it and why it needs to be done had been provided in the context of each department, team and individual's job role. Training had been given. Bill had realized much support was needed and he was motivated to relentlessly follow through. He was going through his own personal pain barrier as ensuring tasks were completed was not his strong point. Bill knew he had no option. He must lead by example and to do that he had to find more time, which meant that he needed to recruit a number two. Recruitment had a cost as it would add to the overheads but Bill had sensed in his own mind that the cost of not investing and continuing with the status quo was much higher. This was not a financial cost. It was a cost to his own health, peace of mind and a barrier to the pace of change.

* * * * *

ACTION LEARNING SET 3

Freddie, Jane and Bill were reflecting on their third Action Learning Set.

"This was the best Action Learning Set meeting that we have had so far. We all had very good coaching conversations today," said Jane. "Completing the preparation sheets in advance makes a big difference as it focuses our thinking on what we want to achieve from the session."

"Everyone contributed as well. There was much humour and some gentle ribbing," winked Freddie. "I had deliberately skipped over explaining progress on my two actions in my feedback from the last session and as Ann hadn't pulled me up I thought I had got away with it. But as we went through my air time, Bill brought up the two actions and I had to confess that I hadn't done them, which is why my problem was in part still there. I was glad you all laughed when I said, 'I thought I'd got away with that!'"

"Remember, we all have a commitment to assist each other, which was one of our Ground Rules," chided a jovial Bill.

"I am glad I went third today," observed Jane. "Ann had to intervene on a couple of occasions to help others nail the Goal (G) but by my air time, I had worked out the Goal for myself. That allowed us more time to explore the Reality (R) and discuss Options (O) which was very useful for me as I was then able to select the appropriate Way Forward (W)."

"That was the same for me too. I smiled when Tom said that he knew his Goal was a little vague and would need some help in honing it down a bit, which we then helped him to do," said Freddie.

"Did you notice that we were almost always using open questions?" asked Bill. "You checked yourself a few times, Freddie, when you realized you were about to ask a closed question but you quickly reframed your questions."

"Thanks, Bill. I admired Tom's approach," said Freddie. "He has struggled with forming open questions but he wrote them out to form them before asking them and after the first air time he was much better at it, even commenting on his improvement himself."

"I think that helped Tom as the number of suggestions he offered was significantly less than the last session," remarked Bill. "I felt that he now appreciates the benefit of asking open questions rather than just providing a solution, although sometimes he still can't help himself."

They all laughed.

"Overall," Bill continued, "I noticed that we only used the laminated sheets occasionally. I believe we are becoming more confident creating our own questions rather than selecting from the list of prompts."

"I still need to refer to my *cheat sheet*," smiled Freddie. "I can't throw it away yet."

"Yes, our open questioning is getting better and we are also more aware of asking leading questions," noted Jane. "In your air time Bill, we each knew of practical solutions so instead of suggesting anything and leading you to an answer, I felt that we were asking you a series of open questions that allowed you to come up with the same solutions that I certainly had in mind. Ann recognized that in her summation so we should be pleased with our progress."

"We should also be satisfied that we largely managed the GROW process ourselves," added Bill. "Ann did not have to interject nearly as much as she has done previously. She did reassure us throughout, as she pointed out when we moved into the different stages of the GROW model. Also, when there were instances of one of us presenting the Goal and the Reality at the same time she reined us back."

"It is helpful, at the start of the session, being reminded what the purpose of Action Learning Sets is, what the GROW model is, how to use it and timings," remarked Freddie. "It helps me gather my thoughts.

I have begun using GROW back at the office but coaching still does not come naturally to me. I need to concentrate when using GROW. It is not easy asking open, insightful questions and to actively listen to what is being said. There is also a skill in moving through the different stages of GROW, spending the appropriate period in each part and asking relevant questions for that stage."

"I agree," said Jane. "We all have very similar issues. It is invaluable to me to be able to work through and resolve difficult people issues with like-minded peers. Many of your problems are my problems, so learning from you on what you have done or will do helps me enormously. I have picked up a few tips on different things to take back to the office."

"Undoubtedly," agreed Freddie. "Being able to discuss major issues in confidence and get resolution is extremely powerful. This deals with the isolation we all feel as leaders."

"I sense that we are also becoming more reflective," said Bill. "We are actively commenting in the reviews after each air time. I thought that we had an excellent final review where we all shared one key learning point from today's session."

Ann had observed a real sense of satisfaction from everyone that the session went well. The high level of trust that had been built between the set members had created an environment for the open, free-flowing conversations in the small group. They had openly discussed financial problems, time management and prioritization, issues within family Boards and problems with fellow directors who were also friends, which made poor performance a more difficult subject to tackle. These were subjects that they could not discuss with those closest to them as, more often than not, those were the people they had issues with.

As Bill observed, "How often do business leaders get the opportunity to share their troubles and woes with a peer group of highly talented and experienced individuals with such a diverse range of skills in such a trusted and confidential environment?"

Jane and Tom had stayed on after the set had finished as both had services of interest to each other's companies. Although David and Ann had stated at the beginning of LEAD that delegates were not there to sell to each other, such was the level of trust that was developing, that the peers were opening trading discussions. Privately, David and Ann were pleased, as local companies buying from local companies particularly within the LEAD network of companies was a business objective that they were keen to see be advanced. However, they recognized the delicate nature of such business activities affecting the learning process. A question they struggled with was how such conversations impact on the development of the cohort as institutional capital. Or is it leakage into social capital as part of extending business networks? Both agreed, though, that this needed to be carefully handled.

* * * * *

MASTERCLASS 4

Ann smiled to herself as she uploaded the message to the Forum. This Masterclass neatly dovetails with the first Masterclass but it will test everyone's thinking.

Maximizing Your Operational Success – Dr John Mackness

> John's session ensures that businesses are able to structure their operations along two themes: order winners and order qualifiers. In essence, are you able to be selected for bidding and are you able to deliver customer value? The session will address balancing what you need to do to win business and what must occur to sustain offering customer value over the long term. Every organization needs to be aligned to delivering customer value – but do you know what this is and how to deliver it? John will seek to illuminate how SMEs can begin to orientate themselves towards such delivery.

* * * * *

"The great thing with LEAD Masterclasses," said Freddie to Jane, "is that we pick up so many good practical pointers in the morning and in the afternoon we can begin implementing them."

"I wouldn't go as far as saying implementing," said Jane. "Some of us need time to mull things over first."

"I had never considered that the way we do business, the Operation, could give us strategic advantage," continued Freddie. "Nor had I thought about running the company from an operations perspective before either. And, what is more, my learning from today can be linked back to my learning from the Business Planning Masterclass. Suddenly, I am beginning to knit things together."

Bill intervened. "I agree. The Masterclass was interesting and enjoyable. It has made me think about the alignment of the different departments in my company to the needs of the customers in the different segments. Previously our strategic approach, if I can use such grandiose words to describe what we do, was a one-size-fits-all. Clearly that is not correct as you cannot treat everyone the same if their needs are different. It's obvious when you think about it. The problem is that we are too busy doing our daily jobs to stop and think about the things that strategically matter. However, we understand the time problem and we are using LEAD to focus our thinking and efforts on the key matters."

"The thing that struck me most," continued Jane, "was the need to make a 'Mafia Offer'[14] – an offer that can't be refused. The conversion of new business prospects into clients has been particularly slow and challenging in recent years, so I am going to address that by creating a Mafia offer."

"Bottlenecks and The Theory of Constraints[15] were a revelation to me," said Freddie. "I recognize that my approach is wrong as I have been foolishly driving everyone to be busy. Understanding what the bottleneck is, or bottlenecks as we may have more than one across the different parts of the firm, and ensuring that the bottleneck is fully utilized is yet another eye opener for me. Before you say it Bill, I'll add it to my growing list of eye openers."

The pair laughed.

Bill moved the conversation on to money, a subject close to the hearts of all the LEAD peers. "Allied to that was the telling observation that the bottleneck actually determines the profitability of the firm. I don't know if I have a bottleneck or where it is. John said that I will have one. But if I don't know what it is then, rather frighteningly, I do not know where we make our money. In terms of time, money and resources, it follows that I could be investing in the wrong things as I should be investing in making the bottleneck more productive."

If silence is golden then the triumvirate had just made a fortune as Freddie, Jane and Bill paused to consider the point that had just been made.

"So, Bill, your key question is, *what is your bottleneck?* Mine is, *what is our Mafia Offer?*" said Jane.

"As you both know, we are working on creating our business plan," said Freddie, "So, my question is, *how could our operations link with competitive strategy?*"

* * * * *

[14] Goldratt, E. (1994), *It's Not Luck*, Aldershot: Gower.
[15] Goldratt, E. and Cox, J. (2004), *The Goal: The Process of On-going Improvement*, 3rd edn, Aldershot: North River Press.

LEAD FORUM – MASTERCLASS REFLECTION

Jane had volunteered to be the LEAD Forum champion and had opened a Discussion Topic.

> I created a Mafia Offer and trialled it with two small prospective clients who needed work doing immediately. The Mafia Offer concept has helped me to look at our proposition from the clients' perspective and to understand the obstacles or hesitations that each felt based on their particular circumstance. Neither company had used our type of service before so the 'fear of the unknown' and reticence to commit finance to something unproven was the sticking point.
>
> Because we were confident in what we could achieve for them, we put our money where our mouth is and have done 'introductory deals' for each – mafia offers that were either risk free, or very, very low risk for the client. Each deal was different but amounted to a similar level of risk and reward for our company.
>
> We won both pitches and the development of trust has been amazing. While it has meant us giving away some time for 'free', it's no more than we would do in setting up a new client in the first few months anyway except they see it, know it and appreciate it.
>
> Jane

An impish Freddie was next to share his learning:

> Well what did I gain? Another rather large list of actions and a larger list of what I'm not currently doing!
>
> I now understand that Order Winners are those factors which maintain and win business, whereas Order Qualifiers may not win business but play an important part in retaining business.
>
> I think there is a significant opportunity to build on our findings from our strategic planning sessions where we have now identified customers' buying reasons. From these we can establish the Order Winners and Order Qualifiers. This has our immediate focus.
>
> We will then examine the ordering and supply process and attempt to identify our bottleneck.
>
> Freddie

THEORY SANDWICH 6   OBSERVATIONAL LEARNING

Description of the next part of the LEADership Learning Cycle and the importance of observational learning to Shadowing in the small business context. Exploring the difficulties of owner/managers being able to observe a variety of notable others, as well as having the motivation to observe and what to observe. Exploring the application of learning from the programme into the SME context.

Becoming a leader in a particular community is greatly shaped through processes of observational learning.

We have outlined in theory sandwich 2 how informal leadership learning can be described as development through experiences where owner/
managers learn, grow and undergo personal change as a result of the roles,
responsibilities and tasks encountered in the jobs (McCauley and Brutus,
1998) and so reflect emergent and accidental events rather than a deliberate and conscious approach to development. We now wish to explore in
more depth processes of observational learning.

Bandura (1986) argues that one of the key capabilities of individuals is
their ability to learn as if they were taking part in the experience. It is a fundamental building block of knowledge that is refined through enactment
in the workplace (Anderson and Cole, 1990). The enactment in a particular context has been explored in the previous theory sandwich with regard
to situated learning. Here we wish to unpack processes of observational
learning that occur within situated learning.

Observational leadership learning is seen to sit within notions of relational learning (Robinson, 2007; Cope et al., 2011). Drawing on this
relational perspective we suggest that a leader's (and a follower's) idiosyn-
cratic lived experience is infused by a culturally embedded understanding of leadership (Meindl, 1995; Gemmill and Oakley, 1992; Uhl-Bien,
2003; Ely et al., 2011) transmitted through the multitude of significant
others. Early formative leadership learning is in the relational context as
a follower – with parents, elder siblings, teachers, first boss (often part-
time employment) and first and subsequent early career line managers
(Kempster and Parry, 2013). Outside such relationships leadership observational cues are informed through the media with regard to such people
as politicians, sporting heroes and stories of past heroic leaders anchored
to images of great triumph (and grand failure).

Steve has generated some interesting anecdotal evidence experienced
with undergraduates. He asked them to identify role models that influence
their understanding of leadership. Some fascinating data was generated
that points to a striking finding: young men tend to highlight distance
role models – iconic figures which they have no relationship with – much
more noticeably than young women. Young women tended to point to
people within their relationships more frequently than men. What might
this suggest? It is too early to say with any claim of certainty but perhaps
young men adopt more romanticized perspectives to leadership (because
they attribute qualities that they have not experienced), while for young
women such romanticized ideas are more grounded in the nuances of close
at hand experiences.

What is unambiguous is that early formative leadership conceptions
are shaped through observational learning. However, this area of observational learning has been the Cinderella of learning theories despite its

formative prominence in our learning of the world (Bandura, 1977, 1986). In Kempster and Parry's (2013) work on observational learning they laid out a theoretical explanation of how observational leadership learning occurs for managers through their careers. Connecting Bandura's work on observational learning with Gibson's typology (2003, 2004) of observational learning Kempster and Parry suggested a model illustrated in Figure 6.1 to explain the dynamic occurring.

The key aspects being shown are:

- Two stages of acquiring understanding of leadership – pre- and early career – which is formative. Leadership understood in 'broad strokes'.
- Next stage of refining – mid-career where the 'fine strokes' are developed, filling in the nuance detail.
- Final stage of affirming – selectively observing people to affirm a perspective of leadership – concluding the painting metaphor, a sense of standing back and admiring the picture.
- The situation makes leadership salient and triggers attention and motivation to observe – wishing to become the desired identity of a leader.
- The proximity of the observed person. How attainable and accessible are the observed behaviour as something to be learned? Hoyt and Simon (2011) examined women role models. They showed that women learned more from close role models than distant. They asserted that women rejected role models in very senior positions as being unattainable.

This suggested theory of observational leadership learning has informed the design of the LEAD programme. As McCall et al. (1988) identified many years back that notable people were a key influence on leadership learning, yet in an SME context, owner/managers have limited role models to engage with (Perren and Grant, 2001; Smith et al., 1999). The key aspects of the Kempster and Parry model have been applied within the LEAD design:

- First, to motivate owner/managers to tune in to observe those leaders around them.
- Second, to make more people available to observe.
- Third, to ensure that owner/managers do not reject possible people to observe that do not fit to preconceived notions of leadership – broaden out an expectation of what leadership might be and therefore what to observe.
- Fourth, to develop skills in observing.

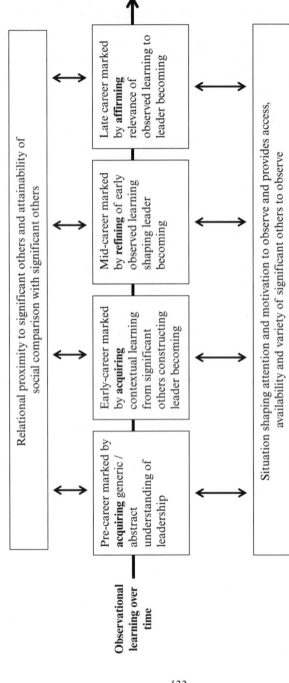

Source: Kempster and Parry (2013, p.3). Used by permission of the publishers, Emerald Group Publishing Limited.

Figure 6.1   Observational leadership learning

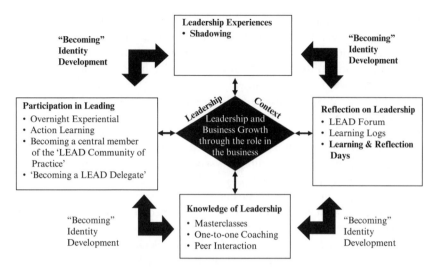

Figure 6.2   LEAD journey, month 4: construction of the "LEADership Learning Cycle" in the context of a LEAD delegate's development from their lived experience

The Shadowing element on LEAD addresses this in part by drawing on the power of observational learning in *Leadership Experiences* (Figure 6.2).

By entering into a different physical environment, Shadowing and Exchanges enable delegates, in pairs or triples, to look at their peers' leadership styles and businesses and compare these with their own. They learn about their own behaviour and learn about their own organization through a fresh pair of eyes and the feedback they receive.

As the variability of contexts and the breadth of individual experience shape leadership learning (McCall et al., 1988), the delegates are encouraged to partner with someone who has a different leadership style or leads in a different industry.

Observation of others is a central feature of participation within situated learning (Lave and Wenger, 1991) where tacit learning is generated. The notion of learning from *their work* anchors learning and development to situations and highlights the importance of reflection-on-action, that is, the retrospective consideration of an action undertaken in order to uncover the knowledge used in a particular situation by analysing and interpreting the information that is recalled (Schön, 1983).

Learning and development through leadership experience predominantly occurs when an owner/manager realizes that previous experience is not sufficient for the situation at hand or that the way the owner/manager previously anticipated enacting skills for the situation is no longer appropriate (Kempster, 2009a). As Shadowing and Exchanges are new experiences for the delegates, these new events allow new behaviours to be learnt for new situations. Breaking routines aids leadership development.

Bandura (1986), in discussing 'attention', warns that what is observed is influenced by conspicuousness and attractiveness, salience and perceived value, preconceptions and prior knowledge. Experienced owner/managers will recognize fine differences that are indistinguishable to the untutored. At the outset, when going into another delegate's business it might look different (for example be a different sector, environment and so on) but delegates quickly realize how many similarities there are as they compare and contrast it with their own business.

There is a high degree of uncertainty and expectation as delegates begin Shadowing, as it is an emotional and anxious episode, which was demonstrated by Freddie, Jane and Bill. LEAD delegates are encouraged to suspend judgements and approach Shadowing with a *tabula rasa* (blank slate). Prior to going in to each other's businesses, the delegates attend a session that focuses on helping them develop their observational skills and they work in their pairs / triples to define what feedback they would like and how they would like to receive it. By asking what they are looking forward to and what their concerns are in advance of the Shadowing day allows delegates to learn that they are not alone with their feelings. The delegates are guided by a simple workbook, which offers them different observational activities to undertake. This helps the delegates to feel equipped for the Shadowing, both in being shadowed and shadowing someone else.

This chapter also introduces the first of the Learning and Reflection Days as the LEAD facilitators focus the delegates on their learning on LEAD to date and the value therein. The purpose of these sessions is to help the delegates engage actively with reflective practice whereby they engage in a process of thoughtfully considering their experiences on LEAD and back in the businesses (and invariably at home). Reflection is concerned with consciously looking at and thinking about our experiences, actions, feelings and responses and then interpreting or analysing them in order to learn from them (Boud et al., 1994).

As with many of the learning interventions on LEAD, the days are designed drawing upon Schön's (1983) concept of reflection-*on-action*. As noted above, Schön (1983) distinguishes between reflection-*in-action* whereby a new problem is experienced and thought about while still acting, and reflection-*on-action*, which is literally that, reflecting on something that has happened. This involves remembering the detail of the incident, how it happened, and the feelings and thoughts that it elicited.

During this reflective process delegates are asked to think about how they might have handled a particular situation differently and what they might do should a similar situation arise in the future.

Reflection-*on-action* is recognized as a way to learn from our experience, and the Learning and Reflection Days provide a structured space to enable the delegates to stop and reflect on their learning and their actions throughout key points along the programme. Additionally they provide the context for peer-to-peer learning as the delegates hear how their peers are learning and what changes and so on they are making in their businesses. Even though they may take a different approach or action to the one(s) they are learning about from their peers, the reflection enables learning to take place for what Pittaway et al. (2009, p. 280) term a "future-to-come". The delegates are encouraged to engage in reflective practice throughout the programme with the intention that they will continue this behaviour long after the programme has ended.

7. LEAD journey: month 5 – July

This chapter focuses on the further layering of the delegates' LEAD learning from another month with its mix of the fifth Masterclass, the fourth Action Learning Set meeting, the third telephone coaching session and their experiences in progressing with Shadowing.

(TELEPHONE) COACHING

"So how is Shadowing going, Freddie?" enquired David.

Today was Freddie's diarized telephone coaching session. It had been a month since the Introduction to Shadowing Day and one of the temperature checks that a LEAD coach takes is to ask how a delegate has progressed since they last spoke.

"Very well, David. I really enjoyed the Introduction to Shadowing Day, which went a long way to settle my concerns. As you know when I first started LEAD, I was not looking forward to this element.

"Jane and I have already met for half a day to plan our Shadowing sessions. We are both very organized people and we want to do the Shadowing as soon as we can. We thought it was best to meet first as we believe that the better we are prepared, the more we will get out of the experience.

"We have identified that staff engagement and the leadership shadow are two key themes from LEAD thus far. Therefore, I have organized a day of back-to-back meetings with various managers and staff from across my company so that Jane can observe how I act in meetings to provide feedback on my leadership. I know I have arranged too many meetings during the day but I want to expose Jane to as many parts of my company as I can as I value her insights.

"Firstly, I will be shadowing her in a Board meeting. I have never been to another company's Board meeting before so that in itself is quite exciting. How I'll be able to remain quiet all day, I just don't know!" laughed Freddie. "I will then observe her running her regular staff get-togethers."

"That sounds like a well-planned approach to Shadowing. What do you want to achieve from the coaching conversation today?" asked David.

Freddie disclosed that coaching had become a valuable tool for him as it helped him focus. He valued the time with the coach and had prepared in advance, sending in his preparation form detailing what he had accomplished since the last coaching session, what challenges he had faced and how he handled them, the new challenges he was facing, new opportunities that were open to him, shifts in awareness and what outcome he wanted from this session.

Last night, Freddie spent an hour reviewing what he had sent and what he wanted to focus on. Looking at what he said he was going to do from the last coaching session, he said to himself, "It's a bit like having a teacher you like at school and not wanting to let him down."

"How stupid does that sound?"

"It's only myself that I'll be letting down. Coaching is a good format for me to come out of my comfort zone. The coach is akin to having a little voice in my ear quite literally saying, 'Have you done that? Why haven't you done it?'

"This forces me to look at the key things and do what I said I would do," thought Freddie.

"What I'd like to talk about today, David, is my weak management team. I have inherited the team and made one appointment myself. I have given everyone opportunities to develop but they are not of the necessary calibre and will not be able to rise to where the business needs to go. Also, the 'old guard' are all slaves to my father's autocratic leadership style and are not prepared to slip the shackles."

During the next hour, Freddie discussed the many key change initiatives that were happening within the company. David guided the discussions, ensuring an appropriate time was spent reviewing progress, sensing that talking about matters would help Freddie form the Platform, the basis of today's coaching conversation. David also challenged Freddie over the process of change and whether the managers were suffering from initiative overload. They weren't. David had seen such change happen at a pace in many other companies. David was satisfied that Freddie was clear in his own mind of what could be changed and by when.

It was evident Freddie was drawing in learning from LEAD such as the marketing planning process, employee engagement questionnaire, appropriate two-way communication and use of open questions, all of which he was integrating within the business. He was encouraged that employees were beginning to see his positive leadership attributes and were coming to him, avoiding his father, as they believed he had the employees' well-being in mind.

As the call concluded, Freddie looked at his notes. He was pleased. He had an action plan for the creation of a new senior management team structure which followed his desired strategy.

* * * * *

Jane phoned a little late and claimed she was struggling to think of an issue. She had completed the preparation form, which David worked through with her, revealing that today's issue was basically the same issue that arose in the last coaching session.

David followed the Solutions Focused approach with Jane again and she was able to come to a conclusion and commit to an action. Jane confirmed at the end the session it had been really helpful.

"I have slipped back a little in my own self-confidence at work. I have had a couple of difficult Board meetings where my performance has been the subject of pointed questions from the shareholders. Instead of creating a plan for growth I am too involved in piecemeal actions. I have a lot on, both at work and at home, and I am struggling to prioritize. I feel I am not getting what I should from LEAD because I do not have time to think about the learning, let alone apply my learning.

"I am going to tackle this head on, David. I have decided to book out every afternoon following a Masterclass to give me time to reflect. This is a small step but it is a major step in the right direction for somebody who is struggling to find time to work on the business because they are too busy fire-fighting in the day-to-day operations."

* * * * *

David was expecting an upbeat Bill on the phone today. His preparation form confirmed that he had recruited his number two, someone to take many of the day-to-day tasks off his shoulders and someone who could start almost immediately. Bill didn't disappoint. He was in an ebullient mood.

"This was a crucial appointment for me so I was brutally honest with her when I interviewed her," revealed Bill. "I told her that I have had three or four assistants who haven't worked out for whatever reasons, that I can only come from my perspective and I don't provide enough support time. I shared with her that I don't think I'm a very good mentor, I don't delegate very effectively and I need to improve on that particularly. I warned her that I was weak on all of those aspects.

"And despite all that she still joined!" exclaimed Bill.

"Now, David, where did those realizations come from? Well, again, it has come from LEAD. Many points have come together for me – the idea of the hero complex where I was doing everything surrounded by sheep, as I saw it, which was my fault. Becoming aware of the cast of my shadow and understanding the consequences caused by my see-sawing polarized styles of leadership – from the autocratic to the laissez-faire leader.

"I said to her it was really important to me that I get this appointment right and it's really important to her that I get it right.

"I can see what I had to do to deal with my sense of being overwhelmed, of not having enough hours in the day and the feeling no matter how hard I work, I cannot get through all the tasks.

"I can see that it's a process – first of all you've got to see what the problem is and the message was strongly relayed to me at the Overnight Experiential.

"After you see what the problem is then you must envisage a solution before ensuring that the solution actually happens. Too many people say '*I know what the problem is*' and '*I know what I should do*', but then never implement it.

"Today I'd like to explore the correct level of support for my number two."

* * * * *

ACTION LEARNING SET 4

"It's always interesting to see where you are on the Jelly Baby Tree and hear your reasons why you have chosen that position," remarked Ann. Before inviting someone to speak, Ann reminded the set members that Action Learning Sets help delegates to solve problems.

"Yes," agreed Freddie. "The Action Learning Set has become very valuable to me. I actually look forward to the format now and I am more at ease with it too. I can't believe it's already our fourth meeting together. I come very much prepared with a couple of things I want to talk about but will decide, when it is my turn, which one that would be. I am always really interested to find out what others think about my issue, bringing value to that through the questioning process."

"I am glad you are finding it beneficial, Freddie," smiled Jane. "Although we have ideas of what possible solutions could be, we are not asking leading questions. Rather we are asking open insightful questions, which allows you to critically think about options that you may or may have not considered."

"We know that you will come up with the end result. We are not doing it for you," laughed Bill.

"I do listen intently and really question myself inside, which allows me to come up with a solution and good plan of action. I know that at the next Action Learning Set I can review my progress with you and proudly say to myself, '*I did that*'."

Ann reminded the set, "In our Action Learning Set, you spoke about your dissatisfaction of the performance of your long-serving sales manager."

Freddie began his review. "He's gone now. I remember at our last session the set was split on what to do next. Even though you were not allowed to say so, I could tell that there were two of you suggesting the need to get rid of the sales manager whilst another was recommending the need to develop him. The latter position was really where I was as well."

"After the session, Tom grabbed me and advised, 'Freddie, you just need to get rid of him. People like that aren't good for your business, pay them off. It might hurt you initially but that's what you need to do.'

"I respect Tom and I admire his achievements in his own business as he has faced such situations. He is someone we all naturally look up to and see as a 'leader'. We had never countenanced his recommendation in my company before, let alone actioned it. We always give people every chance to try and do their job. As you know, I tried performance management but it didn't work.

"So what have I done? I decided to pay him off. Amazingly, once it was communicated, managers and staff came up to me and said it was the right thing to do and questioned why I hadn't done it before. It seems staff recognize the change that needs doing and it is me, the leader, that needs to act more quickly, make the necessary changes and lead the process. This then gives them confidence in me."

"In other words, the followers can legitimately follow the leader," chimed Bill, reminding Freddie of their leader–follower discussions at the April Masterclass.

"It is not for today's meeting," continued Freddie, "but I discussed reorganizing the senior management team with David in my Coaching session last week so there will be other changes. If the behaviour of managers is damaging the business and they are not prepared to change then there's no point in having blockers to progress as it's going to cost more in the long run. I am convinced Tom's advice based on his experiences is correct."

"Following on from last month's discussions on use of open questions, I have learnt quite a lot about myself from Action Learning," said Bill. "I learnt about people's perception of me and what my issues are, such as failing to finish things off.

"The Action Learning Sets have helped me to ask more open questions and now I actually write these on papers that I am taking to a meeting. I write them on the top to remind me to ask open questions. I recognize their importance and I use this approach in my daily discussions with my new assistant, which I discussed with David in my Coaching session last week. She will come in enquiring what to do with a particular task. I now ask, 'What are you struggling with? What are the problems? What do you think?' By the end, she walks out with a solution, her solution. I haven't told her. She figures it out herself and that's very empowering for her.

"Sometimes I just know she's not going to get there so I have to intervene."

"Some people find it very uncomfortable to be asked open questions," noted Jane. "On occasions you don't want to ask someone an open question because you know they are going to feel uncomfortable because you are very firmly hitting the ball back onto their side of the court.

"My secretary will come in and have a moan about various things and the best question to ask is, 'If you were me, what would you do about it?' Then she'll say, 'Oh well, you can't do that because it's going to upset so-and-so and you can't do that because I assume it's too expensive'. In the end she leaves thinking we can do something about the matter at hand. It's understood we can't do everything but progress has been made."

Bill reflected. "So, we've all used the Action Learning Set process to develop ourselves and our businesses. It just helps so much in being able to talk these things through in this way."

* * * * *

Although Jane had reminded her set members about Zones of Debate,[16] Bill sensed that this was a technique that she was not deploying herself. Bill had masked his frustration during Jane's air time as she relayed a "new" issue which in his opinion was a manifestation of an old issue that she had not previously tackled satisfactorily: managing conflict at Board level due to the dynamics of individuals.

Of course, this is one of the most sensitive subjects any business leader faces in their tenure. It's infinitely more difficult to manage if you are the minority shareholder and the issue is the relationship with the majority shareholders compounded by the fact that those shareholders are family members.

[16] Bowman, C. (1995), 'Strategy workshops and top team commitment to strategic change,' *Journal of Managerial Psychology*, **10**, 42–50.

Bill genuinely cared for the fortunes of Jane. The bonds of trust that had been built up over five months, as the set members learned how to cooperate, did count for something.

Bill satisfied himself that meaningful actions had been agreed, specifically that Jane had committed to work with all Board members to define and write their own job roles and responsibilities, which they would collectively review, amend and agree, including authority levels.

Bill was concerned if Jane had potentially misinterpreted the situation with her colleagues. He probed to ascertain why she was feeling a bit demoralized when really she had all the power that she needed to run the organization effectively. In her own words, the staff, who were the followers, viewed Jane as the leader, whereas the other Board members operated in more technical support roles, with little interaction with the staff. Jane had been given the senior leadership role and responsibility to sort out the business but was uncertain if she had the authority to do so.

"I hadn't thought about it in power terms," admitted Jane. "I'll go and read my notes from the Kempster Leadership Masterclass that discussed behavioural power and relational power.

"Freddie will be Shadowing me next month so it'll be interesting to hear his feedback on his observations as he'll see me in a Board meeting, interacting with my fellow directors as well as sitting in on a staff meeting that I run."

* * * * *

Bill wanted to explore another piece of learning from a LEAD Masterclass – Transactional Leadership versus Transformational Leadership – as his coaching Goal (G) today was "What other steps can I take to reduce others' reliance on me?"

Bill did not realize it, as he did not have the vocabulary yet, but he was embracing triple-loop learning. He had realized that he was holding back the organization. He had picked up new techniques and tips from LEAD, rationalized them in the context of his company, modified them to suit, applied them and observed the consequences of his actions. He had witnessed benefits, both at a personal level and for the company. He now wanted to establish what else he could do to improve how he led his people.

Bill could vaguely recall the stuff on transformational leadership.[17] "Successful transformational leaders are usually identified as providing

---

[17] Barling, J. (2014), *The Science of Leadership: Lessons from Research for Organizational Leaders*, New York: Oxford University Press.

a strong vision and arousing strong emotions in followers. They focus on developing the organization through changing follower behaviours, aspirations and stimulation to enhance performance. A transformational leader goes beyond managing day-to-day operations and crafts strategies for taking his/her company, department or work team to the next level of performance and success. Transformational leadership focuses on team-building, motivation and collaboration with employees at different levels to accomplish change for the better. I now appreciate that transformational leadership is critical in enhancing empowerment and during times of major change. Transformational leaders set goals to inspire followers to higher performance levels while providing opportunities for personal and professional growth for each employee."

"Impressive," Freddie commented, "if there was an exam then you've passed!"

"So you could say that they provide the vision of, say, building a cathedral?" said Jane. "We know that an effective leader needs to exhibit both transactional and transformational leadership where a transactional leader has day-to-day interaction with followers in order to achieve organizational goals to attain the desired performance. Using the same metaphor, the leader is getting the followers to smash rocks."

"I liked your use of metaphors, Jane, they're helpful," noted Bill. "In my company, there is a tendency of fee-earners to stick to their narrow roles and look after their own interests. They are smashing rocks, doing the job they are paid to do and in the past I have encouraged them to do that.

"So, how do I motivate people to want to do more for the company, the collective good? How do I enthuse staff, especially fee-earners, to contribute more? How do I convince them to move from smashing rocks to sharing the vision of building a cathedral?"

The set worked together, trying to help their peer resolve his problem. They knew from their own learning from the very first day on the Overnight Experiential that the best leadership is often seen in the smallest behaviours enacted at the right time and for the right reasons. A leader's behaviour has a direct effect on the follower. There is an impact and an outcome. Their task was to coach Bill in determining what behaviours he wanted to develop in himself that would generate the desired outcomes in his followers. As Bill openly admitted, prior to LEAD, his leadership style was a transactional one – rooted in rewards, management by exception and a laissez-faire approach. He was now unshackling himself of these constraints and wrestling with how to develop a transformational leadership style, one that was genuinely his that he could embody and enact.

With the help of his peers, the actions he agreed were to be his next steps forward.

* * * * *

The session had ended and Freddie was walking back alone to his car, licking his wounds after doing twelve rounds with the *heavyweights*. He was reflecting on his air time where he gained valuable feedback on his handling of a major project that had gone wrong during the implementation phase after managers followed an approach he had insisted upon and had enforced.

Freddie admitted to set members that he had not discussed "at length" or indeed invited feedback from anyone involved in the project or the intended users. Nor did he share the purpose of the project. Communication had broken down at an early stage and Freddie therefore lost any cooperation from the users.

"My peer group indicated that I had handled the situation poorly. I can see that now," thought Freddie.

"I must have sounded foolish trying to defend such a poor approach. It was painful as I realized this during my air time but I have learned a valuable lesson on how to communicate a subject matter which is controversial and requires the buy-in of staff members.

"Jane brought up the 'Zones of Debate' model, reminding us that most management teams remain in a Zone of Comfortable Debate, avoiding moving into the Zone of Uncomfortable Debate (ZOUD). This zone also protects entrance to the Intuitive Core, an area where the solution lies but is often masked. Intuitively, we know possible solutions but through fear, lack of confidence, uncertainty or whatever else we dare not raise or discuss our ideas. Well today, during my air time, the set members signalled to me that we were entering ZOUD so I could mentally prepare for some discomfort. They then exposed the Intuitive Core before robustly debating possible options in ZOUD before we returned to the Comfortable Zone where I agreed my actions.

"I lost on points but I have come out the better for it," thought Freddie. "It was also useful to practise the process of going through the Zones of Debate. That's another tool for my toolbox."

* * * * *

MASTERCLASS 5

Ann was excited. Next week's speaker is a well-known and successful sports coach who was able to transfer and communicate the lessons from the sports arena into the cauldron of business. "This will really light the touch paper," she thought.

Subject: Leaders as Coaches – Professor Frank Dick OBE

> Frank will apply his in-depth knowledge on coaching and leadership to the leadership needs of growing businesses. The importance and value of individual contributions will be emphasized through examples of Frank's experience coaching the UK Athletics team and prominent sports men and women. The Masterclass is most entertaining and certainly most stimulating. Frank is an inspiring role model.

* * * * *

The Masterclass concluded with the phrase, "If not you, who? If not now, when?"[18]

Jane and Bill were sitting together at lunch, digesting the last three hours. "Did you notice that the whole room went quiet when the speaker uttered his final words?"

"The enormity of the responsibility and accountability of leadership were captured in those eight words. They were two very powerful questions," acknowledged Jane. "Two months ago," continued Jane, "I asked for feedback on my leadership and management style from my staff using the questionnaire recommended by John Oliver which supported my team's readiness for a more rigorous and demanding leadership stance.

"I am in the process of refreshing and clarifying the vision for the business, reflecting the greater ambition and confidence from the team.

"I had asked for their hopes and aspirations, and found lots of commonality and a shared ambition. I hadn't considered how powerful that was until today's talk by Frank, who spoke of the importance of placing values and vision 'front and centre' all the time and how the leader as coach 'makes it possible for others to achieve'.

"It has furthered my confidence that we are all ready to be more ambitious and that our vision and mission should capture that.

"Frank also talked about the importance of milestones to mark the path to success and towards achieving the overall vision. So my actions are to

---

[18] Dick, F.W. (2010), *Winning Matters*, Abingdon Management Company.

work with the Board to identify milestones over our five-year planning period so that we know what we need to aim for, then articulate clear milestones for the next twelve months, broken down quarterly, that we will share with staff."

"You have taken some business insights from the Masterclass, Jane. I have learned a few things that will help my own development at a personal level," said Bill.

"I was inspired by the idea of developing my own personal plan. As you know, work has challenged my energy levels so I am going to develop a personal plan addressing issues of my health, personal relationships and work–life balance. This will be the basis of a personal development plan.

"I laughed to myself some time ago when you said the phrase, 'It's all about me'. I thought it was too simplistic or too selfish. But you are right. It is all about me. I am going to link up the concept of having my own plan with the dangers of the 'hero complex'. I now understand and appreciate that I am important too. Energy, focus, health and knowledge are all vital in being able to lead effectively. This has two outcomes for me: I have learned the need for a personal development plan and for life-long learning."

"What a fascinating perspective, Bill," replied Jane. "It is also consistent with Sammy's point from the first morning of the Overnight Experiential when she asked us to consider how our behaviour impacts on our people. You are now aware of what leadership means to you in your firm, the influence of your shadow and you are taking appropriate actions to change how you act.

"Bill, you have come a long way from being the red-faced person sitting on his hands, rocking on his chair in frustration at the Overnight Experiential. You should be proud of what you have achieved in five short months. I can tell you that we are all proud of you.

"You more than anyone have addressed Frank's two concluding questions: *If not you, who? If not now, when?* You have taken personal responsibility and changed your behaviour for the good and sooner rather than later. How many others can honestly say they do that?"

* * * * *

LEAD FORUM – MASTERCLASS REFLECTION

As the LEAD Forum Champion, Jane dutifully created the 'What I have learned from today's Masterclass' topic and was first to make a posting:

About a month ago I decided to work from home in the afternoons following a Masterclass or Action Learning Set to try and avoid getting sucked straight back into client and operational tasks and concentrate on whatever revelations I experienced that morning.

It hasn't been possible every time, but it's a step in the right direction (here I am now, sat at home, reading through the LEAD Forum and making plans based on this week's jewels gleaned from my reflections).

I have a long list of 'gems' from the Masterclass that had real resonance for me. Here are my headline 'light bulb' moments:

'Can you deliver better today than you did yesterday?' One to remember: constant goal for improvement, but also, if you had a bad day yesterday, every day's a fresh chance to do things better.

The Leader as a Coach concept was discussed. I've never worked anywhere that had a formal coaching programme for staff, just appraisals and training plans which I can now see are wholly inadequate. I am going to plan how to build a coaching programme for all staff, including ourselves as Board directors.

I'm thinking about throwing out the hierarchical line management chart, which feels a bit forced in such a flat matrix team structure and replacing it with coaching teams instead.

By making these changes there's so much potential to improve the performance of our team – which is very exciting – but also, it could become a point of differentiation from our competitors.

What a great Masterclass. The sporting and coaching analogies made so much sense to me. It is obvious now that my job, as a leader, is to develop the performance of others.

Jane

Freddie was next to reflect:

The speaker was different to all the other big names that had gone before. He was a celebrity, an inspiration to many. As always, I listened intently.

This Masterclass has provided me with inspiration to drive through strong decisions and 'be the best person I can be'. I went back to the office and created a document of the quotes that are ringing in my ears from the session.

For example: 'coach people to make them better than you', 'you don't have to be sick to get better', 'make sure the team know they are working with you, not for you'.

I am sure I will have some 'bad days' ahead so I will stretch over the desk and catch a glimpse of my quote sheet to motivate me. I have already shared the document with my senior management team.

Freddie

Bill shared:

I have never really looked at competitors before. Nor had I considered that we have the same challenges as our competitors so therefore by reacting quicker and being better than our competitors will give us a competitive advantage. In other words, and to build on similar messages from previous Masterclass speakers, we need to understand what is important to our clients then deliver it so that we can steal a march on our competitors. What clients will be interested in will be nuanced and I am sure there will be differences in the various market segments.

I must not feel overwhelmed again by asking this question within my organization. I cannot do the work alone so I must engage my management team on how we collectively address this issue.

Bill

THEORY SANDWICH 7   SINGLE, DOUBLE AND TRIPLE-LOOP LEARNING

Exploration of learning: Transformational learning and single, double and triple-loop learning.

The reflective methods employed on LEAD are intended to allow delegates to learn from themselves as a peer group and engage in exploring the taken-for-granted assumptions that shape their daily practice through questions and discussions. Reynolds makes a distinction between reflection – as making thoughtful use of otherwise un-coded experience that provides the basis for future action – and critical reflection as the ability of an individual to focus beyond the task or problem to "an analysis of power and control and an examination of the taken-for-granted's within which the task or problem is situated" (1998, p. 189). Low-level learning is associated with simple reflection while high-level learning is through conscious and organized reflection (Marserick and Watkins, 1990; Daudelin, 1996).

Thus the depth of conscious awareness distinguishes reflection from critical reflection. And linked to this is the notion of learning levels. For example, Bateson (1973) identified three levels:

- Level 1 – experience and factual information of immediate relevance to a context and not beyond.
- Level 2 – transferable learning recognized by an individual is relevant for the current context and beyond.
- Level 3 – awareness of the conceptions of the world, how they were formed and how they might change: learning that is not situation specific.

Bateson suggested that level 3 is rare. Level 1 dominates everyday learning occurring in a naturalistic unconscious manner (Burgoyne and Hodgson, 1983). The distinction between levels 2 and 3 reflects Argyris and Schön's (1978) work on single and double-loop learning, which we shall explore shortly.

First, though, we wish to examine the notion of transformative learning associated with levels 2 and 3 and in particular the work of Mezirow (1985). Drawing on the work (and philosophy) of Habermas (1971), Mezirow suggests there are three areas to which learning is applied:

1. Work or instrumental action – task-oriented problem solving.
2. Practical or communicative action – understanding social norms.
3. Emancipatory or self-knowledge – understanding ourselves and our identity and how history and biography shapes social expectations.

Mezirow comments that "it is through becoming critically reflective that people become most aware of their learning in three areas as they bring their assumptions, premises, criteria and schemata into consciousness and vigorously critique them all" (1985, p. 25). Emancipation is seeing the norms and expectations, the taken-for-granted, the power structures and political interests, and in seeing how these impact on us (socially produced) we are able to transform them and thus the control they have on us (Alvesson and Willmott, 1996).

The ability to reflect in a transformative manner is argued to be triggered by critical incidents or episodes (Mezirow, 1985). Cope (2003) applied Mezirow's ideas to understand entrepreneurial learning. Examining in depth five cases of owner/manager learning, he showed how critical incidents caused transformational learning to occur and the development of these people's ability to expand their entrepreneurial capacity. Mezirow argues that the transformative incidents lead to a movement from unconscious level 1 learning to level 2 and sometimes level 3. These critical incidents have the effect on us of coming to terms anew with our own histories: "However good we are at making sense of our experiences, we all have to start with what we have been given and operate within horizons set by the ways of seeing and understanding that we have acquired through prior learning" (1985, p. 1).

So the notion of examining the taken-for-granted aspects that we are caught up in as part of the milieu of everyday flux of life is made more visible by critical incidents. Yet these may not be recognized or used for transformative effect. The ability to recognize such levels of learning and consciously examine what is happening and why is where the notion of single, double and triple learning comes into play (Argyris and Schön, 1978). It is a framework that sits solidly behind the pedagogic design of the LEAD programme.

Single-loop learning involves learning what to do and asking *are we doing things right?* In the context of LEAD, listening to and learning the key messages at a Masterclass is an example of single-loop learning.

Single-loop learning assumes that problems and their solutions are close to each other in time and space (thought they often aren't). In this form of learning, delegates are primarily considering actions. Small changes can be made to specific practices or behaviours, based on what has or has not worked in the past. This involves doing things better without necessarily examining or challenging underlying beliefs and assumptions. The goal is improvements and fixes that often take the form of procedures or rules. Single-loop learning leads to making minor fixes or adjustments.

Double-loop learning involves learning why something works, obtaining new insights and patterns and asking *are we doing the right things?*

Double-loop learning leads to insights about why a solution works. In this form of learning, delegates are considering their actions in the framework of their operating assumptions. This is the level of process analysis where delegates become observers of themselves, asking *what is going on here? What are the patterns?* They need this insight to understand the pattern and change the way they make decisions and deepen understanding of their assumptions. Double-loop learning works with major fixes or changes, like redesigning an organizational function or structure. In the context of LEAD, taking new learning (single-loop) and applying that to their organization and seeing what occurs is double-loop learning. Double-loop learning is necessary if delegates are to make informed decisions in rapidly changing and often uncertain contexts.

Triple-loop learning involves principles where the learning goes beyond insight and patterns to context. The result creates a shift in understanding the context or point of view, as demonstrated by Bill in his reflection ahead of considering what to discuss in this month's Action Learning Set. Triple-loop learning will produce new commitments and ways of learning. This form of learning challenges delegates to understand how problems and solutions are related, even when separated widely by time and space – delegates draw together learning from different parts of LEAD from different months to change a fundamental behaviour in order to realize a different outcome.

Triple-loop learning also challenges them to understand how their previous actions created the conditions that led to their current problems. The results of this learning includes enhancing ways to comprehend and change the purpose, developing better understanding of how to respond to the environment, and deepening the comprehension of why they chose to do things they do. Triple-loop learning asks *how do we decide what is right?*

8.   LEAD journey: month 6 – August

This chapter again focuses on the further layering of the delegates' LEAD learning from another month of a mix of the sixth Masterclass, the fifth action learning set meeting, the fourth and final telephone coaching session and their experiences in progressing Shadowing.

(TELEPHONE) COACHING

This was Freddie's penultimate LEAD Coaching session and his fourth and final telephone coaching session. David invited Freddie to share his progress.

"I was thinking the other day, we are just over half-way through LEAD and it is taking more of my time than I thought it would do, but not in a negative sense.

"It is invaluable to learn that the business can cope without me being there on a daily basis. I have found that I can turn my phone off for six hours and the company is still there when I come back. I am more comfortable with the process. It is as if you learn to be a LEAD delegate as you learn to lead better. There is a sense of becoming a LEAD delegate and becoming more of a leader in your business.

"My conversations with my peers have also changed without a shadow of doubt. I am learning a lot more about their businesses and I feel that I am on the inside now because I am familiar with their day-to-day issues or the bigger picture matters with staff or family members.

"You almost throw that familiarity into conversations with them as well. You ask, 'How is John?' Or, 'How are you getting on with. . .'. You are being a lot more amiable. I have known these people for six months now and I am getting a lot closer to them. It's not just a cohort now, not just peers; they are friends, acquaintances.

"Of course, you are not going to get close to everybody as there is going to be three or four in your social circle. But this is not a clique where someone is going to say, 'Look at those four over there, thick as thieves'. It is not that sort of playground mentality.

"I have many examples now where knowledge gained on LEAD is being taken back and being used within the business. So I am seeing the benefits. I suppose in a way it's almost like learning a new language – it takes you a while to pick it up but once you've got it, you know it. You're not going to talk about it all the time but when someone starts talking to you in the LEAD language, you can throw it back. You can use this language in your business.

"I am now comfortable in naturally using Solutions Focused coaching and the OSKAR model. I use Future Perfect a lot now with people and the metaphor of sprinkling magic dust as a signal to begin thinking of a preferred future state to solve the current problem. I ask, 'What do you want? What's your Future Perfect? What do you want out of the situation?' They'll imagine if they went to sleep and someone sprinkles the magic dust and what does the world look like. That is now in our common language, commonly used within the firm and regularly by myself."

Shortly, David would hear that Freddie was clear on today's Platform, the first stage of the Outcome (O). But first, he was keen to share the progress made in the Review (R).

"A lot of things have happened in the last month," said Freddie cheerfully to David.

"We had an 88 per cent response rate from the staff on the employee engagement questionnaire with very good feedback and insights into areas of improvement. The results highlight the need for more meetings and improved communications from certain managers to their teams. This has confirmed my diagnosis, which has allowed me to proactively go back to managers to change behaviours. We have presented the results back to the workforce, which was well received. We shared with them all the findings, including some messages we found difficult to digest but it was important that we were seen to be open and honest. We have started an employee committee and initiated a company-wide newsletter.

"I have also understood the message of the first activity from the Overnight Experiential and I am now not involved in the detail of the day-to-day activities. The managers would like more involvement so my role is now to direct, coach, support and delegate each manager per situation as necessary.

"Jane and I have completed Shadowing, which was a very valuable experience. I probably crammed too much into my Shadowing Day when Jane was here. I shadowed her in a Board meeting.

"The Shadowing itself was great because first of all I had to sit in a room and not say a word all day, which I tend to struggle with. I know I talk too much and do not listen enough. I have now proved to myself that I can remain quiet and actively listen.

"In my feedback to Jane, I was able to ask questions to clarify my observations. I did not want to misinterpret something and make a judgement. I could see something as an outsider and how Jane behaved as a result. Jane confirmed that she hadn't appreciated this was an issue. I acted as a mirror of what was happening in the company. And I did all that without any background information!

"She found it really helpful. She privately told me that she observed the same but she thought she was clouded by her own prejudices and judgements.

"I created ammunition for Jane to go back and use. That was my initial worry in Shadowing – will I be able to add value? And, I did!

"When she came in here I probably had too many meetings and one meeting would go over and then I would be late for the next meeting, which is very unlike me.

"She commented that I had rushed one or two meetings because I had another one fast approaching but I wanted Jane to try and get as much of an overview and insight on me as possible. It was still a very beneficial day.

"Rather funnily, we both discovered that we ended sentences in a particular way. Now I know that, I am trying to stop doing it."

* * * * *

Freddie had rung off, having agreed three actions that would assist him in the appointment of a new senior manager.

Jane was next to call and she was in a much better place this month. She reported that she was more on top of things and therefore had time to step back more. David worked with her logically through the process to create a good action on a very difficult but important issue. Jane was reassured that she could be bolder in her leadership.

This chimed with the outcome of her Shadowing partner's observation.

* * * * *

Bill wanted to continue the discussions of his personal motivation.

"I now recognize that my mental and physical well-being is an important component of my overall leadership but I can imagine that this may be overlooked by many business leaders. It is important not to neglect yourself. This links to your personal, family and business goals."

During the subsequent coaching conversation, it was clear to David that Bill was well prepared, previous Actions (A) had been completed and he had constructed a worthwhile Platform. OSKAR was followed, a timely, rhythmic coaching conversation was had and five Actions (A) were agreed. Throughout, Bill paused, clearly considering his points.

Bill was actively engaged and had many benefits from LEAD. He was critically thinking and reflecting on his learning. He was engaging more with his partners and was working hard to ensure his new assistant was adequately supported.

* * * * *

ACTION LEARNING SET 5

"This is now the fifth Action Learning Set. You are all comfortable with yourselves and you have been exchanging copies of company documents such as handbooks and appropriate meeting behaviours," said Ann.

"Yes, it has become very natural now," replied Jane.

Ann continued. "At this stage, you should be self-facilitating the meeting so my role should be less."

"I can understand why you say that as we are not using the laminated prompt sheets. The stabilizers are off," laughed Freddie. "We are all winning from Action Learning.

"After last month's meeting, I recognized that I needed to have the uncomfortable conversations with my senior management. I have been focusing on managing relationships between some of my managers. My whole emphasis was on not letting internal conflicts get too big. I now realize that was wrong. I have had to learn to have the uncomfortable conversations – you've got to have them and mediate where necessary. I appreciate that I must remove the elephant from the room, get the monkey off my shoulder, whatever the metaphor. In the last month, I have removed another long-serving senior manager who was a barrier to change. I would never have done that before LEAD."

The set members nodded their heads approvingly. Tom had a cactus in his Boardroom which his management team passed around to any individual who was not open to having a difficult conversation on whatever subject. This non-threatening object signalled in a humorous way to an individual to drop their barriers and to engage more positively. Freddie had since bought a cactus and was bringing that approach into his Boardroom too as he assembled his new management team.

Over the next four hours, the set proceeded, surfacing their issues and solving each problem in turn. They agreed who would speak in what order. Open questions flowed naturally. Timings were adhered to. They were all pleased with their morning's work.

"That was another great session," declared Ann. "I observed you were actually mixing coaching models. So although GROW is used in Action

Learning, you were bringing in Future Perfect from Solutions Focused Coaching. The G of GROW is the Goal. Sometimes you asked, 'What's the goal here?' On other occasions, you were asking, 'What does the Future Perfect look like?'

"I like this re-interpretation and, in essence, how you are making the coaching model your own," concluded Ann.

* * * * *

MASTERCLASS 6

"This will be an interesting Masterclass," thought Ann as she posted the usual monthly message to the cohort. "Understanding numbers is so important in business but it is often something owner/managers shy away from. David will bring finance alive for them."

Subject: The Financial Imperative – Dr David Murphy

> David has the astonishing reputation of making numbers fun! A rare gift! There are a number of striking messages on financial management that David will impart. In particular he will explore issues of overtrading – a significant problem of growth businesses, undercapitalization and sources of capital – gearing, health check – business ratios, acquisition and exiting.

* * * * *

Jane was sharing her insights from the morning's Masterclass with Freddie.

"When it comes to specific priorities for my development, improving my financial understanding has become critical. Much of the Finance Masterclass went over my head, I found it difficult to absorb what was said and therein lies the problem – it's a glaring pointer to my inadequacies. I realize that I rely too much on the fact that I have a financial whiz as our Finance Director, and therefore I haven't given finance enough of my attention. I need to make more of an effort to understand it so that I can ask better questions and contribute more fully to the financial decisions about how we're growing our business. Today has been a wake-up call for me to take responsibility for my own learning. I should have a better grasp. Today has been an important lesson."

"Yep I think I'm the same, Jane," replied Freddie. "I too have also relied heavily on our previous financial controller and there lies a historic problem! Our external accountants recently discovered a significant accounting error that occurred before I became Managing Director and which my former financial controller concealed from everyone. There was no malpractice, just incompetence. I was fully reliant on this person doing a job for me. What it highlighted is that you need to have people around you who are competent but also that you need to understand the mechanics of how everything works as well. I have learned that you can promote people from within the organization but you need to be aware that they may be taught by predecessors who didn't know how to do the role properly either.

"I brought my new financial controller along to the Masterclass today. We needed to know some theory about what works in companies like ours. Immediately after the Masterclass, we agreed that we can use the ratio analysis within our organization which will provide us with some valuable key measures for our business. In particular, the debtor days and stock turnover will be very significant levers to pull in our industry during the current tough economic conditions. I will be working a lot more closely with financial information, controls and systems in the future but most importantly I will have an open and transparent relationship with my financial controller to enable the appropriate management and reporting."

"I am fortunate to have the opportunity to learn from my Financial Director, as well as colleagues on LEAD," continued Jane. "In particular, I must identify what questions, measures, language and methods to interpret the financial data that I should use to help me to assess, benchmark and improve performance. After LEAD started, I established a Senior Management Team of key operational people and I will now focus them to establish, monitor and be accountable for a set of KPIs – Key Performance Indicators. This is a new process for us, and I will need to provide guidance, support and encouragement if this is to be embraced by the team as useful and positive, rather than bureaucratic and oppressive."

Freddie added to Jane's insight: "I know from my experience over the last few months how employee engagement is integral and instrumental in achieving high performance. I am building my own new management team too and they recognize this intuitively. At the inaugural meeting they suggested a series of meetings with staff so that we can involve, inform and listen to each other as we 'sign up' to clearer accountability to each other in the pursuit of high performance.

"I need to consider, *what range of leadership approaches do I have for dealing with different people and teams in different situations? What are the appropriate financial and non-financial measurements for my business?* Finally, I know I have a new senior management team but *are they aligned to the goals of the business?*"

* * * * *

LEAD FORUM – MASTERCLASS REFLECTION

It had been a few days since the Masterclass and there had only been limited reflections on the Forum so David used his "Pokey Stick" to stimulate discussions.

"It seems telling that less is being said – does this reflect the nature of the subject?"

Bill shared the following:

> Finance is one of my strengths but it is a weakness of many of my partners. Every month detailed financial information and Key Performance Indicators are circulated to all fee earners including their individual performance against target and the firm's overall performance.
>
> The circulation of financial information has enabled me to work alongside the partners, in effect coaching them, and we have reduced the work-in-progress by more than 20 per cent so improving cash flow. A habit of interim billing has also being created.
>
> I strongly recommend focusing on this area.
>
> Bill

No comments were made by Freddie or Jane.

**THEORY SANDWICH 8   HUMAN, SOCIAL AND
INSTITUTIONAL CAPITALS**

Description of three dimensions of capital within a Community of Practice that develop owner/manager leadership.

We have spoken on a number of occasions with regard to the importance of Communities of Practice and the process of situated learning – see theory sandwiches 2, 3 and 5. What LEAD is beginning to contribute to management learning is how a Community of Practice (CoP) can be created in a leadership development programme (Kempster and Smith, 2014). By building a CoP, we suggest it enables a three-dimensional perspective to developing owner/manager leadership. Such a three-dimensional approach relates to the three capitals that we introduced earlier. Importantly evaluation of the LEAD programme has shown that a significant impact occurs on first, the owner/manager as human capital, and secondly, on the business as social capital (Wren and Jones, 2006). Learning with LEAD develops the delegate and their business (Gill and Harris, 2014).

Additionally, we have seen that a LEAD programme CoP develops as the third dimension, institutional capital (Leitch et al., 2013), though they do not explore how this capital is developed. We provide an illumination through the data of Freddie.

HUMAN CAPITAL – LEADERSHIP LEARNING

One of Freddie's first learning experiences at the Overnight Experiential was from the leadership timeline exercise which he populated with incidents and experiences from an early age. He quickly discovered that the majority of his leadership experiences were based on negative memories. He now understands that he developed his own leadership from learning from the mistakes of other leaders that he has worked with in the past, thus creating his own style. This is why he believes that he sometimes comes across as too placid and not as authoritative as he should be as a leader, as he has seen very aggressive styles of this leadership not working.

He was startled when he realized how little support he had received from his family that were involved in the business. His father and directors had never taken him to one side to coach, nurture, praise or reprimand when required.

Jane is also developing her human capital as she realizes that feedback cannot all be positive. She is also developing a clarity of purpose to avoid swinging wildly from a nurturing leadership style to providing the answers. She is developing a more suitable balance, and with it, is growing in confidence as her approach is welcomed by staff.

Freddie, Jane and Bill all discuss how developing the skills to ask open, insightful questions and actively listen are allowing them to engage better with their staff.

SOCIAL CAPITAL – COMMUNICATIONS AND EMPLOYEE ENGAGEMENT

The final activity at the Overnight Experiential provided Freddie with a very steep learning curve and a realization of his own business. He posed several questions to himself: "How do staff feel in my organization? Are we carrying out mushroom management? Do we ask them for their ideas? Do we communicate with them effectively or indeed at all? Are they bitter towards management due to a negative response to the questions posed above?" The answer to this last question was yes, which was a bolt out of the blue as Freddie did not realize that was happening.

Freddie connected this learning with that from the May Employee Engagement Masterclass to build a new communication structure within his business. An employee newsletter is now completed bi-monthly and sent to the employees' homes. Conducting a leadership questionnaire has helped to let the employees anonymously have their say on their manager's performance. The newly formed employee committee has allowed the 'voice' of the workforce to be heard and provided some very valid points, issues and ideas for the company. Directors have encouraged managers to relay essential information back to their teams after the Key Decision Makers meeting; this wasn't happening before as information channels were blocked.

These action plans have all been brought on by the realization that communication wasn't working at all in his organization. The company endured a strict hierarchy with major barriers to cross-organizational communication with long-standing directors struggling to communicate between themselves, meaning that any interaction and exchange with staff at any level was minimal. The performance of these directors is now under scrutiny. Previously, poor performance was not addressed.

BOTH HUMAN AND SOCIAL CAPITALS – LEADING IN-GROUPS AND OUT-GROUPS

From the April Leadership Masterclass, Freddie linked Leader Member Exchange (LMX) theory (Graen and Uhl-Bien, 1991) with his organization, discovering he had very distinct sub-groups. The financial controller and sales manager with access to a wide range of information were in the "in-group". A sales office manager, interiors manager and operations manager were in the "out-group".

Freddie had heavily relied on the information provided to him by the "in-group" and made big decisions based on their knowledge and facts. Although he would listen to the "out-group", they were on the periphery. This, however, has been to the detriment of the business and the two members of the "in-group" are no longer with the company due to the provision of inaccurate information.

Freddie learnt a harsh but very valuable lesson from this experience and on reflection, he spent too much time relying on and listening to the "in-group" when the "out-group" were holding key operational information which hadn't been tapped into. After his recent encounter with the LMX theory he realizes being too close to an "in-group" alienates the "out-group" and does not promote employee relationships. For future reference he will be extremely careful not to harbour strong links with certain managers who are on the same level as each other to avoid creating groups which would not be beneficial for relationships within the company.

INSTITUTIONAL AND HUMAN CAPITALS – PERSONAL RESPONSIBILITY

Freddie recognizes that he cannot do it all and that he needs a capable management team around him. Leaving managers to manage on their own is not suitable either. During the course of LEAD he has discussed replacing poor-performing senior managers with his peers inside and outside of Action Learning Sets as well as with his coach. This is something that has never happened in his company's history, but because peers that he respects said it was the correct course of action, he has changed most of his senior management team.

* * * * *

THE THREE CAPITALS AND FREDDIE'S LEADERSHIP DEVELOPMENT

Freddie has developed his human capital, that is, improving his knowledge, skills and capabilities (Leitch et al., 2013). This is evident through the acquisition of new knowledge he says he has gained from the learning interventions and the other owner/managers, which he has put into practice and plans to continue to do so. He has developed new skills such as open questions and listening, which has changed the way he leads and manages and uses to "fix" what was being run poorly within the business. Reflective practice is also a skill he is working on, reflecting back to events, during meetings and using this skill to reflect forwards in order to prepare himself and his staff for when they meet. He also highlights how his confidence has increased and identifies with being a leader with his own chosen style, realizing that he has learnt from what he sees as mistakes from other leaders in the past. In parallel, he has developed his business, creating a business plan for the first time in the company's 100-year history. He has implemented key strategies as the future heartbeat of the organization to enable a realistic growth plan.

Secondly, Freddie has developed social capital, that is the relationships between individuals and organizations that facilitate action and create value. He recognized he needed a capable management team around him and subsequently changed most of the senior team, replacing those who were poor-performing. Freddie is also mindful of his future behaviour and relationships with managers and highlights how he will be careful not to create groups that are not beneficial for the company. Communication has been an area Freddie has clearly worked on throughout the company.

The implementation of an employee engagement strategy has addressed the previous highly directive leadership practices and has allowed social capital to develop, giving a "voice" to the workforce which, in turn, has enabled issues and ideas to be circulated. Blockages have been addressed and communication has been encouraged between directors and managers to relay essential information back to their teams after the Key Decision Makers meeting. Additionally, Freddie has built up strong social capital with his LEAD peers, recognizing the trust and openness he has with them as well as the wealth of information they can share.

Thirdly, institutional capital is developed through the creation of the LEAD CoP, that is, the formal structures and organizations which enhance the role of social capital and go beyond enriching the human capital stock of individual leaders (Anderson, 2010). This has been enabled through the expanded network of Freddie's LEAD peers; business leaders who did not know each other previously, coming together to create a CoP. Freddie recognizes this peer group has been a huge aid to his development. Leitch et al. (2013, p. 358) argue that the development of the reservoir of social capital (in this case, the LEAD peers) transcends the boundaries of each individual firm, which provides the platform for the development of institutional capital. For Freddie, it is the structures and the processes within the LEAD CoP that enable institutional capital, which, in turn, has an effect on his own leadership development and his business. He recognizes that his peers have been the greatest support group he could have hoped for and he networks/socializes with them outside the programme. Freddie also highlights how, through his own development, he can see the benefit to his peers' organizations too. Shadowing another business has given him insight into how he can add value to another organization, with the resultant gain for the whole community.

Although Freddie is just over halfway through the LEAD programme, his leadership development brings together human, social and institutional capitals, showing how institutional capital can be developed through the establishment of a CoP (in LEAD) that can enable the development of owner/manager leadership through nurturing and enhancing human, social and institutional capitals.

9. LEAD journey: month 7 – September

This chapter describes the delegates' reflection on Shadowing, introduces the Exchanges and discusses the delegates going into another's business to undertake two projects on leadership and business growth. The final coaching and Action Learning sessions take place with the latter being self-facilitated. The delegates experience another Masterclass.

REFLECTION ON SHADOWING AND INTRODUCTION TO EXCHANGES

"Times have changed," thought Freddie to himself as he parked his sports car and quickly set across the familiar path through the now recognizable sports fields by the lake towards the shimmering metal and glass reception that held the LEAD meeting rooms within.

"It was only six short months ago when, full of trepidation, I took my first faltering steps along this very path on my LEAD journey. Yet today, I am genuinely excited about standing up with Jane in front of our peers to tell our story, to share our learning from our Shadowing experience. We have both benefited from being in each other's organizations. The experience was so enjoyable.

"Times have changed," mused Freddie again. "It was only four months ago that I ducked giving a speech in the April Leadership Masterclass. Today I am going to volunteer us first!

"Now, that is a big difference in how I behave!

"I wonder how David and Ann will organize the day. I am very interested to hear about our peers' learning. We are all moving into a new zone where no one has been before. I sense, too, that we are about to move up into a new gear and increase the speed.

"How times have changed," contemplated Freddie. "I am more familiar now with LEAD and how to critically think and reflect on my learning, though one aspect remains a constant . . . I'll continue to do what I have done from the beginning . . . trust the process."

* * * * *

"The delegates know the form now," said David to Ann, "and it is great to see they take advantage of the time before a session to arrive early."

The morning sunlight was flooding the refreshments area and the pair were now mixing with the cohort. David and Ann's preparations were complete. Everything had been set up. They were ready. All around them peers were deep in discussion, swapping stories, waving arms and sharing jokes. There was much laughter.

"It is just as it should be," thought David as he motioned the delegates next door. "They have become a community. I am looking forward to hearing their individual contributions which will enhance others' learning."

Ann was first to address the whole cohort at the start of a full day, a special day.

"The beginning of month 7 is another pivotal stage in your LEAD learning journey as you reflect on your Shadowing experience and are introduced to the Exchange projects.

"It is a special day because it is one of the few occasions on LEAD that you come together as the full cohort where only yourselves are present. It provides you the opportunity to catch up with peers and speak to others outside your Action Learning Set that you do not see as often.

"It is special because you have the time during the day to look back, reflect, value and share with your peers your insights from your unique experience that is Shadowing.

"It is special because you will not only crystallize your own learning but will help the development of your peers, because as leaders, we can all learn from each other's experiences and learning.

"You will see that I have displayed your 'By the end of Shadowing I would like. . .' quotes from the Introduction to Shadowing Day three months ago to remind you what you thought you wanted from the process. Now, how closely did your experience match what you thought you would get from the shadowing process? Take a few minutes to write down your thoughts."

Ann then distributed a handout with questions for the delegates to work through on their own considering what they learned during Shadowing, getting them to refer back to their Shadowing workbook.

Finally, the delegates went back into their pairs and triples to discuss how they were going to present their learning of the Shadowing experience and produce a poster or something similar to aid their presentations.

"Think about what your key learning points are and why, and how your peers will benefit from what they hear and see. The more creative you are in your presentations the better," concluded Ann with an encouraging smile.

As Ann spoke, shock and concern quickly spread over Bill and Jane's faces. "We're going to have to draw?"

* * * * *

An hour later, Freddie and Jane were first to present their reflections on their learning in a 7-minute burst followed by questions and answers.

"Firstly," said Freddie, "it is such a privilege to be able to go into someone else's business. I found the whole experience enlightening."

"Yes," added Jane. "It was an eye opener for us both. I particularly enjoyed the Shadowing because it provided a critical, unbiased view of how we behave within our business. The process allowed me to become more aware of my leadership shadow and work on my leadership style.

"The first key learning point for us was to trust our instincts. What we both thought were the right changes to make for the better were the right changes. This is energizing. It also brings clarity.

"We both also observed that balance is key," said Freddie. "There needs to be consensus and the appropriate challenge with the use of open questions rather than people dominating discussions. We both observed others getting the balance wrong.

"Allied to this learning point is the importance of freedom of speech which requires 'coaching for extraordinary results'. I submit that this is a LEADism, a phrase for the LEAD lexicon," laughed Freddie.

"Neither of us were aware of our next learning point," noted Jane. "This was a blind spot in the true sense of the Johari Window. We both have an annoying habit of ending a sentence with a specific word that we use to infer an understanding of the point we have just made. Actually, we lazily use our favoured word to finish what is actually an incomplete sentence. We both observed our partner's teams struggling to understand the meaning of a sentence. We were creating gaps in understanding and inviting others to fill them, which of course they were doing in different ways leading to confusion."

"Next for me," said Freddie, "is not being aware of the power of our leadership role. Jane's major shareholder was pulling the strings when actually she has the power as her managers and staff follow her vision. It is her structure. So she should draw power from both."

"Finally, we both have difficult people in our organizations and there will be a bumpy ride as dealing with them is far from over," ended Jane.

"There was an impression in my firm that I was introducing change at a considerable pace," continued Freddie. "I have a clear idea of which staff are reluctant to change, evident through conversations. I am engaging those that wish to drive change in their area. I can build on and take strength from Jane's observation that I have a positive and engaging manner with staff which they respond to.

"From the Leadership & Management questionnaire that staff completed a few months ago, I know that they see me as authoritative, as well as being consultative and approachable. From Jane's feedback, I have the room to turn the authority up a notch as I come across too lenient at times.

"How easy is it for staff to know when you are pleased or disappointed by observing your body language? We know from LEAD that we should not read too much into body language as it can be misleading; however, I need to be mindful of how I hold myself as inadvertently and unconsciously I am sending out the wrong message. Finally, Jane observed that I can also increase my use of open questions during the Key Decision Makers' meeting and coach others to use open questions too. *Coaching for extraordinary results* is my new mantra."

"Creating the posters has been fun and it makes you distil all your learning into the key points in such a short space of time. It's an eye-opening technique," said Jane. "It wasn't easy, especially trying to find the right image to match to the learning point that was to be communicated but it is good to reflect on the Shadowing experience and filter the take outs. I have learned so much about myself and now I need to do something with these insights."

"Well done Freddie and Jane. A round of applause everyone. Any questions or comments anyone?" asked Ann.

"Just an observation, Ann," said Bill. "I have looked forward to today with some trepidation. We both made so many notes and generated so many ideas, and I was finding it hard to distil what I experienced both as a shadower and being shadowed. By focusing on the key learning points and why, really does get you to consider your learning experience, as demonstrated by Freddie and Jane."

After a few questions about Freddie and Jane's experiences, next to speak were Bill and James.

"James and I have had three days together, firstly a few hours preparing ourselves, then a day in each other's companies and a final feedback session to each other. It was interesting, refreshing and I had another eureka moment," exclaimed a buoyant Bill.

"I felt as if I was in the Wizard of Oz film as I got to look behind the curtain but I didn't see a disappointingly small person; rather I got to see a larger image, a bigger picture of what was going on both in someone else's business and in mine too. The opportunity to go into someone else's company at a high level was fantastic. I would like to do it again. Although our businesses are completely different and we have different leadership styles, it was amazing to find that there was so much in common – good and bad!

"The importance of planning was a key learning point from my interesting and chaotic Shadowing day with James. We had a 20-hour day which he said was typical! There was no planning except the times and locations of the meeting. There was no clear purpose of what each meeting was there to achieve, no notes taken at any of the meetings, so no planning forward, no outcome. We went to a particular job which was good actually because, in a nutshell, it exemplified everything that was wrong with what he was doing and all his skills were being deployed to fire fight effectively.

"He has shadowed me and we have met to feed back to each other. He genuinely listened to what I had to say and he knew about 90 per cent of my observations. What he will do about it is another question!

"Receiving his feedback was extremely useful, particularly the validation of what I thought was happening. James stated that I am still too prescriptive and not asking enough open questions. He observed that the company was far too reliant on me, that I was still doing too much and my partners were not challenging me. There was a lack of any strategic input that feeds directly into the leadership of the firm.

"What is astounding is that our businesses are very different but so much is similar. We are both isolated, separate, adrift from our organizations. I am separate but in the midst of everything, doing stuff; James is separate and out on an organizational limb where everyone covers for him."

"We found that when we were in our businesses we were too task focused and thus could not see what was going on. We had no overview."

"It has been a great experience," echoed James. "Our respective businesses reflect each other."

Bill interjected. "And that was my eureka moment. I could plainly see that James's firm was a mirror of himself when I was in his organization. The way his business performs is an embodiment of James and he knows it. Yet, despite the chaos and confusion, his people adore him. There was a throwaway comment made by a key member of staff that stuck with me. 'It is as if he is always on stage, he is always smiling, joking and relaxed. So if he can withstand the pressures from clients then so can we. We can get by'.

"Up until this point I thought it was processes, not people, that matter. Here, before my very own eyes, the people were making the difference despite the chaotic processes. James's team members were helping each other out whereas my staff are still leaving things for me to do.

"Imagine if we as leaders manage the people to manage the processes? They know how to do the job better than us so let's inspire them, let's give them the direction, support and freedom to make the difference. We need both the people and the processes but our behaviour as leaders has greatest impact on our people. That was the point that Sammy was making throughout the Overnight Experiential. I have spent a lifetime focusing on the processes, not the people. Not any longer!

"I realized from the April Leadership Masterclass that managing by walking around matters, and the importance of having the appropriate narrative for the off-stage moments. James observed that I still need a strategy to do this more naturally and more effectively when engaging my staff. My water cooler moments and impromptu chats with staff need to be more fluid. Also, I must not assume people understand what I am talking about. I need to check that they receive the message and understand the meaning. We all know we should do this but how many of us actually do it? That was a powerful reflective point for me.

"Whilst I thought I'd become more self-aware and had made changes on LEAD to date, I haven't gone far enough. I must change more."

"Fabulous openness and candour, Bill and James, and some key learning points to take away and do something about. We'll take a couple of questions before our next presenters," remarked Ann.

* * * * *

"It is interesting that David and Ann made us work with different people from those that we had just partnered with or are within our Action Learning Sets to discuss the emerging themes from all the Shadowing presentations," said Jane.

"Yes," replied Bill. "Speaking to those that I do not normally see was of benefit. It disseminated our learning across the cohort and initiated a discussion to further refine these into common learning points."

"It is incredible," continued Jane, "that everyone had leadership issues, whether it was unobserved interactions between senior managers in meetings, managers not contributing in meetings or being brought into discussions. Behaviours at meetings and lack of clarity or structure of senior management team were all mentioned. So many of these issues were similar, irrespective of the size of company or business sector. I am not alone with these issues. I am not the cause. This is a confidence boost in its own right."

"It is rare to get such an honest appraisal in business," noted Bill. "There was no agenda, the feedback is priceless!"

Bill paused and turned his head slightly for a few seconds, staring into the distance clearly searching for something in his mind before re-establishing eye contact with Jane. "I've taken a lot of strength from confirmation of the known issues and that we can indeed trust our instincts.

So many of us raised having more belief in our own abilities. I feel more self-confident. We are all more self-aware now. It is up to each of us to adopt the appropriate leadership behaviour and implement the necessary change."

"I agree," replied Jane. "Shadowing has re-energized me and given me the confidence to use the power that I have as a leader. Like many peers, I must address the elephant in the room and face my demons."

"The power of the outside observer is considerable," noted Bill. "Shadowing has reaffirmed and reinforced issues from other parts of LEAD. We all have agreed further actions that we must do."

Bill then paused again. He was wobbling as some self-doubt momentarily crept back. "My concern is who will hold me to account? The answer is of course me, but Coaching and Action Learning both finish this month. I have used these sessions as monthly prompts to ensure I do what I said I was going to do. That comfort blanket is about to be withdrawn. As you know, one of my weaknesses is not following through."

Jane smiled and reminded Bill of the quote from Frank Dick, the Coaching Masterclass speaker, who in July said, "If not you, who? If not now, when?"

"As leaders we need to take responsibility and be accountable for actions in our purview. We cannot procrastinate either. Both cast the wrong leadership light. Remember that you have another four months of LEAD left including the Exchange, plus you have the strength of the wider LEAD cohort too that will always be available to you. You are no longer alone. We have each other as a support unit. Our Action Learning Set can continue; it is down to us to organize meetings. The bond of the overall cohort is a strong one, as evidenced today, and its power will give us strength of conviction. I am sure of that."

"You are right, Jane," smiled Bill, reassured by Jane's words of encouragement.

"It was interesting to see how others approached creating their posters and displaying their learning," said Jane, changing the course of the conversation. "The process reveals so much about ourselves. Some people have taken a very practical approach, while others were very detailed. Everyone now is so relaxed, there is so much banter and humour.

"I am glad I went first with Freddie as it seemed to give me more time to concentrate a lot more on what you and the others had to say," concluded Jane.

* * * * *

David drew a line under the Shadowing experience and moved the cohort into the next phase of LEAD – conducting the Exchanges.

"The purpose of the Exchanges is to provide an opportunity to learn from each other's organizations, learn about your own behaviour and learn about your own organization through a fresh pair of eyes.

"The Exchanges enable you to look at your peer's leadership style and business and compare these with your own. They provide a valuable opportunity to give and receive feedback, to and from LEAD delegates.

"The Exchange process involves you going into your partner's organization and carrying out two projects – one on business development and one on leadership development. This is akin to director level consultancy. The Exchanges will enable you to learn how to observe what is going on in another organization, look at an organization through a fresh pair of eyes, relate your learning back to your organization and give and receive feedback based on the learning from the experience.

"The Exchange process provides an opportunity for self-reflection about your own leadership style and the culture within your business. You will also learn about the ways another business operates and see if the different perspectives and practices can be beneficial to your own business.

"The Exchange consists of you and your partner swapping with each other and carrying out projects whilst in each other's organizations. You will agree which two projects you wish your partner to carry out in your company and vice versa. You will also agree how long you will exchange with each other."

David then took the delegates through the project pages of the Exchange workbook to ensure that they were fully aware of what was expected of them and what deadlines they had to adhere to. David then invited the pairs and triples to agree a date for the first exchange and decide which two projects they wanted their partner(s) to undertake.

"Now what I'd like you to do is write on a post-it note what you would like to achieve by the end of the Exchanges, come up to the front, put it on the flip chart and share it with your peers. This encourages you to think about what you might hope to get from the process and, by sharing it, broadens understanding and learning about each other," said David.

With a final comment from David and Ann of "Good luck and have fun!" the delegates headed off into the late afternoon sunlight, briefed on the next stage of their journey.

* * * * *

ACTION LEARNING SET 6

"I will miss these sessions as Action Learning Sets have been amazing for me," said Freddie. "I never thought I'd hear myself say those words because at the beginning of Action Learning I found it very difficult. I didn't think it was going to work for me as all I wanted to do was give answers and press my opinion on others. It seemed too difficult to ask open questions.

"But I stuck with it, I have acquired a new language and have been putting it into action. Staff at a lower level obviously don't see me very much so I have begun educating my new management team to speak to staff in a better manner. I am not saying that they are doing anything wrong but as I sit in a meeting I am looking at other people's performance and wondering how they think they are performing."

"Freddie, I felt the same," disclosed Bill. "I have found Action Learning very difficult but it gets easier with time and the process of LEAD. It also gets more fruitful and valuable.

"My nature and my job is to provide solutions to people so asking open questions was anathema to me. It was metaphorically difficult to sit on my hands and remember how challenging that was for me to do when Sammy instructed me to do so at the Overnight Experiential."

Everyone laughed with Bill, sharing in his uncomfortable learning event from six months earlier.

"However," continued Bill, "as tough as it was, by asking open questions, we often found that the issue or problem that the presenter brought to the session was not the problem. There was another deeper issue. By thinking what open question to ask and how to form that question it made me think more about what the actual problem was. There was much value in discovering that, so much so that I now use the Action Learning process in my firm."

"That's a giant step forward," noted Freddie. "I agree that often we had similar problems, it was just that we perceived them differently.

"Due to LEAD, I am now self-critical, constantly reflecting on every meeting that I have, which in turn has aided me to evolve in my role as Managing Director. An example of this is the Key Decision Makers meeting which I chair. I ensure that I am well prepared going into the meeting with a set agenda and forward this to managers to add content/ points before the meeting. As this is an important meeting, it is vital that I listen intently and answer succinctly any questions posed. Prior to LEAD, I was a poor listener. I also asked closed questions rather than the open questions I have been coached to use in Action Learning.

"I always take time to reflect on how the meeting went and evaluate what went well and what didn't go so well, how I felt about the meeting and whether I was happy with the results from the meet. I will analyse the meeting with my directors to gauge the feeling from within the meeting, which is a good indicator for staff morale and well-being at the present time. An action plan is then devised along with minutes and a 'to do' list with more feedback on my own performance from the managers on how I could improve my performance and how they can improve their performance.

"I have found reflection extremely beneficial, which has helped build my confidence and performance over time.

"I now constructively challenge everybody and everything. We were interviewing the other day and I could tell the others wanted to give the candidate the job because they were asking closed questions. Afterwards I sat down with them to reflect how they could have interviewed differently. That would not have happened a few months ago. Indeed I too would have been asking closed questions.

"I feel as if I have jumped up a few rungs on the performance ladder as I attempt to become a better leader, a more effective leader, to be the best I can become. That's why I am at the highest point I have ever been on the Jelly Baby Tree," concluded Freddie.

"I feel as if I have gone full circle," said Jane, "so I am going to choose the same Jelly Baby that I did six months ago. Why? Although I have gone full circle, I have gained real insights. I have learned and examined but I recognize I have yet to implement the desired change – Shadowing confirmed this for me. LEAD is an awakening but it is not a fast thing for me as I need time to reflect, process and then act. I know that the time to act is now and Shadowing has given me the confidence to do so."

"Over breakfast this morning, I thought about where I was on the Jelly Baby Tree so that I would have my answer ready," said Bill.

"I am like Freddie, both in a similar place on the tree and in our respective development. As I said a few moments ago, Action Learning has taught me the power of the open question; that what I see as a problem may merely be a symptom; that my character demands that I always seek and offer *my* solutions rather than helping others to explore problems and find their *own* solutions; and that self-generated solutions are more likely to be appropriate and successful. In short I needed to listen more and talk less."

With the final round of Jelly Baby Tree behind them with the ensuing mirth, Ann reminded the set that she expected the closely bound peers to self-facilitate the morning session.

"I'll go first this time," stated Bill, "but before I do I'd like to share this box of Jelly Babies with you all. We have spoken about them for so long I thought it was about time we tasted them too!" Everyone laughed as Bill passed the box of sweets around.

"My issue is how can I learn and capture the lessons from LEAD and apply them to my day-to-day routine? Should I be describing the Future Perfect? Creating my personal vision, my dream? My goal is to maximize the return on investment in LEAD to realize the desired change in my personal life."

Just as so many times before in each of the Action Learning Sets, the presenter concluded their air time with actions that they agreed that they would do something about. Bill was pleased.

Ann noted that the next two who spoke brought issues that they told the others they really, truly had no idea how to solve and would be very grateful for any input. Again the apparently unsolvable was resolved through the power of Action Learning by the set members.

In the final wrap up and reflection, Jane shared, "Ann, you are very good at nudging us to recall relevant models, tools and examples from various parts of LEAD. I'll miss that but I plan to go through my LEAD binder and bring out all my key learning to date. That will help me to focus and implement the necessary changes."

"I'll miss someone regularly asking how I am progressing with my actions," noted Bill. "Going forward, it is up to me to hold myself to account and I will set and diarize six weekly goals so that I can keep moving towards my vision. I am also going to explore having a coach outside of LEAD and indeed, as one of the Masterclass speakers suggested, I may use a different coach for different scenarios."

"I suppose two boxes will be ticked this month with the completion of Action Learning and Coaching," reflected Freddie. "It's been a successful process so far and I am looking forward to completing the final sprint. It's taken a lot of my time away from the office to acquire this new learning. I say that in a positive sense as it has demonstrated that I don't need to be in the office nor do I need to call my managers either. Indeed, now that Coaching and Action Learning are finished that gives me a day every month to implement strategies that I've been considering from the programme.

"This will sound strange but I wanted to share it with you. Every night I take my dog for a long walk. My mind is so full of things that sometimes I can't think clearly. After a couple of kilometres my mind shifts into a different state – a more reflective state that helps me to problem solve. This thinking on the move prompts me to take actionable steps back in the business, so a similar approach may help you too."

"Thanks everyone for your contributions," concluded Ann. "I observed lots of joking today, indicating how comfortable you are with each other.

I heard lots of praise for actions taken, lots of story-swapping in the break, lots of pulling together of your LEAD learning and suggestions on what to do next.

"You have come a long way together in a short period of time. I understand you aim to meet as an Action Learning Set after LEAD. I am glad you see the benefit and I wish you well."

* * * * *

(FACE-TO-FACE) COACHING

"Good to see you again, Freddie," remarked David. "Welcome to the final face-to-face Coaching session."

"I can't believe it is our final session. Time has flown by," replied Freddie. "We have spoken about many different issues including tools, techniques and models that I've learnt during LEAD."

"Last month we had a business Masterclass on Finance. We discussed your issues around finance during our coaching sessions. I see from your preparation form that you never raised this in Action Learning. Please share your reasoning with me."

"It wasn't that it was sensitive," said Freddie. "The discovery of mistakes in financial reporting by my previous financial controller happened during LEAD but I felt there were other things where the Action Learning Set could provide more value. This issue was something which was beyond my control as it happened before I came into my role and the consequential internal matters were too specific for any external person to be able to help with.

"Nor was it a sense of embarrassment. Though imagine you are doing really well and suddenly the biggest stick strikes you and you realize that you are not as good as you thought. That was how I felt. Further, you discover that the person you've had at the helm of finance for many years was not competent and had not reported errors. My natural optimism immediately disappeared and was replaced by a deep pessimism.

"I was fully reliant on someone doing a job for me. What it did highlight was that I needed to have capable people around me who I could trust implicitly but also that I need to understand the mechanics of how everything works as well.

"So you can promote people from within the organization but you need to be aware that they may be taught by predecessors who didn't know how to do the role properly either. So I had a double whammy – a major accounting error and realization that a so-called trusted manager deliberately misreported figures whom I subsequently had to remove.

"It was a very difficult time for me. My father saw it as an opportunity to criticize me and my approach again. We took the ex-controller through the disciplinary process correctly, he was dismissed and subsequently he is taking us to a tribunal which will absorb a phenomenal amount of my time. He is already throwing anything that he can, trying to make it stick. The whole experience is a major character-building episode for me. I have never been to a tribunal. We should win, and if we do it will show that there is a fair world out there. If we lose though, it will knock me for six.

"Obviously some of the things I picked up from LEAD and the people I've been speaking to – yourself and a few others – are helping me through this experience. There's been a couple of other LEAD peers' companies who have had financial issues too. I have spoken to them and I have taken strength that I am not alone. The whole peer group is very good at providing timely support."

"So others experience difficult times too in their businesses," noted David.

"Yes," replied Freddie. "The pressures that Tom has had with his family within their company, how he's conquered those and managed to avoid issues within the family are an inspiration. Their challenges are fast approaching me as well. It is as if you solve one outburst and then another one springs up and starts spraying water over you."

* * * * *

Jane and David had just completed another productive coaching session. Jane always prepared for the sessions so David was using the remainder of the available time to get Jane to reflect on her learning on LEAD and what she planned to do next.

"I have been anxious of revealing my inadequacies, and while I trusted the cohort and always revealed my weaknesses, it has proved to be a rollercoaster in confidence. I have had some of my lowest points on LEAD, the first Action Learning Set springs to mind, so being on the programme has made me face and address some difficult issues.

"My confidence has grown over the course of LEAD," disclosed Jane. "LEAD has reassured me that some of what I am doing is correct but it has also highlighted the areas where I need to change how I lead. Principally I need to become tougher and be prepared to direct more than I do. Although I have to implement many of the changes, I do believe that I have significantly improved my leadership qualities.

"I have taken bits from each of the LEAD elements. My initial apprehension was overcome at the Overnight Experiential. The Leadership Style Spectrum highlighted that I am just too consensual and that I look for agreement too much. I need to become more assertive and directive, which has been further highlighted in Action Learning, Shadowing and from the leadership survey that I introduced after the Oliver Masterclass. I've received the green light from the company to initiate the desired changes. I can see all that now, hence my increased confidence and reassurance.

"I need to find the appropriate balance between direction and engagement. How much of it should be me leading the way versus engaging the others to reach these goals? I now know that my role in the business is to set a clear vision and help the others to achieve it. I have a meeting with my team shortly and I have set the agenda as 'Vision Delivery'.

"I must better understand the concept of power and mentally be able to separate it from control. From Shadowing, I appreciate that in the eyes of the followers I have power as they see me as the leader but the main shareholders have the control. Bill said an interesting thing in Action Learning, 'You have earned the trust, now spend it'.

"So that is my next development challenge."

* * * * *

David was listening to Bill's reflections since the last session. He was impressed that Bill had changed his views on the OSKAR coaching model and now wanted David to put more information about it on the LEAD Forum.

"There is no doubt face-to-face coaching is better, but over the phone was good too. Coaching has taught me the value of finding time to talk about myself occasionally and to someone with a 'critical' eye – I mean that in a positive sense, not a negative one. In particular I liked the idea of seeing the Future Perfect and then working backwards to where I am now – but crucially not being despondent because a lot of the time there are a lot of good things in place already. So the journey from today to the Future Perfect may look a long one but when you know you are half way there already it spurs you on.

"I simplified OSKAR in my mind seeing it as 'where am I now' – often pretty good, so thumbs up – and where do I want to be, and then tiny steps to get there, none of them impossible but the first step pretty hard due to not knowing what to do, hence the need for coaching. I also felt I needed a reward for every step rather than seeing the final goal as the only reward. This motivated me so each step seemed an achievement in itself.

"After the first coaching session, I diarized an hour a week – Friday – to plan the following week ahead; an hour a week to 'tour' the office and chat to staff and finally, in a later session, to hire a 'wingman', an assistant who is more than just a worker, to be in my team. I've kept to both the weekly planning and the tour and I've got a great 'wing woman'.

"I have made giant strides because of Coaching. My daily meetings with my assistant are transformative. I have now succeeded in finding a way of working with my assistant that is good for both of us and motivates her. We agreed that we would meet for as long as it takes each day. Sometimes we'll have an hour, sometimes we'll have ten minutes. It doesn't matter. It's in the diary every single day at nine o'clock. Some days we don't meet if there is a nine o'clock company meeting or if I'm at one of the other offices at nine o'clock. Key is that it is in the diary every day and therefore if I've got something I'm procrastinating over then I must consciously move it forward. I do not book appointments to clash with this meeting.

"Also my door's open and she will pop in between two and twenty times a day. I believe it's really important to be open and honest in the dialogue. I follow up more, I recognize good work, I adapt my leadership style to the situation and I try to give out as many tasks to her as I can. I am actively trying to let go and not control as much as I once did.

"Despite being offered an excellent role with a competitor, my assistant has stayed with us. She has provided excellent feedback on my leadership. She says that I am the best boss she has ever had! This confirms that spending regular time with key staff members is time well spent. Our daily meetings have become embedded learning and part of the department's culture.

"I have taken energy and confidence from various parts of LEAD and I'd like to show you a personal model, my personal and business plan that I have created that I believe adds value to my life.

"The 'Solutions Focused Wheel' is my attempt to bring all my learning together so far. I have been feeling overwhelmed by all the fantastic bits of information that I have had. So I had to bring it into a concept, a way of living, a leadership culture, a belief system rather than a list of twenty pithy things to say about leadership, which frankly is neither use nor ornament.

"Prior to LEAD, I could only see linearly so lists were good for me. Now I am starting to see patterns and I am able to draw things together so creating a leadership concept is important and useful for me and my business.

"The hub of 'The Wheel' is the Future Perfect and the outer rim is my current position in terms of every aspect of my life: health, business (external: clients and internal: the organization). From the rim, spokes lead to the hub and on each spoke is a goal/milestone.

"I have identified my Future Perfect and imagined the person I can be, fulfilling my potential and leading my business to do the same. Personally this means focusing on my private life, health and well-being and future learning. In the business context it focuses on how the individuals that make up my business can each fulfil their potentials. This is not just in terms of their direct contribution to the business because I believe that if in their private lives they achieve fulfilment that will contribute indirectly in the business in terms of creating a healthy working environment, reduced absenteeism, less stress etc."

"This is a great piece of work, Bill. I can see you are beginning to contextualize what you want to become and what steps you can take to achieve your goal. One immediate observation is that there is a lot of information already on the model. How can it be simplified so that patterns and linkages can be more easily observable?"

"That's a very good question," replied Bill.

"That *is* a very good question," repeating himself but in doing so giving himself some time to pause, think and reflect on what he was actually trying to achieve.

"What you are saying really is that it is the *process of preparing* 'The Wheel' that is key. As each aspect is considered in isolation a solution in one area may address many points in different parts of the model.

"Let's take an example. If I've got to speak to everybody every day as it is really important then how do I do that? You know I'm not very good at doing things like that so a solution could be to put it in my diary and make myself do it every week. I could put that under a heading of 'Improve Communication' or something trite like that. However, where the value lies is not just in recognizing its significance in that context but appreciating the importance of actively listening to others, understanding what is going on, obtaining good feedback and learning about people.

"This coaching session has really helped as I now appreciate that it is the actual process of addressing the points individually and identifying the linkages that are key rather than fitting in every bit of information."

* * * * *

MASTERCLASS 7

"I am really looking forward to listening to this Masterclass speaker, and a lady too," thought Ann as she sent the message to the cohort that the slides were available on the Forum.

Subject: Emotional Intelligence in Leadership – Pauline Clare CBE

Pauline was the first female police Chief Constable in the UK. Pauline will start by sharing her own experiences as Chief Constable of the Lancashire Constabulary. She will describe how the organization went through significant change during the period 1995–2002 including cultural, people and structural changes. Pauline will then introduce a key ingredient for making organizations and companies more successful: Emotional Intelligence.

* * * * *

The cohort had agreed to spend an hour together after lunch to collectively reflect on the morning's Masterclass.

"We should have thought about doing this months ago," said Bill. "Using the power of all delegates' minds to focus on and share their learning from the Masterclass is inspired. Great idea, Jane."

"Thanks, Bill. I thought it was so refreshing to hear from a female leader and someone who has come from such a male dominated sector."

"For the first part of the morning she spoke to everybody with no slides, and in the opening hour, nobody asked her any questions at all. Why?" asked Freddie rhetorically. "She was inviting questions. I felt I had to weigh in to talk about what it is like to try to change a culture. This is something that I am trying to do in my business so I was seeking top tips."

Freddie continued. "Before LEAD, Emotional Intelligence wasn't really a subject I would have been hot on or would have actually valued hugely. But for me I can see it's a massive thing. It's maybe the ability to read people's minds and understand what they are thinking. I plan to use Emotional Intelligence in my everyday business life now in dealings with staff but also with customers.

"I understand I must take the staff on a journey and get the best out of them. To do that you need to know what's inside and Emotional Intelligence will help me do that now. As Pauline said, 'Emotional Intelligence does not cost anything'."

Jane was next to speak. "My Action Learning Set feedback reaffirmed what I know about myself but have been reluctant to confront – I need to improve my ability to balance a nurturing and supportive approach that helps to engender loyalty and the development of others with greater discipline and detail if we are to achieve the specific goals and results the business requires.

"I am overly reliant on 'resonant' leadership,[19] but an element of 'dissonant' leadership is necessary in order to achieve desired outcomes. I found it a valuable exercise considering myself in relation to each of the six leadership styles. I recognized my own predominance of affiliative and democratic styles, with infrequent forays into visionary and coaching

---

[19] Goleman, D., Boyatzis, R. and McKee, A. (2002), *The New Leaders: Transforming the Art of Leadership into the Science of Results*, London: Little, Brown.

traits. However, the absence of pacesetting and commanding styles within my repertoire, the two dissonant styles, has led to an imbalance.

"It is this that my team are recognizing when they signal a desire for me to be 'tougher'. I need to experiment with this, to know when an emphatic demand is required to drive a sense of urgency, and to set demanding goals that stretch individuals to achieve their 'personal best' performances."

Bill interjected. "If you can do that then you'll make the breakthrough in leading that you desire. Just as Sammy said right at the beginning of LEAD on the Overnight Experiential, it is down to us to make the changes in our behaviour if we want a different outcome. You can all remember well how Sammy made me reflect on my behaviour."

Everyone laughed. Here was a group all at ease with each other, supportive of the changes that all were at various stages of accomplishing and genuinely interested in each other's welfare. The smiles on the faces, the nods of approval and light-hearted banter were all signs of a group of like-minded leaders whose lives had been enriched through a shared experience.

Freddie cut in once more. "I've enjoyed both forms of coaching on LEAD and I was concerned that both of these elements have now finished. This Masterclass has helped me to build a perspective on the importance of coaching by emotional contribution. I have learnt that empathy is a crucial skill in engaging with staff. As we know from the May Employee Engagement Masterclass, it is important to give credit when credit is due. Recognizing contributions and appreciating staff goes a long way and is something that I have been poor at in the past.

"I have realized that Emotional Intelligence can be used as a very powerful tool en route to successful Employee Engagement and I will be reflecting on how I handle delicate situations within the workplace and how the employee reacts with a greater consideration on the personal relationship.

"And what better time than now to put these lessons into practice? I'm off back to the office. See you, soon."

Bill and Jane continued chatting to each other.

"As you know, Jane, my personal energy levels suffer from time to time. So, I was interested in *how do I build personal energy levels for greater resilience to overcome difficulties and to achieve high performance?*" said Bill.

"The question of *how much time should we spend between work, family and on ourselves?* intrigued me," replied Jane. "I now know what the balance is and what I would like it to be."

"One final challenge I've taken from the session was *how to enact Emotional Intelligence so that it comes naturally,*" concluded Bill.

* * * * *

LEAD FORUM – MASTERCLASS REFLECTION

Freddie jumped in first and opened the topic this month:

> I thought the speaker provided a thought-provoking session on Emotional Intelligence. I realize I need to find out more about the six leadership styles. It was very valuable that we all had taken an extra hour to reflect on the session. I've had a few additional thoughts since then that I thought I would share with you:
>
> Firstly the quote, 'Actions of one person (the leader!) directly affect the performance of the staff'. Obvious I know, and a message we've heard consistently throughout LEAD, but this has been very true of my organization in previous years!
>
> There was certainly a theme around 'empathy'. This has only been drip-fed into my business over the past two years as I have pushed affiliative and democratic styles of leadership. After the Masterclass I now believe that we have had too much of this and need to also focus on the visionary, pacesetting and commanding leadership styles (taking the bad bits out of the last two).
>
> 'The Emotional Quotient (EQ) is as important as IQ' is an assumption I had not thought about before. Another statement which I took home in my back pocket!
>
> Freddie

> Hi everyone
>
> Thanks for starting the discussion, Freddie.
>
> I brought a guest along to this Masterclass who is a fellow director and is my number two. We had never spoken about leadership styles before so being able to share our thoughts has been a big step forward. She couldn't believe there were parts of the leadership model that I lacked confidence in. She was not aware of my lack of confidence and indeed observed a more rounded leader in me.
>
> There are times when my confidence wavers and I hope that others around me have the answer.
>
> I need to draw strength and power from the attribution my followers give me about my natural leadership style and remember that it is the followers' perceptions that matter.
>
> Jane

THEORY SANDWICH 9 SELF-EFFICACY OF LEADING: THEORETICAL IMPORTANCE OF EXCHANGES

Exploring self-efficacy and the extent or strength of a leader's anticipatory belief in their own ability to complete tasks, reach goals and attain performance in leading in the small business context.

In the context of LEAD, self-efficacy provides a link between lived experience and the interpretation the owner/managers make of experience to form judgements, beliefs or expectations in his or her capability to accomplish a certain level of performance of leading in a particular context. Activities that are valued and desired are weighed against the person's ability to achieve them. If perceived as important, the person may invest effort to improve capability and thus enhance their self-efficacy. We suggest that there is a link between the salience of leadership, the identification with leadership and self-efficacy, directly leading to enhancing capability to become a better leader and improved business performance (Ling et al., 2008; Kempster, 2009a). This will be explored further in theory sandwich 12.

The significance of context to individual learning is central to the leadership roles of Freddie, Jane and Bill and their engagement and interaction with their firms. Their learning is shaped through an emphasis on what is considered important and salient to them individually within their companies.

Returning to the important work of social learning theory (Bandura, 1977, 1986 and 1997) and the broad theory of social learning, a concept that persists for all of us throughout our lives is the notion of self-efficacy. Bandura asserts, and few have questioned such an assertion, that its pervasiveness is fundamentally due to interrelationship of behaviour, cognition and environmental events. These three aspects form a process of reciprocity and exchange where each is informed through the others.

Let us give an example. You (the reader) have wished to play golf for many years. You have seen it on television many times and have accompanied friends on pleasant walks around various golf courses. You purchase a bag of clubs and head with excitement to a practice ground on the nearby golf course. With the ball placed on a tee and a 7 iron in your hand you swing – you've seen it thousands of times. You miss the ball. A few more swings, you hit one and it scurries along the ground. A few more swings and one actually flies high. A few more swings and along the ground they go but you've not missed one for many swings. At last more and more fly into the air. All very exciting. This then is self-efficacy in action. The cognition of what to do is clear as a result of observational learning – the environment. But behaviour – the coordination of swinging and hitting the ball – is at first unknown. From your behaviour (swing) you see the result (ball sitting on the tee or scurrying along the ground). This has impact (or learning) with regard to cognition. You rethink the swing (particularly when your friend advises you not to move your head up and down and not to sway from side to side) and you modify your behaviour. The ball flies in the air (environment provides feedback) and this is captured in cognition. And so on in a reciprocal interrelationship.

This is the same for leading. Leading after all is an act, a behaviour. It is undertaken in an environment and there are impacts from the behaviour in the environment that shape cognition. The cognition may be that "I'm leading well, they are excited". Or perhaps "no one appears to be following me". These reciprocal exchanges between cognition, behaviour and the environment set up expectations of performance. How well do I expect to be able to hit the golf ball? How well do I think my performance of leading will be? Self-efficacy then is "people's judgments of their capabilities to organise and execute courses of action required to attain designated types of performances" (Wood and Bandura, 1989, p. 391).

Bandura qualifies this expectation by contextualizing the value of being able to perform the activity to an individual. "The relative influence exerted by the three sets of interacting factors will vary for different activities, different individuals and different circumstances" (1986, p. 24).

So if golf is not important to you, you would not invest significant time, energy and commitment to becoming better at it.

The same is true for leadership. If leadership is not highly valued then the performance anticipated and the results obtained would not cause much concern. After all, you might say to yourself (cognition) that "people are born to lead so what can I do?" This immediately limits expectations of performance. If, however, intervention occurs (for example committing to undertake a programme on leadership!) there is recognition that leadership is a valued outcome to which effort is required to enhance self-efficacy of leading. This does connect to another important aspect of salience which has been touched on throughout the book – which we shall revert to shortly.

Self-efficacy then is a significant link between thought and action. In Kempster's research he showed that "an individual manager's self-efficacy of leading is argued to be shaped by both pre-organizational experiences and notably their organizational career" (2009a, p. 73).

In the context of the delegates going through LEAD, and in particular Freddie, Jane and Bill, their pre-organizational careers have shaped their approaches to leading but also their expectation of their performance of leading in their own business context and expectations of being able to lead outside of this context.

So valued activities are those that we seek to improve our capability at performing. Bandura (1986) suggests there are four sources that construct self-efficacy:

1. "Direct experience – personal enactment of leading reflected as learning by doing.
2. Vicarious, observed experience – comparison through modelling of others' performance.
3. Verbal persuasion – examples of which are instructions, coaching or feedback.
4. Emotional arousal – hardships and low confidence have the effect of lowering self-efficacy" (Kempster, 2009a, p. 74).

Taken together, these four aspects have been used to shape the LEAD programme design. However, caution in designing a programme to enhance self-efficacy has to be the watchword. Bandura makes clear a salutary lesson: "To succeed at easy tasks provides no new information for altering one's sense of self-efficacy whereas mastery of challenging tasks conveys salient evidence of enhanced competence" (Bandura, 1977, p. 201).

Artificially seeking to create challenges is likely not to have an impact on self-efficacy. The key is to anchor challenges to real, live, on-going contexts. Such development reflects the research of Davies and Easterby-Smith (1984), who highlighted how self-efficacy of leading and managing is enhanced through engaging on a variety of experiences and responsibilities. "The greater the authentic challenges to leadership learning, the greater the likelihood of a manager enhancing self-efficacy" (Kempster, 2009a, p. 73). It's not just the variety of experiences that enhances self-efficacy but also the people to observe in a variety of situations – returning the point to the value of observational learning in theory sandwich 6.

However, for self-efficacy of leading to be increased there has to be a desire to increase such capability. This moves us to the phenomenon of salience – how pronounced a particular entity or concept is. In one of the Leadership Masterclasses the speaker concludes the session with the words "Up your salience. If leadership is not salient then simply put, all the rest is of little value".

The argument is that the mind can simply not examine everything at the same level of attention. Many things become generalized into schematic understandings – knowledge structures that help us make sense of what's happening and assimilate this into a history of what's gone before. That is, assumptions are made about phenomena that go beyond the information presented (Catrambone and Markus, 1987). Such generalizations allow us to cope with the astonishing array of data we experience every day. Schemas cause us to "fill in the gaps" of missing detail – hence generalizations (Gioia, 1986, p. 346).

When a concept is low in salience to someone it can be interpreted as being aschematic – limited knowledge on the subject leading to very broad assumptions to fill in the gaps. An aschematic view of leadership would be someone metaphorically applying "one tool to all problems" – one style to all situations. Where leadership is most salient, attention is endlessly drawn to the many manifestations – most prominently people around us (Kempster and Parry, 2013). The consequence of leadership being highly salient for a significant period of time is the corollary of an advanced and nuanced schema on leadership. A person becomes adept at identifying the subtle cues in the environment to guide sense-making, such cues that would be overlooked by the aschematic leader.

So observational learning becomes greatly advanced in terms of desire to attend to observing people and motivation to observe. This positive reinforcement loop can be applied to Kempster and Parry's (2013) model illustrated in Figure 6.1 and outlined in theory sandwich 6.

However, that's not all. When leadership becomes salient, we observe with much greater attention and this has a marked impact on aspirational leadership identity (Stryker and Statham, 1985; Markus and Wurf, 1987). We spoke earlier (in theory sandwich 5) on the development of identity and how this has an impact on behaviour and touched on the work of Ibarra (1999).

We return to her work here as she usefully connects process of observation, role enactment (past and present), anticipated sense of becoming with identity salience. Ibarra illustrates a process of refinement of practice (her word is "repertoires"), moving from leadership role generalization (formative stages of schematic development on leadership) to discovering what constitutes a contextualized and relevant leadership role performance, to developing an identity to align with situated relationships where notable people are compared to themselves in their contexts. Ibarra argues that the process of developing repertoires, through continual interaction of observation, experimentation and evaluation, both internally and externally, provide an explanation of how the self "becomes" (1999, p. 110).

In the first theory sandwich we outlined the structural limitation for leadership learning in the owner/manager context – the restricted variety of contexts and restricted variety of roles and the restricted number of people to observe. Alongside these restrictions is the low emphasis placed on leadership as a valued identity. Yet all of these aspects are compounded by the low salience of leadership to be studied in the flux of events.

Returning to the Masterclass speaker's final call on leadership learning: "Up your salience!" Two aspects for measures of the LEAD programme as a research-led solution to stimulating SME growth through leadership are an increase in the leadership salience and a significant strengthening of the owner/manager's identity with leadership. A salient leadership identity would emerge as a result of the design. A corollary would be enhanced self-efficacy of leading. We illustrate examples of these changes through the story of Freddie, Jane and Bill.

From theory sandwich 5 in Chapter 5, in SMEs there is very little evidence of a strong sense of self-efficacy of leading amongst owner/managers, which gives rise to questions as to their confidence, competence and capability to lead in contexts other than in their own business (Kempster, 2009a). This is evidenced by Freddie and Jane in their Shadowing experience, as they moved from a feeling of trepidation, self-doubt and lack of confidence to having an enlightening and enjoyable experience gaining awareness of what leadership meant to them in the contexts of their own companies. This then gave them the springboard to undertake the Exchanges in each other's companies, developing their own leadership self-efficacy (Barling, 2014) and improving their leadership effectiveness.

Exchanges provide delegates with two leadership experiences, helping them to see how similar their issues are, no matter what the business. Delegates undertake two projects of their partner's choice providing a short report on their findings. One project is on business growth and the other is on organizational development. The Exchanges combine much of the learning on LEAD to give the delegates the opportunity to put it into practice (Figure 9.1).

Rich experience of leading in a variety of contexts greatly enhances an individual's belief in his/her capability to lead (Kempster, 2009a). LEAD

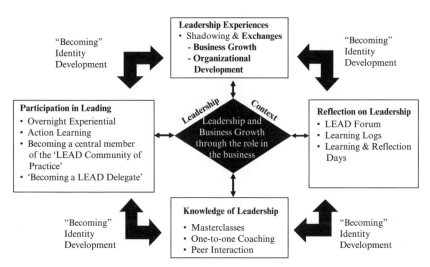

Figure 9.1 LEAD journey, month 7: construction of the "LEADership Learning Cycle" in the context of a LEAD delegate's development from their lived experience

provides confirmatory evidence of leadership or otherwise from alternative contexts.

Salience is a significant catalyst for leadership learning and a deepening relationship with leadership but has less of an effect in SME (Kempster, 2009a). This is addressed on LEAD through Exchanges, which allow an external trusted partner to unearth what people within an organization hold as important, whether that be explicit or tacit, and feed back these findings to their LEAD peer. This in turn may provide powerful insights into underlying causes of leadership learning. If leadership is personally salient to an owner/manager then he/she invests personal effort and commitment to become the identity of a leader, that is, they are increasing their leadership self-efficacy.

Freddie himself notes a sense of becoming. "As you learn to be a LEAD delegate you are learning to lead better".

10. LEAD journey: month 8 – October

In this chapter the delegates begin their experience of undertaking two Exchange projects on business growth and organizational development in their partner's firm and gain more knowledge from another Masterclass.

MASTERCLASS 8

Ann smiled. "Another female Masterclass speaker and this time on managing conflict. This will get them talking."

Subject: Conflict in Business – Professor Carole Howorth

Carole is Professor of Entrepreneurship and Family Business and founded her first business at 19, a family firm which continues to this day under the direction of her sister and niece. Carole will give an insight into conflict at senior management level in family and non-family businesses and how to manage it.

* * * * *

Autumn had set in. The rain was falling steadily, the wind was blowing, the leaves on the trees were changing colour and some were now falling slowly to the ground, carpeting all below. It was a little after two in the afternoon.

"It is good to meet up. It seems as if we have not seen each other for a while," noted Jane.

It had been a month since the cohort was last together, the longest period that they had been apart since LEAD commenced just over seven months ago. The delegates had again organized to meet for an hour after the Masterclass to reflect on a subject specifically selected for them as it had been the most discussed on the programme: managing conflict.

"...*be explicit in what you want...have a long term plan....don't just muddle along.*"

"Those words resonated with me," said Bill. "I never considered having a ten-year vision. Due to LEAD, we have created and implemented a strategic and commercial five-year plan, but ten years seems a long way off and many things can change. It would be good to talk with my business partners about succession plans and our roles for that timescale and beyond. Similarly, to establish more policies for the 'if and when' as we are all getting older."

"'Play together and socialize as a senior management team' struck a chord," observed Jane. "We often talk a good game and have some great ideas about doings things outside of work but plans fall by the wayside due to pressing short-term commitments. I need to ensure we put things in the diary and stick to them. The results when we do socialize are always positive."

"For much of LEAD we have discussed the importance of ensuring employees are involved in change processes and asking for feedback etc.," commented Bill, "so I found it interesting to hear Carole's suggestion that decision by committee leads to compromise and compromise is not the best choice. I concur as I find business teams aim to find the best solution whereas committees aim for an acceptable compromise."

"I was quite taken by the notion that positive conflict is good," said Jane, "as it can be constructive, address more issues and allows for a collective view on the solution. Collaboration is the goal – you win, I win. Not only can it lead to more developed ideas and opportunities but it can create more openness and trust amongst a team. I am going to work with my team to establish guidelines for positive conflict that encourages the necessary uncomfortable discussions."

"You are unusually quiet today, Freddie," remarked Jane.

"Interestingly I didn't feel that I took that much from the Masterclass, but I have listened intently to what everyone has being saying and our discussion has been very intense and quite animated. I don't recall another Masterclass which has invoked a more passionate discussion so it shows that the session was more useful than I had initially thought.

"The use of Non-Executive Directors being a key to success has prompted me to consider if I should bring a NED or NEDs into my business with very different perspectives and personalities. It may help avoid homogeneity and promote constructive discussions. I am building my new management team now so an outsider's view could be helpful."

"Managing conflict this month, leading change next month. I can't wait for the next Masterclass rollercoaster," said Bill.

"Before we go, how are you all getting on with the Exchanges?" enquired Freddie.

As expected, the peers were at different stages from yet-to-start to completed one project to both Exchange projects completed and date agreed to give feedback. One enthusiastic pair had completed everything: Freddie and Jane.

"For those of you who have yet to start, here are a few top tips," said Freddie. "Preparation is everything on the Exchanges. Jane and I met up twice beforehand in each other's business and agreed a plan of what we each wanted to achieve and how to do it. This was extremely beneficial. I also practised using the workbook on myself to improve questions and avoid repeats.

"It is still a big unknown and there is a positive nervousness that is actually a good thing to have, otherwise it may spill over into a cockiness. I felt as if I almost became an employee of Jane's in order to get the projects done in a manner that would assist Jane and me.

"The Exchanges are another one of the raw materials of the LEAD recipe book," smiled Freddie.

"You and your LEADisms!" laughed Bill.

"You recall we shared our leadership timeline at the Overnight Experiential. The final pointers I could give you, Bill, on your leadership Exchange project are to consider *how are your leadership attributes different from your company values? Does improving your attributes establish the values and the desired culture of the firm?*"

"I hadn't thought about that in such detail," replied Bill. "I would like to know, *how far leadership is distributed within my firm. Whether my managers, staff, my followers, embody the desired leadership attributes.*"

* * * * *

LEAD FORUM – MASTERCLASS REFLECTION

Bill opened up the discussion topic:

> I thought I'd share some wider learning for me that has helped me make sense of my LEAD learning.
>
> There is a danger of learning one thing from each Masterclass and leaving them in separate silos. I believe it is important to bring it all together and because of my preferred linear learning approach, I have found it difficult.
>
> It may well be that some of you think like me in a linear way and in my opinion to address that is where the power of reflection comes in.
>
> It's not about the fact we have just had our eighth Masterclass that you reflect on Masterclass 8. It's about reflecting on Masterclass 8 and then thinking, where does the learning from Masterclasses 1 to 7 come in? And similarly, the other aspects of LEAD and the key learning points you build up. It is this realization that has made me go through all my LEAD hand-outs and notes and re-read the things I have written down.
>
> Funnily enough, I have written down leadership experiences which I had forgotten about and thus should have implemented by now!
>
> I've a bit of work to catch up on!

Freddie was up next:

> I want to build on Bill's observation. We have all been making our own personal reflections throughout LEAD, some which we have publicly shared on the LEAD Forum, some in Action Learning or in discussions when we meet. I guess most of our notes are in our LEAD binders.
>
> Bill's comment made me go back to my notes again and I am pleased that I have implemented a number of different tools, techniques and models and I am now integrating them into the business.
>
> I want to share one with you which we all saw on the first morning of the Overnight Experiential – the DO–REVIEW–PLAN–DO Kolb Learning Cycle. Unknowingly I have been following this model. Since I have re-read my notes that model means more to me now so I am consciously going to use it more.

THEORY SANDWICH 10   BIRD'S NEST AND MARBLES

Exploring the notion of holistic learning development in the SME context and describing the theoretical importance of layering learning using the LEADership Learning Cycle – Lived Experience.

LEAD's design deliberately covers a broad range of leadership, business and organizational needs to assist owner/managers in numerous different situations and stages of development. It is unrealistic and impossible to cover every topic but subject selection is wide, with its focus on being practical and useful. Changes in Masterclass subjects are made to reflect individual cohort needs.

Many delegates identify that the uniqueness of LEAD lies in the combination of the different elements of LEAD with the quantum and frequency of these elements over ten months, their interaction with like-minded peers on the programme and the focus on both self-development and the development of their business. Delegates can contextualize their learning as LEAD is both personal and peer-based whilst being practical and business relevant. Delegates are encouraged to directly connect learning from the individual elements of LEAD with themselves as well as to their business contexts. There is a layering of learning and a growing sense of *becoming* in terms of learning to be a LEAD delegate, being a central member of a LEAD Community of Practice and ultimately to an increased identification of being a leader in practice.

This layering of learning is akin to a bird building a nest where each carefully selected twig is a chosen piece of learning from a LEAD element that is connected to another. The cycle is repeated, with the bird going round and round building its edifice until eventually a nest is constructed in a shape that meets the need of the particular bird. We submit that this is

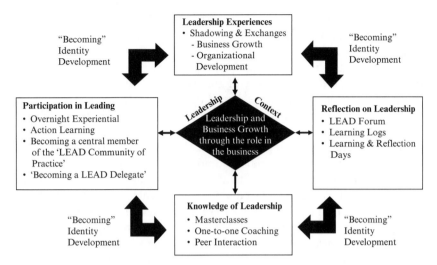

Figure 10.1 LEAD journey, month 8: "LEADership Learning Cycle" – lived experience

how a delegate constructs their leadership learning (Figure 10.1). It may or may not be pretty but it is beautiful in the eyes of a delegate – identifiable and consistent with their definition of leadership in the context of their business. Each nest, a delegate's LEAD learning journey, is unique to the delegate, fitting where they are with leadership as a concept, with where they are with their relationship with their business at that moment in time. This speaks to Bennis (1989, p. 1): "Leadership is like beauty, it's hard to define but you know it when you see it".

Freddie and Bill are clearly constructing their nests more quickly than Jane. By her own admission, Jane's learning style is different, preferring to experience all parts of LEAD to understand what the wider leadership canvas looks like for her before making fundamental change. That is perfectly fine and a small proportion of learners report the same (Gill and Harris, 2014).

In Freddie's case he has reflected on his leadership timeline, drawing out key learning; he has joined together strategic planning where a business plan is a first for his firm with an employee engagement strategy including desired leadership behaviours, a communication network and appropriate recognition systems. He is deploying his newly learned coaching, questioning and listening skills in his quest to be the best he can become. By reflecting back on the Overnight Experiential he has begun to appreciate the DO–REVIEW–PLAN–DO learning cycle.

Bill is similar and has begun to construct his Solutions Focused Wheel – his cohesive philosophical whole – an action plan with milestones on his journey to realize his leadership, business and personal goals.

In contrast to the "bird's nest" metaphor for the design of LEAD is the "marbles" metaphor. Each of the aspects of the design of LEAD could be seen as separate mechanisms. Different providers could be employed to do each. This could be most cost effective in terms of efficiency. The providers of their bit could shine up their "marble" to be the most glorious gleaming object. Yet there lies the problem and the power of the metaphor of marbles and bird's nest. However beautiful the marble is in comparison with the ugly misshapen twig, the marble simply cannot integrate. Stretching the marble metaphor further, forcing integration causes damage to one or a number of the marbles. In a sense the reaction can be conceived of almost competing for attention. In contrast the bird's nest beauty is in the integration, not the separate bits – the bits are needed, but alone are not of much value. The old axiom that the whole is greater than the sum of the parts applies here. In systems language (where this metaphor is taken from Checkland and Scholes, 1999) there is an emergent property generated by the integration of the system elements. They suggest such emergence in learning systems can be seen as the 5 "E"'s:

1. Efficiency – the utilization of resource.
2. Effective – achieves broader overall purposes (e.g. growth).
3. Efficacious – does what it says it would do (e.g. make leadership more salient).
4. Ethical – in the manner it is conducted (e.g. no abuse of insights from the programme).
5. Elegant – the system design makes good sense (we hope this reflects the LEADership Learning Cycle).

It is interesting to question the application of 5 E's to the design of leadership development programmes. Despite huge sums of money invested in leadership development every year (typically reported to be in excess of £50 billion), Bolden (2011) notes that there is much debate in the leadership industry as to the efficacy of this investment.

In our decades of experience we see too many training programmes fall foul to zealous providers polishing their wares looking to keep to timetables rather than having the learners' development to the fore. Yes, delivery is important, but crucial to the success of leadership learning is joining up the pieces – co-constructing the leadership practice. Highly polished delivery methods are not as critical in making the desired connections between the different learning elements and between the learning and personal/business contexts.

We would assert that of significant importance is the need to integrate the three capitals together in leadership development: human, social and institutional. With an eye on all three in an integrated design (which reflects Checkland's 5 E's) we advocate that evaluation would have a clear focus on what to measure and begin to go beyond the often cited truism that leadership development is more a leap of faith. If designs are research-led and thoughtful in terms of integration anchored to delivering enhance-ment to the three capitals, there would be a palpable shift in conversations regarding the ROI (return on investment) in the leadership development industry.

* * * * *

11. LEAD journey: month 9 – November

This chapter describes the delegates' findings and reflection on the Exchanges plus they gain more knowledge from the penultimate Masterclass.

EXCHANGE PRESENTATION

The weak autumnal sun was yet to break through the early morning mist that hung in the avenue of trees in the approach to the LEAD rooms. Feeling the chill in the air, Freddie pulled the collar of his jacket up as he got out of his car as he began the now familiar walk. Leaves lay everywhere, piling high in a blaze of red, yellow and orange. Recalling his childhood, Freddie couldn't resist and kicked out, scattering the coloured mounds.

"Oi!"

Caught in the act, Freddie quickly looked around and espied the wrecker of his amusement. The voice belonged to a familiar face. It was Jane.

"That looks like fun," said Jane as she too aimed her foot at a nearby pile.

"You all set?" asked Freddie.

"Sure am!" replied Jane. "We're as ready as we can be. We have both made lots of notes and supplied each other with a summary of our findings plus we have gone through it with each other."

"Very true. I feel quite relaxed. I trust the format so I no longer feel anxious, which is quite different to the stomach churning walk this used to be."

The pals laughed.

A far tenser Bill was inside speaking with David. The pair had been in discussion a few times over the last couple of weeks as Bill wrestled with what to do with some of his findings from the Exchanges.

Bill had an emotional Exchange as he discovered his Exchange partner, James, and his brother had major differences in the future direction of their business. Neither could speak to each other calmly any longer, so much so that they were effectively working independently, to the detriment of the firm and to the overall well-being of the staff.

In separate one-to-one meetings with Bill, both brothers broke down in tears, in despair as they unburdened themselves of months and months of torment, anxiety and uncertainty. Neither knew what to do next. The business was operating in a leadership vacuum. Unwittingly Bill had walked into a minefield. Staff too were caught up in the poisonous atmosphere.

Bill's Exchange had not gone to plan. He found himself listening intently to all those he met and interviewed. To get the most from the Exchange, he knew he had to adapt quickly, to think on his feet and utilize his learning from Action Learning to ask open insightful questions to advance discussions, explore options and identify routes forward. He also listened empathetically, deploying Emotional Intelligence techniques he had picked up from the recent Masterclass.

Bill was now having an impromptu coaching conversation with David. He cared about James and, by extension, the future of his firm. The bond of trust that they had built through LEAD was strong and Bill was exploring what he could do and should do to support his Exchange partner and what to reveal in his learning today without disclosing any of his findings.

To his relief, a reassured Bill agreed a way forward with David.

* * * * *

"Good morning everyone and welcome to your second Learning and Reflection Day as you look back and reflect on your learning from the Exchanges," said Ann.

"The main purpose of today is to encourage you to reflect on your Exchange experiences and to consider what you have learned and how you can apply it and use it to make progress. It is important to understand that the day is about looking at your learning, not the specific outcomes of your Exchange projects. These should have been fed back to one another prior to the session.

"You will see that I have displayed your 'By the end of Exchanges I want. . .' quotes from the Introduction to Exchange Day almost three months ago to remind you what you thought you wanted from the process. Now, how closely did your experience match what you thought you would get from the Exchange? Take a few minutes to write down your thoughts."

Ann then distributed a hand-out with questions for the delegates to work through on their own, considering what they had learned during the Exchanges, and getting them to refer back to their Exchange workbook.

Finally, the delegates went back into their pairs and triples to talk through how they were going to present their learning of the Exchange experience and produce a poster or something similar to aid their presentations.

This time the delegates were prepared for what Ann was to say next.

"Think about what your key learning points are and why, and how your peers will benefit from what they hear and see. The more creative you are in your presentations the better," concluded Ann with her familiar encouraging and reassuring smile.

Grabbing coloured pens, crayons, scissors, glue, flip chart paper and piles of magazines, the Exchange partners went off to find a quiet corner to prepare their visual masterpieces.

* * * * *

Bill began. "It's human nature to want to show your business off in the best light. The first key learning point came when I asked myself, 'What am I worried about James seeing in my business and, if there is something I am concerned about, why don't I sort it out now?'

"Similarly, before the Exchanges, I reflected on what I said at the Overnight Experiential about the 5 per cent per month I spend reflecting, and if I know what needs addressing, *why am I not doing it?*

"Just the thought of someone coming prompts you to think, but actually, you don't have to have someone come in. Just look, reflect and be honest with yourself. So that's the first thing.

"Having said all that, the reality was James and I were sitting on things that our staff and both of us as leaders knew were not right and we hadn't done anything about it!

"Secondly, being open-minded is important. Your Exchange partner is coming in, you have to trust them to be honest as they could tell you something you didn't know.

"James told me that people were genuinely speaking very positively, that they felt that I did too much and a couple of good specific points came out. For example, some of my staff didn't know where I was sometimes. I thought I wouldn't be missed for a while. Actually, I needed to inform them when I was going out of the office, so I've addressed that.

"Next learning point was, don't assume people know because they don't. I thought I had communicated the plan and progress against the plan but the message had not got through. I now need to hold 'state of the nation' briefings more regularly and use support staff more effectively who are under-utilized and would like to help out more to improve communication.

"Going in to James's company was phenomenally interesting, illuminating and I really enjoyed it. I examined the relationship between James and the key members of staff, personality issues and the approach to work. His staff are tremendously loyal to him, work hard for him and want to go the extra mile for him. Some are frustrated with him in quite a jokey sort of way – 'You know. . .Oh, James is James. . .He won't change. . . ha, ha'.

"In the branding project, I had to think on my feet because it became apparent with the first person that I would have to go off script otherwise it was just going to be a wasted opportunity. So, being prepared is important but being flexible is vital."

"I agree, Bill, and that is a difficult thing for me to admit to," said James. "The Exchange has made the biggest impact on my thinking and made me think differently. I realize I need to prepare more – with clients and staff. I must take the time in my mind to listen, be objective, see the other side and use the techniques I have learnt on LEAD.

"The Exchange process enables barriers to come down, which allowed me to be open to new ideas that in the normal day-to-day are not altogether visible.

"The mutual trust that developed was brilliant. Rarely, if ever, in business do you get the chance of unfettered access to someone else's business and vice versa plus receive unbiased feedback.

"I felt that it was a privilege to be able to go into Bill's business. The preparation for the Exchange gave me the confidence to go into his company and suggest changes. Who would have thought I could do that? I didn't! It has given me more confidence to tackle the issues identified back at my office as I know that others are looking to me to do so.

"I would like to repeat the process as I got so much more from this approach than expected. Someone looking within your business that understands what you are trying to achieve and can give you honest response with no hidden agenda is priceless."

"I agree, James. The Exchange allowed me to really get under the skin of your business and understand what makes the business and the staff tick. In turn, this allowed me to make comparisons to my business, which was useful in identifying ways to add value," concluded Bill.

"Thanks Bill and James. Any questions?" asked Ann.

After a few questions about their experiences, next to speak were Freddie and Jane.

"Firstly, we have improved our creativity, our thinking outside the box, catchphrases and pictures," joked Jane.

Freddie continued. "Jane has been so inspired by the Strategic Planning Masterclass she asked me to do the strategic planning project. If she had asked me to complete it a year ago, I would have run for the hills! However, after listening to the McDonald Masterclass and completing a similar exercise with success in my own organization and gaining much confidence in the area, I had the conviction to do it and in effect become a coach in another business for the day. Firstly I interviewed everyone as planned, did some analysis identifying gaps in market knowledge then presented the findings back to them, helping them to understand what it meant to them in the context of their roles.

"I taught them some new tricks," laughed Freddie.

"The feedback to Jane from her staff was very good and she believes that they picked up key learning points from the day. I have learnt new knowledge from a Masterclass, put this learning in to practice, reflected on the learning and evaluated what it means to me. I have then taken that learning and new knowledge and applied it in another company. I rationalized the findings and gave a short report to the Board in the business.

"It's amazing the growing sense of confidence, capability and know-how that I have obtained that I never had last year that I drew on during the Exchange. Just like Bill said earlier, I reflected in real time, making sense of things, thinking on my feet, tuning in and focusing on a speedy adaptation using my intuition in an organization I am not familiar with. This has also helped me to master the subject matter and provided me with a comparison of how my staff differ to Jane's in a positive and negative manner.

"The Exchange with Jane was important for me as her lack of bias would be vital in discussions with the employees. Prior to the Exchanges we discussed Jane's own development needs and we agreed that it would be good for her to deal with hardened, time-served, long-standing employees – a body of people she had no experience of professionally so she would need to quickly find common ground to make the projects worthwhile. This would be a test in itself for her."

"Yes," said Jane. "I struggle to deal with difficult people. Although during LEAD I have grown in confidence, which has allowed me to have difficult conversations with my fellow Board directors and face my demons, this was different. I was deliberately going to meet difficult people to try to engage with them and open them up. I knew it would be a test of how I would react in a different working environment.

"All the meetings started slowly but eventually I managed to get them to speak. The problem was that senior managers had not spoken to them in the past. They felt like mushrooms and they had experienced 'mushroom management' – kept in the dark with the proverbial thrown at them from time to time. They knew Freddie was trying to do things differently for the overall good, but they had yet to hear the vision and direction and Freddie was not visible. He was masked by the middle managers who were not communicating. The various departments were silos with impermeable walls and Freddie had an over-reliance on key staff to transmit messages.

"Our learning is people want to be led; they take security from it. They recognize they need managing but they want leadership, both transactional and transformational, with an appropriate balance.

"In both our businesses we concluded that we had the wrong balance. We realize that we have over-empowered and that more direction, more guidance is required. Although LEAD has made us both more confident, actually we are still not confident enough to ask the necessary searching questions. So, we must develop further and become more resilient.

"A major learning point for both of us was that key decisions within the business which aren't made will follow you around. For example, Freddie did not remove a sales manager when in reality he and the staff knew that it would be the best decision for the business. This unwittingly follows you around until ultimately the right decision is made. This was the same for me with a junior family member in my business in a position he was not capable of holding. What we learned is that instinct backed with facts is enough to be bold to make the judgement call earlier rather than later.

"The final learning point, as James said earlier, we have had insights from our people, so we now need to do something about it. We must not procrastinate or duck our responsibilities.

"To conclude, the Exchanges have provided us with a sanity check. Our businesses are poles apart in size and sector but we are similar. Our people are loyal, they care, they are passionate but they seek clarity of vision, they want to be challenged and are prepared to take responsibility and be accountable. The only thing that stops it from happening is our leadership. We can do something about that and we must for the good of us, our companies and our people."

"That is fabulous and neatly marks the end of the Shadowing and Exchange process," said Ann. "What you have achieved is unique and we encourage you to continue to shadow and exchange with one another to continue your learning.

"Next month is the final Learning and Reflection Day where we get you to reflect on your learning throughout your LEAD journey. In advance of the session, please complete all your Forum reflections, review your binder and organize your thoughts ahead of sharing your learning with your peers.

"Also next month is your Graduation evening where you will receive your certificate for completing the LEAD programme. Please let us know who will be accompanying you – family, friends or colleagues from work – to recognize and celebrate your achievement. In addition there are four peer awards – business growth, staff development, leadership improvement and peer support – where you can nominate a peer."

"Can I suggest something?" said Freddie. "Why don't we create a topic on the Forum where we can record what our accomplishments have been since we commenced LEAD? That will give us all the opportunity to blow our own trumpets, allowing everyone the chance to properly consider who to vote for."

"That's a brilliant idea, Freddie. And are you volunteering to open the topic?" smiled Ann.

* * * * *

Back outside in the autumnal afternoon, Freddie and Jane had their eyes on the piles of leaves.

"Shall we scatter them again?" an impish Freddie asked.

"Yeah, why not?" laughed Jane.

"Freddie, you are a self-confessed shy guy who wasn't sure of your own value as a leader a few months ago amongst all these larger companies who you thought were all doing successful things. But you stepped forward this afternoon and volunteered to create a Forum topic on performance. What inspired you?"

"If you're voting for something then you've got to have some background to it. We don't actually know what everyone has done during LEAD. We hear snippets of stories. I know some people better than others and I have a feel for what they have achieved but I don't actually know. This evens the playing field.

"I wanted to ensure people voted. Selfishly, I hope some will vote for me so I have to tell them what we actually achieved in my business. I've done OK. They can also look at what I had written over nine months on the Forum. But this allows me to give them a context – putting it down in writing and saying *well this is what I've done* is a strong statement of achievement for us all.

"I also believe I have something to shout about – I can proudly blow my own trumpet because we achieved much and sometimes in very difficult circumstances. I have made some major inroads into my business. I wanted to inspire others to think, if Freddie can do this then so can I – the Clares, the Marks and the Sams who wouldn't have done it unless someone had said *look go and do that*.

"I think we are all very comfortable with each other now and no one is going to judge in a derogatory manner what we have said about ourselves. Everyone would take it in the right style and vein that it was intended for. It'll be a bit of fun – one of our Ground Rules, remember?"

* * * * *

LEAD FORUM – BLOW YOUR OWN TRUMPET

"Hi Everyone," began Freddie on the Forum, "note to self, stop saying good ideas out loud in case it ends in an action for me!"

> As we discussed, the idea of 'Blow Your Own Trumpet' is for you to share with your peers what you have accomplished since you started LEAD. It is your opportunity to share your successes, your achievements and give a context so we can appreciate the magnitude of what you have implemented. This will enable us all to complete our Award Nominations for the Graduation – the form is attached to this topic as well as in the Resources section so you really can't miss it.

* * * * *

MASTERCLASS 9

"The delegates enjoy listening to fellow business leaders so they should enjoy the insights that will be shared from our next speaker," thought Ann. "That's all the details and slides on the Forum for them now."

Leading Change: Knitting It All Together – Stewart Barnes

> This Masterclass addresses how to lead change whilst engaging and taking people with you. Stewart seamlessly knits together the corporate view from the CEO/MD and Board with the business view at the Senior Management Level and below and how to achieve consistency throughout your organization. It dovetails a number of key themes from LEAD such as leadership effectiveness, strategic planning, culture change and employee engagement, demonstrating how to bring your learning together to maximize its effectiveness.

* * * * *

The cohort had hung back for an hour after lunch to reflect on another high octane session.

"Crikey, what a Masterclass," said Bill, "an avalanche of strategy, leadership and team empowerment packed full of top tips, goodies and delights! There is a lot to reflect on what to knit together and how."

"I agree," replied Freddie. "My first reaction was *where am I going to start?* But having reflected quite a bit over the whole LEAD experience I'm beginning to see a way through, not least because through the coaching, I have started some of these things but not finished them. Like a lot on LEAD, much of today's Masterclass content has come across as self-evident, obvious, common sense and yet I am not doing it. This was not really what I was expecting when I started LEAD!"

"I took much strength from the fact that all the businesses featured today had a similar sales turnover to mine so the Masterclass is not about big company stuff," said Bill. "The models, tools and techniques are relevant to all small–medium-sized companies."

"Yes," replied Freddie. "The tools are more advanced than you would normally see in companies our size but I believe that is where the competitive advantage lies with senior management teams understanding and using them. After all, most business leaders are too busy with their heads down inside their companies. That implies they are not taking advantage of reflection or obtaining new knowledge outside their organization. And if the senior leader is not doing it then their management teams, if they have them, are probably not either."

Jane spoke. "It was intriguing to hear how many times you have to repeat and reinforce decisions to make things happen. I can now view this reluctance to change as innate human behaviour, not belligerence or stupidity. This makes it much easier to deal with resistance, both within the business and personally."

"Relentlessly following through is not easy," sighed Bill, noting his weakness to complete tasks. "Implementing any change is hard enough but to find that when your back is turned staff go back to their old habits is soul destroying yet it is natural human behaviour. I need to work on getting staff to make a small change and embed it to get the change done month in, month out until it eventually becomes second nature. If they don't do it regularly, they forget it. If the leader does not enforce it then they return to their old ways. I need to work on this."

"Within our senior management," said Freddie, "we are of the firm belief that we could not have successfully implemented our recent changes without having set the foundations in place. Success and high growth comes from the very top. Senior leaders cannot do it on their own so need to surround themselves with great people who must not have a chink of light between them. Senior management must stand as one. This is pertinent in our business as the teams would sniff out if one of us was not in line with the vision.

"There was much emphasis on the importance of appropriate business and financial reporting and improved controls," declared Freddie. "They are a game changer for us. Having put a Management Team in place, we realized very quickly that we can raise our game. We identified a lack of useful reporting available at our fingertips and have embarked on creating a 'KPI Dashboard' that links to why our customers buy. This is based on our learning from three Masterclasses: Strategic Planning, Operations and

Finance. Not only is this improving our business knowledge, it gives us a direct indication that our strategy is effective and our tactics are efficient."

"Did you pick up on the importance of developing the ability to move up and down the Leadership Style Spectrum at the right times?" asked Jane.

"I did," replied Freddie. "On the Overnight Experiential, Sammy made us think about where our preferred position was on the spectrum, where our staff think we are and where we want to move to as a result of LEAD. Stewart overlaid the situational variable. I am working hard to quickly assess the different situations and challenges I face, and use the right leadership skills to tackle it. It is working, and it's having an impact on my staff and their awareness to solve problems themselves. Proper empowerment! This will help in creating the right culture – an appropriate way of doing things round here."

Bill paused before speaking. "Most of our companies are growing and in many instances our LEAD learning has given us confidence to further increase growth and move towards whatever high performance looks like for our companies in our market segments. The pace of change is likely to be greater than that faced previously by individuals and teams. I understand that this is likely to be difficult for staff to change so quickly, so as leaders we must either create a crisis or engender a sense of urgency. Whatever we choose, we need to focus on the top 20 per cent of staff. We heard this message in the Employee Engagement Masterclass but now it has a context in leading change."

"As Marketers," said Jane, "we're often asked by clients, 'What should we do in Social Media? What do you think of our advertising / website? What marketing should we be doing? What should our marketing budget be?' These are all promotional marketing issues that can't be answered properly until there is a proper marketing strategy or business plan – points we regularly communicate to clients. So hearing a Masterclass speaker say, 'Strategy first and for that strategy to be led by customer insight' was music to my ears."

Bill continued. "My thoughts are beginning to turn to *how do I develop a culture of high performance? What does power look like in my company? How do I build learning into my organization?*"

"Enough of all that learning stuff, we have more important things to consider," interrupted Freddie, waving his arms and gathering the cohort together. "Before we go, next month there is a social event in the town. I have been to their Christmas get together before and it is really good. Should we get a couple of tables for us all to have a meal and a few drinks together? It should be fun. It is the night before the LEAD Graduation so we can have a double celebration."

The cohort thought it was a great idea and gave Freddie the thumbs up to organize it and send out the details.

* * * * *

LEAD FORUM – MASTERCLASS REFLECTION

After a few days of reflection, Freddie shared the following on the Forum.

It was a shock to find out that the 20–60–20 rule happens at every level. This was a body blow for me as it applies to my hand-picked Senior Management Team of five! Of course I hope I am the top 20 per cent. Having thought about it, my technical manager is the bottom 20 per cent. So my learning is that I must ensure he is on board with all decisions and messages. When he walks outside the board meeting there must not be a blink of light. Outside, he is viewed as top 20 per cent in his function (it's odd how people attribute things). Therefore my role is to coach him to stay on message. But, of the time spent individually with the senior managers, I understand that I must proportionally spend the least amount of time with him.

I am making great inroads into identifying where we make money. Firstly we have found that we make more profit by selling certain products over other ones. We have introduced sales and profit mix measures. It has already given me an excellent insight into our product offering that I'd not previously considered. This wasn't something I would have thought of but I can already see a huge benefit and will be undertaking this across all the business streams.

Freddie

Bill commented:

Reflecting on the 20–60–20 rule, I seem to spend 80 per cent of my time with the bottom 20 per cent. It's clear I need to change but that involves in part an element of trust as when reviewing this, those within the bottom 20 per cent are often client facing. If this is the case and I don't focus on them, is there a reputational risk? My view has always been that you are only as good as your weakest member – that clearly needs to be flipped on its head.

Situational Leadership came up in Coaching and I must confess that it has helped me tremendously. The ability to walk the Leadership Style Spectrum and understand how to manage an individual on a particular task with the appropriate style is of enormous benefit. The observation for me is that you are always learning and I have found this to be a really engaging topic that I want to explore more and develop further. It is clearly an advantageous skill.

Do I relentlessly follow through on tasks and objectives and hold my team to this? Simple answer is not enough. It's easy to get caught up in the whirlwind and lose sight of some of the things I have committed to. I must try harder.

Do I always push the team to be excellent? Again not enough. Sometimes I am guilty of accepting good as good enough but if we really want to achieve high performance then I need to up the ante with my team.
Bill

Jane's reflections were:

For me the key takeaways are:

1. As we move the business forward I must stay cognizant of the change curve and plan to get through it quickly. There is a big difference between realizing the need to change and doing it.
2. Understand and utilize what differentiates us from our competitors in both the strategic direction of the business and the marketing approach to exploit it. We raise this with our clients but have not been applying it to our business.
    See you soon, Jane

THEORY SANDWICH 11   REFLECTION AND REFLEXIVITY

Exploring awareness of taken-for-granted assumptions and purposes.

In addition to the delegates' experiences of LEAD, it is often their tacit knowledge of running their own companies that contributes to the circulation of ideas and exchange of knowledge through peer-to-peer learning. As discussed in theory sandwich 3, tacit knowledge as conceptualized originally by Polanyi (1966) envisages it as a way to know more than we can tell. Wenger (1998, p. 47) acknowledges that tacit knowledge includes what is said and what is left unsaid and because it is often what we take for granted, it tends to fade into the background. Similarly, Nonaka and Takeuchi (1995) argue that more attention should be paid to tacit knowledge held by individuals.

Paying attention to tacit knowledge, delegates engage in reflective and reflexive practice throughout LEAD, as discussed in theory sandwich 6. Reflection is learning from experience, that is, thinking about something after the event (Cope, 2003). Reflexivity, in contrast, involves a more immediate, dynamic and continuing self-awareness. Reflexivity is reflecting on the consequences of reflection, action or inaction. The delegates engage with reflection and reflexivity throughout the programme. Sometimes this is immediate, as Freddie notes, as he had to reflect in real time, to make sense of things, and sometimes it is a process that takes longer, sometimes with forethought as Bill recognizes, as the

Exchanges were an opportunity for him to think about someone coming in, which prompted him to reflect. The process isn't discrete either, as Freddie recognizes; he has reflected quite a bit over the whole LEAD experience and about how he needs to finish some of the things he has started.

Reflective practice is the capacity to reflect on action so as to engage in a process of continuous learning (Schön, 1983). It involves paying critical attention to the practical values and theories that inform everyday actions by examining practice reflectively and reflexively, which leads to developmental insight (Bolton, 2010). The Exchanges give delegates the opportunity to observe, be reflective and reflexive and gain such developmental insight. Bill's Exchange partner, James, recognizes that this part of the programme has had the biggest impact on his thinking, making him think differently, and he identifies actions that he will undertake, such as more preparation, taking the time to listen and be objective and using the techniques he has learnt to hear "the other side."

Reflective practice is an important tool in practice-based professional learning such as Work Based Learning, which is discussed further in theory sandwich 12 and the Epilogue.

Work Based Learning recognizes that individuals such as the LEAD delegates mainly learn and develop from their own professional experiences rather than from formal teaching or knowledge transfer. Work Based Learning brings together theory and practice as through reflection and critical thinking, delegates are able to identify relevant tools, techniques and models then apply them within the context of their workplace (Figure 11.1). This combination of reflection on past actions and events with existing knowledge draws out new knowledge to create a higher level of understanding. On LEAD, this translates into greater salience and insights into leadership as delegates learn to become a leader.

Reflective practice provides a tremendous development opportunity for those in leadership positions. Leading a team of people requires a delicate balance between people skills and technical expertise, and success in this type of role does not come easily. Owner/managers engage in self-limiting behaviours because of the small business context (Perren and Grant, 2001; Smith et al., 1999). Reflective practice provides owner/managers with an opportunity to critically review what has been successful in the past and where improvements can be made.

As the three cases demonstrate, LEAD supports the establishment of new behaviours as it encourages reflection, critical thinking and adult transformative learning. Delegates have acquired a body of experience throughout their life or frames of reference that define their world (Mezirow, 1997). The LEADership Learning Cycle is a process of

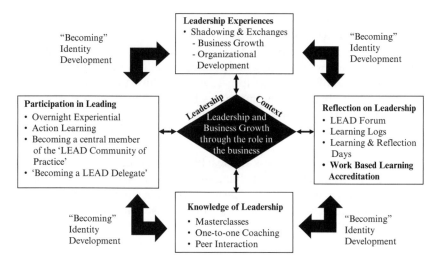

Figure 11.1   Work based learning within the "LEADership Learning Cycle" – lived experience

questioning and rebuilding these pre-determined frames of reference. The goal is for a leader to maximize their professional potential, and in order to do this, there must be a process of critical reflection on current assumptions, which we submit the LEADership Learning Cycle provides for owner/managers who wish to become better leaders.

REFLEXIVITY IN PROGRAMME DESIGN

The principles of collaboration and the co-construction of knowledge rather than expert and acolyte models (E-Quality Network, 2002, p. 6) underpin LEAD. There are discussions in the broader literature of management learning and educational research in general that focus on the need for reflection and reflexivity on the part of students and tutors (see Reynolds 1999a, 1999b; Reynolds and Vince, 2004). As discussed earlier, LEAD is underpinned with a social constructionist approach to learning and advocates that relational dialogue is key in the construction and circulation of knowledge.

This view, Beaty et al. (2010, p. 589) argue, demands and requires critical reflexivity to examine both the nature of knowledge being developed and identities constructed. Supporting the arguments that call for reflexivity, we submit that designers of programmes, facilitators, tutors and so on need to be aware of their role within the learning community in which they reside (see Smith, 2011).

Wenger (1998, p. 9) argues that we must become reflective with regard to our own discourses of learning and to their effects on the ways we design for learning. Cunliffe (2004) writes: "If we accept that management education is not just about helping managers become more effective organizational citizens but also about helping them become critical thinkers and moral practitioners, then critical reflexivity is of particular relevance" (p. 408).

Indeed, LEAD focuses less on teaching owner/managers to become leaders explicitly and more on helping them to develop their critical thinking skills in order to be able to develop their leadership capabilities. It is essential that we as management educators are also critically reflective and reflexive.

* * * * *

12. LEAD journey: month 10 – December

This chapter focuses on the conclusion of the ten-month long programme with the final Leadership Masterclass and Final Learning and Reflection Day where delegates reflect on their learning journey ahead of inviting their families and friends to the LEAD Graduation Ceremony and Peer Awards.

MASTERCLASS 10

"This session will stimulate the delegates' thinking on leadership," thought Ann as she uploaded details of the final Masterclass.

Leadership Challenges – Everest: The Hard Way – Sir Chris Bonington

> In an inspirational manner, Sir Chris will relate his mountaineering experiences to clarifying the essential need to balance leadership and management to achieve success. Through an examination of case situations, Sir Chris will outline a situation, explore the characters involved, detail his thinking prior to taking action . . . and then stop the talk and ask the cohort to think through the problem and suggest their way forward. Sir Chris will then compare suggested ideas to his decision and the outcomes that followed. There will be a number of cases following this format. As the talk proceeds the delegates will be encouraged to make the connections to their own business contexts.

* * * * *

"What a way to finish off the Masterclass series with such a distinguished and inspirational speaker, amazingly skilled and phenomenally brave," said Jane.

"Yes," replied Bill. "Moreover, getting the opportunity to sit with him and ask him lots of questions over lunch was fantastic.

"As soon as he spoke, I was immediately captivated and I zoned everyone else out. In my opinion he was a great leader, someone who had done it. He was very natural in how he felt about leadership. That sounds quite superficial but he didn't come out with really great one-liners or some great rules of leadership or some inspiration or quotes. I just got this huge sense from what he said and his demeanour that he appreciated how important leadership was and that he thought about it very, very carefully.

"He also said that 'the end does not justify the means'. He left this colossal impression on me that leadership needs integrity. I recall from our first Leadership Masterclass in April that this was the number one trait in numerous pieces of research.

"As a mountaineer, he had a very simple defined goal – he wanted to get at least one person to the top and, in many ways, that is a simpler stated goal than often what we have. As business leaders we're not quite sure what our goal is, or we know what it is but it's very difficult to define.

"For him it was very easy to define and as such it would be very easy for him to say, 'Right, I don't care what we do, all I've got to achieve is this goal and we're effectively going to sacrifice whatever to get there'.

"But he understood that the team needed to come together again. They would have future goals, future challenges and therefore he wanted to make sure that not only was the goal achieved but also the process built a stronger team and that those, as a team and as individuals, would go on to greater roles personally and greater goals collectively.

"So that was quite an odd lesson in many ways but I thought the integrity of leadership was very important.

"He disclosed there's some people that he didn't frankly get on with particularly well; there's others he did; there were people he admired without particularly liking them on a personal level but he knew everyone's strengths and weaknesses. He obviously thought about his team members a great deal and he cared about them as individuals even if he may not have agreed with their views on things."

"What I found really interesting," said Jane, "was his gentle, calm personal characteristics that I recognize in my leadership. I am overwhelmingly reassured that I do not need to change my personal traits to become a better leader. He was not loud or aggressive. Prior to LEAD I thought a strong leader of a successful expedition would need those traits.

"He also spoke about using his gut instinct, which was based on his experience of successfully using gut instincts in the past. Trusting his gut instinct led to successful experiences, which built a bank of knowledge that informed future decision-making.

"In a key moment of conflict when his decision-making was being questioned he used his calm personable style to engage the whole team to listen to the challenger. He had planned for years for this moment and his instinct was that the suggestion would not work. Nevertheless, he went to check out for himself the new information that the challenger had advanced. Through open questioning and active listening he diffused the situation so that all in the party could discuss calmly and rationally the new option before they all agreed that the best route forward was still the original plan."

"I am going to miss the stimulation that the Masterclasses bring," said Freddie. "I have found them very beneficial to me and my business. For example, if I had missed the Strategic Planning, Employee Engagement or the first Leadership Masterclass in April then I would not have made the giant strides that I have in such a short period of time. The learning has such a knock-on effect too as it has impacted what I have done on Coaching, Action Learning and Shadowing and Exchanges."

"I agree, Freddie," replied Bill. "And here we are today, still picking up new learning points as we think about leadership in a different manner. Learning about leadership is truly a continual process. That thing we heard about that seemed a little odd – 'leader becoming' – from one of the early sessions now seems to make sense. Not simply born or made . . . but becoming and that becoming is more than just me but many that I have the privilege to share time with."

* * * * *

LEAD FORUM – MASTERCLASS REFLECTION

As the Forum Champion, Jane was keen to open the final topic:

> We all better appreciate now how reflection is an important part of LEAD and in developing our leadership. I am not sure I quite saw it like that when I volunteered to be the Forum Champion all those months ago which is an interesting observation in itself.
>
> Here are my three key learning points from the final Masterclass:
>
> 1. Be confident to look and take the hard challenges – try new techniques to new routes.
> 2. Do not fear failure – adversity draws the team together.
> 3. Commitment, drive and passion can help you to achieve your goals. If you believe in your business then your clients and employees will believe in you.
>
> See you next week, Jane

Next up was Bill.

> I had a long chat with Sir Chris at lunch and came away with the strong impression that he is a gentleman and a diplomat. This was apparent in the way he managed the proposal to change the route to the summit by cleverly steering

the decision to his preference (the original route) by asking the group the right questions.

However, the team selection process might have been handled differently as naming teams A and B was guaranteed to upset the members of team B. I am sure that we have all been in positions where we have lots of stuff going on and are focused on burning issues and we forget people's feelings.

Ability is important. I do not have all the answers but someone in my company does. Let them take the lead at the appropriate time.

Bill

Freddie was forthright as always.

I was gripped from start to finish. I never once thought about the leadership challenges that were faced with such an activity and even more so the lengths and depth of planning for this event. This journey was all about the planning, and without it, it never would have happened. It reinforces the importance of planning within business.

What was also interesting was the on-going adjustments made to that plan throughout the course of the journey and how much emotions impacted (or could have impacted) on the decisions made. Yes, we have to be aware of the impacts of our decisions but sometimes I believe we make the wrong decisions because of shying away from facing the emotional elements attached with the impact of such decisions.

His story made me realize how selfish I am and has seriously made me question whether my selfishness will prevent me from being a high performing leader. I am not sure that I would have taken that decision not to make that final push because I think my own personal satisfaction and fulfilment would have prevailed. Maybe my age has something to do with this and as I get older, I hope that I will think less about my own fulfilment and more about that of others.

Caring for the team. Sir Chris mentioned that he made sure that he cared for the team. He ensured that he was in regular contact with them and involved them in the strategy. I think this attribute is very important in leading a success-ful team. If team members do not feel included within the group then they are likely to underperform. Communication between team members is important and also they must be made to feel they are part of the success. With the strong echoes of the Employee Engagement theme of LEAD, positive input must be recognized and rewarded.

Freddie

* * * * *

FINAL LEARNING AND REFLECTION DAY

"Who'd have thought it'd be such a lovely day in December?" said Freddie to Jane. "It is as dry and bright as our first day together almost ten months ago. I remember that well as I walked as slowly as I could from the car park, such was my level of trepidation. Now I have a spring in my step. The walk is still a blur. I don't take in the surroundings as I make my way here. The difference now is that my head is full of positive thoughts and opportunities to consider."

"It is sad that LEAD is coming to an end, Freddie. I'll miss it."

"True," replied Freddie, "but take heart that our Action Learning Set plans to meet quarterly and the first date is in the diary. We also have our Christmas meal together next week."

"It has been a fantastic year," said Jane. "We have all got on, no one has argued and there is such a high level of camaraderie built up amongst us. I'm glad you organized bringing us all together. Something had to happen."

"Thanks, Jane, I am pleased my self-appointed social secretary role has been so successful! Everyone is turning up!"

"Freddie," started Jane, "I am worried that I haven't achieved all that I could have on LEAD. I have been exposed to lots of fantastic people and there have been so many great learning opportunities. What have I changed? What have I done? How have I used what I have learned? I don't think I have done a good enough job.

"Some, like Bill for example, have methodically gone off in a certain direction moving faster and further than me. I am deliberate. I am not the fastest. That is me. I need to take things on board and think about them then contextualize. That is who I am."

"Great insight, Jane," noted Freddie.

"I know I am judging myself harshly. The pace of LEAD and the pace of my business in parallel do not always match. My process of change is not a radical one. LEAD has been a start for me, an awakening. It has given me a platform to build on. For me my leadership journey does not stop next week when LEAD finishes. I am more self-aware, I am better equipped and I have a bagful of practical, useful tools. My team have noticed changes in me and I have shared my journey with them where appropriate."

Freddie reflected on what Jane had said. "I am proud of what I have achieved on LEAD. I can imagine David and Ann will have us creating a poster reflecting our LEAD journey today so I want mine to be a master-piece. It puts a different spin on events with our family and friends coming to the Graduation next week and being able to see our outputs. I am going to put a lot of effort into things today."

* * * * *

"Good morning everyone," greeted David, "and welcome to the Final Learning and Reflection Day where you will make sense of your LEAD journey and value what you have learned. You will hear and learn from your peers about their journeys.

"Perhaps some of you may be apprehensive about LEAD coming to an end but your learning will not stop when the programme stops and we will help you consider strategies for the future and establish the next steps to continue your learning and momentum after LEAD.

"Today is an informal celebration of your learning and along the way we'll keep to our ground rule of having fun!

"Anything you would like to add, Ann?" Ann stepped forward to run the next part of the session.

"Well, it's ten months since you joined LEAD and you have come a long way since then. Close your eyes and think about how you were feeling when you first came on LEAD. Think of an adjective to sum up how you were feeling then. Write it on a post-it note. Turn to your neighbour and talk through what you were feeling then and why you decided to come on LEAD."

The room became abuzz with the peers swapping their story. After ten minutes, Ann spoke again.

"LEAD takes you on a journey and you are in a very different place at the end of the programme to where you were at the beginning. Reflecting on the journey is a fantastic way of analysing learning and celebrating your development. We now want you to make a visual representation of this in a creative and fun way to help you reflect in depth about how you coped with the trials and tribulations you encountered, what has helped you and what you are going to do next.

"Your journeys will be displayed as part of the celebration of LEAD at the Graduation – this helps your family and guests understand what you have been doing for the last ten months. Small businesses and families are so often intertwined and LEAD often indirectly helps people that never even attend a session. Independent research[20] shows that 83 per cent of delegates state that LEAD has helped them in their personal lives."

Ann then unveiled and explained an example of a journey from a previous delegate.

"Firstly, draw a path which will represent your LEAD journey. The LEAD journey could have started before you joined the programme, so locate LEAD at an appropriate position on the path.

"You will be revisiting the journey throughout the day to populate it

---

[20] Gill, A. and Harris, G. (2014), 'Evaluation and impact of the LEAD programme on owner/managers of small- and medium-sized enterprises in South West England from 2011–2014 using mixed methods', Cheltenham: GillFoxJames Ltd, unpublished.

and note barriers, challenges and opportunities which you faced and are still facing.

"Tell me, what were your expectations when you came on LEAD?"

After a few minutes of collating the various points, Ann then handed out the delegates' original LEAD application forms and asked them to compare their answers to what they thought then and what they said they wanted from LEAD. Ann then invited them to reflect on any difference and to consider just how far they had come and what had changed during LEAD.

"On your journeys, draw something that represents what you wanted at the beginning of the programme.

"Your journey poster is now beginning to take shape so for the next hour think about the different elements of LEAD and what you encountered along your LEAD journey. Write a few words about the relevance of each element to you and mark the key learning on your poster. Capture the thunderstorms as well as the good stuff."

People disappeared off to various corners to create their posters. Some worked on their own and some in pairs or groups, appreciating the wider social support. There was a lot of laughter. Quite a few had brought in boxes of sweets to share, including a box of Jelly Babies which initiated a humorous reflection of the tree of the same name.

* * * * *

Ann brought everyone together again.

"By sharing your journey, each of you will be able to learn from each other's experiences. This helps with the feelings of isolation. You know by now that you are not alone and others have the same issues. Sometimes it is only when you hear a peer's experiences that the 'light bulb' moment occurs.

"Who wants to go first?" asked Ann.

A keen Freddie volunteered, jumping to his feet, bringing his *masterpiece* to the front and proudly sticking it to the board.

"After I take into account my learning achieved through schooling and university, nothing has provided me with as much new knowledge and experience as what I have gained during the past year on LEAD. It has brought me out of an inner comfort zone and helped develop myself as an individual, both from a personal perspective and in business.

"One of the first learning experiences was from my leadership time-line, which I populated with incidents and experiences from an early age. This was an invaluable exercise as I quickly discovered that the majority of my leadership experiences were based on negative memories. I now understand that I developed my own leadership from learning from the mistakes of other leaders that I have worked with in the past, thus creating my own style. This is why I believe that I sometimes come across too placid and not as authoritative as I should be as a leader, as I have seen very aggressive styles of this leadership not working.

"What was also quite startling to realize was how little support I had received from my family who were involved in the business. My father and directors had never taken me to one side to coach, nurture, praise or reprimand when required.

"My LEAD journey has provided me with the basis to form a new structure within the organization. Before I started the programme I had certainly approached a cliff and realized I needed further learning, knowledge and peer support to help increase my skill level as a Managing Director in my company. I felt isolated in my environment and required an added impetus to help change my organization. After establishing some new knowledge with some very beneficial Masterclasses, I went back and reflected further on the Overnight Experiential, which really opened my eyes to consider what was broken about the organization. This helped me enormously in putting my new learning into practice to 'fix' what was being run poorly within the business, namely communication up and down the company and between departments.

"I recognize that I cannot do it all and that I need a capable management team around me. Leaving managers to manage on their own is not suitable either. During the course of LEAD I have discussed replacing poor-performing senior managers with my peers inside and outside of Action Learning Sets as well as with my coach. This is something that has never happened in our company's history, but because peers that I respect said it was the correct course of action, I have changed most of the senior management team.

"Due to LEAD, I have found myself constantly reflecting on every meeting that I have, which in turn has aided me to evolve in my role as Managing Director. An example of this is the Key Decision Makers' meeting which I chair. I ensure that I am well prepared going into the meeting with a set agenda and forward this to directors and managers to add content/points before they meet. As this is an important meeting, it is important that I listen intently and answer succinctly any questions posed. Prior to LEAD, I was a poor listener. I also asked closed questions rather than the open questions I have been coached to use in Action Learning.

"The peer group that has been part of the LEAD programme has been a huge aid to my development. Having access to such a network is immeasurably important and I have learnt a wealth of information from just listening to other owner/managers, chief executives and managing directors. This has been the greatest support group I could have hoped for and I plan to continue to network and socialize with these personalities with personal and business gain for us all.

"I have worked with my new management team and we have created a business plan for the first time in the company's 100-year history.

"One of my weaknesses has been my lack of knowledge of financial accounting. I have been conscious of a gap in knowledge and made it my business to familiarize myself with financial models over the past year in particular regard to balance sheets, cash flow forecasting, debt ratios and stock turnover. As a company we are in the process of compiling some of this crucial information which will now form part of our monthly Board meeting.

"Shadowing and Exchanges helped increase my confidence further by 'living' in another business for two days, realizing that my new knowledge and learning could also help another organization. I found myself coaching others.

"I am more self-aware, others aware and aware of how people perceive me. I'm more aware of my leadership shadow.

"I now feel that I have arrived at a major crossroads in my working career with implementation of key strategies being the future heartbeat of the organization, with growth and expansion of the business not just a pipe dream but a reality. I have gained much experience, knowledge and learning over the past year and will be putting this further into practice over the coming years as I take the right path forward."

As Freddie paused, the cohort burst into thunderous applause. With a reddening face and a steely resolve, Freddie concluded, "Today has been a good reflective lesson as it ties much of LEAD together. I realize I have come a long way, learned much and benefited a lot. I now need to implement my learning."

"Wonderful," remarked Ann. "You have come a long way in a short period!"

"Thanks," replied Freddie. "I'd like to think I would have arrived at this point on my own. Truthfully, I am not sure if I could. Certainly LEAD has given me the confidence to dramatically increase the speed of change aided by new knowledge, tools, techniques and top tips that I have learned along the way."

"Who'd like to go next?" asked Ann.

"I will," said Jane.

"I have tried to encapsulate my significant moments but there have been so many that I have struggled to finish my poster.

"I agree with Freddie that today has been a really good process. I am already thinking of where my LEAD journey goes next as I want it to continue.

"At the beginning, I was at a crossroads and I didn't know how I got there and was unsure what to do. I could see that LEAD was not business as usual and would bring fresh ideas and new perspectives by meeting others. That had a big attraction.

"For months and months I have been on a confidence rollercoaster. My highs and lows including my lowest ever point have been on LEAD. LEAD has made me face my demons over many months and with the help of my Action Learning Set, my coach and Freddie as my Shadowing and Exchange partner I have found my own solutions to deal with difficult situations. This has led to my 'A-ha moment' where the light began to dawn that it is me that has to change my behaviours.

"I have become better at adopting a coaching leadership style, which I have consciously encouraged my team to adopt too.

"I have grown in confidence and I feel confident enough to trust my own hunches especially now I realize through Coaching, Action Learning and Shadowing & Exchanges that my direction was right.

"I have also learned that the more I do the correct things, the more rewarding it is and the more you get back as you see your teams flourish.

"LEAD has helped me see that a coaching leadership style is one that I am comfortable with and that I can and should do more of it. I recognize that I need to get the balance right and use a more directive style at the correct time in the right circumstances.

"While there were specific tools I began experimenting with throughout the programme, I only reached a level of confidence to put changes into action at the end of LEAD. For me, each stage of LEAD is like a chapter and I needed to read the whole book through once before I was able to share the story with conviction.

"One of the strengths of LEAD is that it is a ten-month long programme and that it all knits together. Sometimes, without you realizing, you have changed for the better, becoming a better person and a better leader.

"Even though I volunteered to be the champion, I didn't enjoy using the online Forum but I did find the process of reflection required to update it very beneficial. Making time to absorb, reflect and articulate learnings helped me to recognize the changes that I needed to make, that required me to progress.

"LEAD has reignited my leadership. It has enabled and encouraged me to look critically but positively at my own managerial and leadership per-formance within my organization. Importantly this is not in isolation. The opportunity to interact with other leaders from a variety of businesses in a structured way has helped to build my own confidence in the knowledge that I am not alone in wanting to improve or in the challenges I face. The way the LEAD cohort has formed into a close and open team has been a mark of the programme. LEAD has helped me to stand back more from the day to day, to give more time to prioritize and to prepare for meetings.

"And LEAD is a very enjoyable experience."

The cohort greeted Jane with a loud cheer and a round of applause. Yes, there had been tears on her very personal journey but there had been many more smiles and throughout Jane demonstrated unflinching support to her LEAD peers.

Next to present was Bill.

"Throughout LEAD, seeds are sown that, for me, germinated later as other things needed to happen first to create germination. So I have worked very hard at drawing together all my learning and applying that to me and my business. I then reflected on what that told me, which I used to create further improvements.

"With the agreement of my partners, I have undertaken an overall review of the business. This was partly to create personal accountability for myself as historically I am very poor at completing tasks. I agreed to report my findings and recommendations plus I wanted to generate buy-in from my partners.

"My investigations were very wide-ranging and there was always a danger that I would jump to initial conclusions and then seek out only evidence which supported those conclusions. I consciously set about a very careful reflective process. I attempted to strike a balance: as each investigative action ended I reflected upon it in isolation *and* in the context of the other investigations I had undertaken. This followed my approach to LEAD: after each Masterclass, Action Learning Set, etc. I would reflect upon it *and* my other learning.

"The failings of the firm were, at least in part, due to failings in my leadership. This was a negative concept, but following reflection I saw it as very positive because it also meant that the solutions to those failings were within my power as the leader.

"I have learned from LEAD that simple improvements in communication would improve staff morale: employees should be trusted with more information, they would be and feel part of the business planning process and they would more likely 'buy in' to the business plan. With a better understanding they would feel confident to contribute more and they would be and feel more valued. My investigations confirmed this – my partners and staff wanted this! I was holding the organization back.

"Listen! The learning from Action Learning Sets was that I had to improve my listening skills and genuinely listen to others to hear, understand and appreciate what they are saying. Most notably, Action Learning

Sets taught me how to form and ask open questions; and I've learnt so much not just answering questions but listening to other questions and answers on issues that were often my issues.

"Next, delegation: I now realize that I should only do what only I can do and also that I must let go of responsibilities, trust my colleagues and delegate effectively. This would reverse the crowding out that everyone felt as they were used to me jumping in and taking over.

"I have taken that further through one-to-ones with all the partners where we formulated succession plans after subsequent discussions at an away day when all the partners met off site to discuss personal and business plans.

"Each department now meets monthly with a template agenda to ensure that key issues are addressed and I attend them regularly to be seen to be providing the necessary support.

"I have diarized three 'all of staff' meetings per annum. The aim is to give more information about the business plan and the financial position of the firm. The nexus between financial success of the firm as a whole and rewards for staff was stressed and a bonus scheme introduced. From my learning from the Marketing Planning Masterclass, a cross-selling initiative was introduced where the best referrers are rewarded and praised.

"The appraisal system has been overhauled: more open questions are included and all managers have been trained in how to conduct appraisals and the importance of appraisals was promoted. An automatic six-month review was introduced so that action points arising from appraisals are followed through.

"Another positive outcome is increased self-awareness especially of my own limitations in learning and the personal need to self-challenge. This has led to reinvigorating my passion for leading the firm by recognizing the obligation and opportunity to achieve the vision and mission of the company for the benefit of all its stakeholders.

"In many ways my learning experiences through LEAD have been transformative. I recognize that learning is a continual process. I now see self-awareness as essential and better appreciate my strengths, my weaknesses and my preferred learning and leadership styles."

Bill paused and smiled before saying, "I have come a long way since the Overnight Experiential when Sammy told me to be quiet, sit on my hands and allow others to speak. That was a chastening experience."

The cohort laughed and clapped. *Bill has truly changed.*

Bill nodded, accepting the warm acknowledgement from his peers and continued. "The concept of reflection is paramount. By use of various techniques that I have learned on LEAD, my overriding goal is to embed reflection and become a reflective practitioner. I aim to utilize learning opportunities especially from clients, mentors and colleagues; create accountability to enhance self-discipline and create a learning environment. You'll remember the conversation we had on the first morning of the Overnight Experiential when I disclosed that I spent 5 per cent of my time on such activities and there was a sharp intake of breath when many of you declared that you are not doing that. Well, I am going for it. I believe the approach I've outlined will move me towards spending the majority of my time reflecting, strategizing, generating ideas and concepts as opposed to spending my day focused on actions and tasks.

"I remember Sammy talking about the DO–REVIEW–PLAN–DO continuous learning cycle. She said most leaders are 'doing' and undertake very little reviewing or planning and that LEAD is all about taking the time out to properly explore the learning cycle. When she went through that at the time, it didn't mean much to me and it was months later when the meaning struck me. Now it is a crucial part of my development and on-going thinking.

"Which takes me back to what I said at the beginning. There are so many great learning points on LEAD you cannot view them in isolation. You have to find a way of making connections to generate the learning. You then need to contextualize and apply them to you and your company then you need to step back and reflect to consider the outcomes and how to improve.

"I often get my LEAD binder out and talk about it. I love sharing it because I think there's some really useful things and I speak to my staff about it and I've used it in staff meetings. I am so pleased that one of my equity partners is coming on the next LEAD cohort. It will be good for her and for me. I want to be questioned and challenged. I want to metaphorically feel the breath of someone else on the back of my neck. Someone chasing me for the very first time. It'll keep me on my toes to further improve my performance.

"I believe I have improved as a person as a result of LEAD. I have definitely improved as a leader. I understand the need for leadership and that it is a responsibility rather than a right or a privilege. It is the most important thing in business.

"Leadership is about more than just getting people from A to B. It's about making sure they want to get to B. But we all want to get to B as B is the right place to be in the first place. So helping them along the way is important. It's very complex, it's very difficult sometimes, and sometimes it's obvious what needs doing but it needs that thought and attention to detail and listening to people, listening to clients.

"Leadership is something you're constantly learning. You change as a person, a business changes, the environment surrounding the business

changes, you've got to change every day and leadership is required to identify those changes and lead the organization to meet the challenges that are
constantly being thrown.

"There's no such thing as a period of consolidation, it just doesn't
happen. There might be in one specific area of the business but overall
the business is constantly changing, constantly reacting to changes and
circumstances and we've got to keep doing that and there are lots and lots
of things that we need to do.

"I came on LEAD seeking a Eureka Moment but privately not expecting to find one. I have had many. Thank you."

As he finished, Bill was greeted by a wall of sound as his peers loudly
clapped and cheered.

"That's an amazing journey, Bill," said Jane as Bill sat down. "If we
go back to the Overnight Experiential and the Leadership Style Spectrum
where we all jokingly said you were so autocratic that you should be in a
different room. Where would you put yourself on that line now?"

"Good question," thought Ann to herself. "It is testament to Jane to
remember the incident, make light of it and connect it with Bill's story
today. And she has the confidence to ask such a searching question."

"Thanks for reminding me," groaned Bill with a wink. "I would still be
towards the autocratic end. That is my preferred leadership style but I'm
much more open to listen and to learn because I'm much better at delegat-
ing than I used to be and prepared to share the leadership tasks around
more.

"So I would say that I'm more inclusive and democratic than I was but
I still lead from the front. I consciously know I need to let go more and
continually communicate. It's back to being self-aware, understanding
your leadership shadow and not being a hero leader."

Over the next hour all the delegates shared their learning journey. The
room was buzzing with achievements, successes, new insights and some
low points, major issues that needed dealing with and solutions to how
they were addressed. There was a real sense of end-of-year celebration.

Ann invited the cohort to capture their good news stories and create a
news sheet that each Action Learning Set could share amongst themselves
and display at the following week's Graduation.

"Too often delegates talk about how hard things have been and what
goes wrong at work so this is a chance to celebrate the good things and
publicize them," said Ann.

With an intensity you could touch, the peers set about capturing their
stories in a blaze of colour and animation before retelling their tales, Set
by Set.

"'Setting the Ground Rules for Success' is my title," said Freddie.

"Picture a board of talented directors in their individual fields of work but not working together at the right level to lead the business. LEAD gave me an insight into setting clear ground rules for meetings to encourage a listening culture and full participation by everyone. Each meeting agenda starts with the reminder of the rules. All agree that the meetings have not only improved but with it so has the decision making – better informed decisions and shared decisions. It is work in progress but a definite step forward."

"'It's Good to Talk as Long as Someone is Listening' is my catchy tabloid title," laughed Jane. "Action Learning has taught us the benefit of asking open questions to encourage a thought-through process. We have learnt that it is just as important to listen to gain the most benefit in all situations."

"We're on fire here," exclaimed Bill. "Under the heading 'MP invents Wave Machine' it reads: the main perception of a leader by their followers is off the main stage, so what better place than by a wave machine (aka water cooler). Talking with his team in the informal setting of the wave machine has worked wonders at a local professional services company. MP (Managing Partner) invented his wave machine to assess, through discussion, the moving tides of motivation within the business. The waves produce free and sustainable energy – great ideas from employees, allow the MP to share his vision for the future, building momentum and crucially empowering the team to have confidence in their ability. New high tide marks have already been achieved."

"Corny, Bill, but very funny," laughed David.

"One of our ground rules," said Ann, "was to have some fun and your LEAD headlines have truly embraced that and embodied the spirit and learning of the programme.

"I'd like you now to think about your challenges ahead and what opportunities you have. Think about one plan you have and also one puzzle you still have – something that does not have a straightforward solution. Write one each on a post-it, come up to the front and share them with your peers. These are good reminders for you that your LEAD journey does not end here.

* * * * *

Ann was walking around the room handing out LEAD postcards, blank on one side apart from a postage stamp.

"We will be posting these back to you in three months. Write on the back the address of where you want it to be sent, somewhere you will be in three months. Write your individual and collective actions for the coming months, for example, set up an Action Learning Set meeting, do another Exchange, start the accreditation process, enrol on GOLD etc. What are the next steps on your journey?"

As she collected the postcards, Ann asked, "What else do you want to add to your posters?"

To conclude, David returned to the learning objectives that the cohort agreed at the beginning of the day and went through and ticked off each one with a whoop of delight from the delegates.

"Congratulations everyone," said David with emotion and a sense of pride in their achievements and contributions. "You have very eloquently and pictorially made sense of your LEAD journey, valuing what you have learned and sharing your key points with your peers who in turn have learnt from your journeys.

"You have all considered strategies for the future and established the next steps to continue your learning and momentum after LEAD. For those of you who wish to do so you can get your learning assessed to obtain a Postgraduate Certificate, the first stage of a Master's degree. During the last ten months, you have demonstrated that you are independent learners.

"So today has been an informal celebration of your learning, and judging by the amount of laughter in the room, you have all had a lot of fun.

"You have learned a lot more about each other today and for those of you yet to do so, you have until the end of the week to send us your nominations for the four awards.

"We will all see you next week at the Graduation where we look forward to welcoming you and your families to the celebration of your LEAD learning."

* * * * *

GRADUATION

Everything was arranged. The stage was set. Seats were neatly laid out in rows with places reserved at the front for the would-be LEAD graduates, with their families, friends and colleagues seated behind. The area was cloaked by boards filled with the delegates' individual learning journeys, their LEAD newspapers that they constructed and a surprise – a montage of photographs that had been taken throughout their time on LEAD, which was also being shown in a slideshow on the main projection screen.

The four piece jazz band was quietly playing, adding to the relaxed early evening atmosphere. Smartly attired waiters and waitresses were at the ready with trays of champagne glasses and soft drinks. David and Ann were chatting with the guest speaker, awaiting the arrival of the delegates and their guests for the two-hour long celebration.

True to form the delegates arrived a few minutes early, introducing their husbands, wives, partners and children to the other delegates.

"I have heard so much about you. It's a pleasure to meet you!"

"It's great to put a face to a name."

"It is fabulous to be invited along this evening. I never normally go to business events so it's great to be involved."

"It's a lovely occasion and such a great way to mark what they have been doing together for the last year."

The room was charged with excitement and laughter. There was much discussion and a sense of expectation. Some delegates were looking up at the screen. Fingers were pointing at the photographic loop on the giant screen.

"I didn't know that happened."

"Gosh, I can't remember my photograph being taken."

"Look! We're there with Sammy! It seems such a long time ago now."

Other delegates had taken their guests to their LEAD posters.

"I thought you'd been working hard this year?" teased Freddie's wife. "It looks like all you have been doing is drawing!"

Delegates were also intensely reading their peers' posters. It was their first chance to closely see each other's LEAD journeys.

"I didn't realize that you did that," said Bill to his Exchange partner, James.

At that, the jazz band finished playing "Take Five" and David and Ann began to usher the delegates and their guests to their seats.

"Good evening LEAD delegates, ladies and gentlemen, boys and girls," announced David. "Welcome to the graduation of the LEAD cohort and to the celebratory 'passing out' ceremony for those who have completed the LEAD programme where the delegates graduate with a 'certificate of completion'. We will also have some fun with our own peer awards. Before we invite our delegates up to receive their certificates, I am delighted to introduce our guest speaker for the evening who will say a few words on leadership in small businesses and the importance of learning and reflection."

* * * * *

The evening quickly flew by. After the guest speaker had finished, the name of each delegate was read out in turn, who then came to the front and was presented with their LEAD certificate by the guest speaker and had their photograph taken along with David and Ann. Every delegate was loudly applauded as their name was read and as they received their certificate. The LEAD Graduates and their families beamed proudly. It was a great moment, a personal triumph.

"As LEAD Graduates you now become part of the LEAD Alumni joining a select club of owner/managers who approach work with highly developed abilities of self-reflection and critical learning with the self-awareness to deploy those abilities in the workplace," said David.

"And now for the awards," continued David. "All of the delegates have shared their achievements on the online LEAD Forum, which has allowed them to nominate their peers. There are four awards.

"The first award is the Staff Development Award which recognizes the LEAD delegate who has implemented change in their organization in order to develop their staff. The winner is . . .

"Tom!

"Tom has committed to making his LEAD learning clear to his team members and has spent a lot of time working on employee engagement and developing staff internally to cope with the responsibilities of their roles. A number of his LEAD peers have commented that Tom is keen to cascade his learning down throughout the company and has clearly insti-gated a number of initiatives to engage, train, evaluate and recognize staff. Tom has had to face up to and make the difficult decision of removing under-performing staff, drawing upon his reserves when faced with people questioning the decision-making process. Tom's staff have remarked on Tom's increase in confidence as a leader and we are sure he will continue to develop his leadership skills for the benefit of his staff and the business."

A surprised Tom came to the front to receive his award, a framed certifi-cate and book. He then had his photograph taken again with the LEAD team and guest speaker.

"Our second award is the Business Growth Award which recognizes a delegate who has implemented their LEAD learning to further grow their business. The winner is . . ."

David paused and looked around the room to build the tension.

"Freddie!"

"Wow!" exclaimed Freddie, jumping to his feet while, and most surpris-ingly, wiping away a tear of joy. "I didn't expect that."

As Freddie came up to accept his award, David said, "It has been a challenging year for Freddie's business but he has risen to the challenge by appointing a new senior management team, implementing a business plan for the first time in the company's 100-year history and in parallel he has addressed poor communication, inappropriate management behaviour and created an Employee Engagement strategy that has been embraced. He is also launching a new product line in a new division. Freddie has truly demonstrated that he has been working on the business and has brought alive and realized his Future Perfect. Freddie has acted decisively and his LEAD peers have tremendous respect for what he has done."

Photos taken and with his award certificate and prize under his arm, Freddie returned to his seat, winking at his wife and mouthing, "See, I have been busy this last year!"

"Our next award is the Peer Support Award in recognition of the LEAD delegate who has been nominated by his or her peers for the support he or she has given throughout the programme. The winner is . . .

"Jane!

"Jane received many nominations from her LEAD peers and the consistent message has been that she is always willing to help and take time out for people. One peer said, 'Jane is always positive and sees the best in everyone which is a trait I admire in her'. Within her Action Learning Set, members have commented that she was very supportive of the others and would often approach them outside the Set to say that she had been thinking about what they had shared with the group and offered suggestions. Jane made her peers feel like she really cared about their issue and has demonstrated a high level of emotional intelligence.

"Jane, please come to collect the Peer Support Award."

"I can't believe that they have recognized me," an astonished Jane said to David and Ann. "I didn't expect to get an award. I am so pleased my husband is here tonight to see this as he listens so attentively to my frustrations from work."

"Our final Award this evening," said David, "is the Leadership Improvement Award in recognition of the LEAD delegate who has shown the most improvement in his or her leadership capabilities. And, the winner is . . .

"Bill!"

The announcement was greeted with a whoop and loud cheer.

As a bashful Bill came forward, David said, "Bill received many nominations from his peers who have commented on the improvement in his leadership qualities and subsequent positive changes to the company. According to his peers Bill identified that he is a process rather than a people person and so started making changes to his behaviour to ensure that there was an equal balance of both. Bill engages more with staff now, plans his time to walk the floor and understands that not being the centre is key."

"That concludes the official part of the ceremony.

"LEAD Alumni, you must follow your path no matter where it leads.

The road is long, the journey will be hard. But do take strength from your experiences – you have listened and you have observed; you have learned, applied your learning and you have become more effective leaders. It is our privilege to have worked with you.

"I'll now invite all the graduates to come to the front for a group picture. More drinks and canapés will be served. If you have not already done so please do read the graduates' learning journeys and listen to all the stories. Enjoy the rest of your evening. Thank you."

The ten months concluded with rapturous applause.

"This is why improving leadership matters in SMEs," said David to Ann, "and how it can be fostered as an asset and a point of differentiation between businesses."

David and Ann had witnessed over the ten-month period that through LEAD the delegates had participated in a range of experiences that the delegates themselves recognized had greatly assisted their leadership development. The delegates had reported a greater confidence and that the peer network addressed the sense of loneliness. The delegates were con-tacting each other outside of LEAD to further support each other. They were also beginning to trade with each other, such were the levels of trust that had been built. David and Ann had observed how the delegates had wrestled with the concept of leadership, their predominant style and the greater involvement of their staff in the running of their firms. Leadership now had meaning to them personally and it had a meaning in the context of their own businesses.

"The questions that the Alumni have asked of themselves we need to pose to other business people," said Ann. "*What impact does your leader-ship have on your organization? What changes do you want to make to the way that you lead? What changes do you want to make to your organization?*"

THEORY SANDWICH 12   THE LEARNING AND THE
**   CHANGES**

A continual aspect of LEAD is to research the learning and to inform the pro-gramme design in order to meet the ever-changing needs of the delegates. This chapter presents the results from this continual practice showing the impact of the original design principles and what was done to enhance the learning capability of the delegates.

The stories of Bill, Jane and Freddie have given much insight into a journey of learning. There seems little doubt qualitatively, as illustrated throughout this book, that the programme has had much impact on the delegates and their business for the vast majority of participants. Additionally the programme has been thoroughly examined through three large-scale evaluations looking at the personal, business and economic impact of the programme (Wren and Jones, 2006, 2012; Gill and Harris, 2014). The latter focuses on SME owner/managers participating on LEAD in a different geographical region delivered by the private provider, QuoLux, and uses mixed methods including quantitative and qualitative approaches, with further validation through focus groups. The assessment identified an overwhelmingly positive set of statistics.

- 100 per cent of LEAD delegates state they are a better leader.
- 100 per cent are more effective and more confident.
- 97 per cent believe their business has grown or will grow as a result of LEAD.
- 83 per cent claim that LEAD has helped in their personal life.
- 75 per cent state colleagues have seen a difference in them.
- 59 per cent of delegates who did not know each other prior to commencing LEAD were now trading with each other.

The delegates stated that the top eight reasons for doing LEAD were to:

1. Be a better leader.
2. Grow the business.
3. Learn new approaches / techniques.
4. Meet like-minded business people and share experiences.
5. Overcome any personal shortfalls.
6. Address the loneliness of being at the top and obtain external support.
7. Gain formal training on leading their business.
8. Build and improve the senior management team.

Some of the key changes in a delegate's business and leadership included:

1. Increase from 50 per cent to 95 per cent of delegates having regular monthly management meetings.
2. Increase from 52 per cent to 86 per cent understanding priority of target markets / profitability.
3. Increase from 53 per cent to 89 per cent having a business plan.
4. Decrease from 75 per cent to 14 per cent focusing on poor performers.

In addition, analysis of secondary data, that is, published financial information and internal management reports, found that the average growth of a LEAD delegate's company the year after participating on the programme was 27.1 per cent, with delegates reporting growth in employment of 12.8 per cent.

From the findings it can be concluded that learning with LEAD develops a delegate and their business and that LEAD can be viewed as an essential leadership development programme for any SME owner/manager who wants to be really successful.

The delegates have clearly enhanced their self-efficacy, having given sufficient effort on LEAD to succeed in specific behaviours: 100 per cent of delegates report that they are more effective, more confident, and are better leaders; 97 per cent state that business performance has improved dramatically. Consistent with Barling (2014), this suggests that self-efficacy is more specific than self-esteem or self-confidence and a stronger predictor of performance than individual skill levels.

We suggest that the three cases demonstrate a link between the salience of leadership, the identification with leadership and self-efficacy, directly leading to enhancing capability to become a better leader and improving business performance (Ling et al., 2008; Gill and Harris, 2014). Moreover, we propose that leaders with high-quality leadership behaviours – such as transformational or leader–member exchange – expend greater levels of energy to fulfil their leadership responsibilities and that leadership self-efficacy is a useful predictor of leadership effectiveness (Barling, 2014). Leadership self-efficacy is also associated with significant higher levels of collective efficacy amongst followers where teams that work directly with a person who is attributed with being a transformational leader share a belief of *we can do it*.

Research and learning from experience continue to inform the design of LEAD and there have been a number of changes to the programme. Ongoing research has enabled business themes such as Employee Engagement to be more fully aired. There has been a change in LEAD Coaching to include more face-to-face sessions and a move towards co-constructed coaching, which more closely resembles the coach–coachee interaction in an SME environment. There has also been a major change in the structure of the online LEAD Forum, providing delegates with an easier interface to ensure greater online usage and sharing of learning.

The importance of the Community of Practice and the role that the LEAD Facilitators play in enabling the delegates' learning has been recognized. LEAD Facilitators now carry out inductions individually in the delegate's place of work and act as coaches in both Coaching and Action Learning. These changes allow for a deeper understanding of each delegate's business issues and a better appreciation of context.

Delegates learning from LEAD can now be accredited to obtain a

Postgraduate Certificate as the first stage towards achieving a Master's degree. This challenges the notion that SME owner/managers do not wish to obtain professional qualifications, consistent with Wren and Jones (2006, p.33).

LEAD has been established in a different part of the country as a full-fee programme demonstrating owner/managers are prepared to devote a significant amount of time and money to develop their own leadership skills.

Informality and a social element are important to owner/managers and this has been built into the LEAD programme in the form of social events during the programme and post-LEAD, with a formalized LEAD Alumni that meet regularly, maintaining the established bonds of trust.

Finally, the research by the authors has led to an adaptation of Kempster (2009a) LEADership Learning Cycle through Lived Experience (Figure 1.1) and the formation of a new learning cycle in becoming a leader (Figure 12.1) that better reflects the structure of LEAD. Figure 12.1 includes Work Based Learning accreditation within the Reflection on Leadership dimension as this form of meta-level learning is available to LEAD graduates post-LEAD. This is discussed in the Epilogue.

The cycle of learning is suggested to integrate together the key causes influencing leadership learning identified in the three cases, with the informal naturalistic experience of leadership learning and development described in the extant literature (McCall et al., 1988; McCauley and Brutus, 1998; Conger, 2004). As each situated curriculum is bespoke rather than prescribed, emphasis is on the process rather than the content.

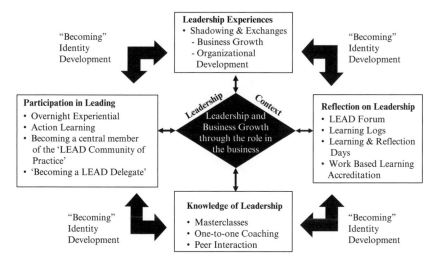

Figure 12.1   "LEADership Learning Cycle" – lived experience

A key skill of a LEAD Facilitator is to understand the role of enabling the situated curriculum, namely when to intervene and what to intervene about (Kempster and Smith, 2014).

Consistent with Elliott (2008), Freddie, Jane and Bill have shown by participating in a leadership development programme there is a strong social learning manifestation. The delegates speak of social comparison: how do I compare to the colleagues sitting next to me? There is an overt sense of growing in confidence through hearing that their problems are similar. It is this social learning within a Community of Practice in a process of a situated curriculum which is key in stimulating a development in the owner/manager's sense of identification with leadership (Kempster and Smith, 2014).

* * * * *

13. Ambitious implications

This chapter addresses the real concerns of SMEs, being the backbone of modern economies and how developing the leadership in small business is vital to economic growth. We explore how ambitious owner/managers, leadership development practitioners, universities and policy-makers need to realize the significant potential from developing leadership for owner/ managers.

The evidence is available and it is most clear: leadership has a major influence on growth of small and medium businesses. This is not equivocal. Our research in this book is but one of a portfolio of commentaries based on evidence that repeat the same call for attention to the development of owner/ manager practice in leading (Phelps et al., 2007; Levie and Lichtenstein, 2010; Cope et al., 2011; Smallbone et al., 2015). For example a comprehensive project was undertaken by the UK Government as part of the Council for Excellence in Management and Leadership (CEML) activities to examine this issue (Perren and Grant, 2001). The Government's interest in improving the management and leadership skills of the SME sector speak to the following: SMEs represent 47 per cent of the UK's total turnover in the private sector, employ 60 per cent of the UK workforce (BIS, 2014) and have over 1.75 million managers practising within them.

If changes in practice can occur to these 1.75 million owner/managers in the way demonstrated by the data presented from the three evaluations of LEAD (presented in theory sandwich 12), then growth in UK PLC would be considerable. This is an ambitious statement and similarly an ambitious vision. But is it so unrealistic? There are three major obstacles that need to turn into *major ambitions*: owner/managers; providers of leadership development; and policy-makers and the various intermediaries. In this chapter we examine each in turn, starting with policy-makers.

HOW AMBITIOUS ARE POLICY-MAKERS?

The major conclusion of the CEML work was that a major mismatch existed between demand and supply (Perren et al., 2002). The report

generally critiqued the confusing array of initiatives that the government
and associated agencies had created to develop leadership in SMEs:

> The Government is largely responsible for the volume and fragmentation of
> organisations and initiatives in the area. Indeed, the inflexibility of funding
> regimes often appears to encourage the development of new initiatives even
> if there are similar schemes already in operation. The aim may have been to
> respond to perceived needs, but instead it appears to have resulted in a tangled
> and confusing assortment of dislocated organisations and initiatives. Indeed,
> the term "initiativitis" has entered the vocabulary of many policy-makers and
> intermediaries (2002, p. 7).

The influence of this review seems to have shaped government policy.
Attention was given to seeking to address this confusion of offerings
and to refocus on stimulating interest among small business owners – a
demand-side approach based on empirical evidence of "what works".

The Regional Development Agencies responded to their master's
wishes with a series of "demand-led" initiatives (which were understandably supply-side with a help accent on engaging universities to embrace
research-led approaches). One initiative was the creation of regional leadership academies; for a review of this, see Thorpe et al. (2008).

In parallel was the creation of LEAD, with an explicit research-led
design and a pilot of four cohorts. After evaluation LEAD was given
a £10m budget for roll-out across the North West of England through
a series of providers engaging with over 1200 businesses and respective
owner/managers.

Then the credit crunch hit, change of government, Regional Development
Agencies scrapped and the birth of the Local Enterprise Partnerships
(LEPs).

So there has been great ambitious endeavour. Can this approach return?

This seems highly unlikely as the economy digs itself out from the
"deficit". The role of policy-makers is not to forget what has been learned.
For example the Northern Leadership Academy outlined clearly "what
works" in terms of leadership development and will sound most familiar:
a situated approach to development that is centred in the context of the
owner/manager that focuses on enabling owner/managers to explore their
issues and apply learning, revise learning and seek out more learning
through supportive mechanisms – such as mentoring, coaching and action
learning (Thorpe et al., 2008).

Arguably the role of policy-makers is to engage major institutions
(notably financial institutions) in embracing a partnership with universities and privately-owned leadership development practitioners: a
sense-making role to convince such institutions that it is in their interest

(and make it their interest) as major stakeholders in society (as well as being embedded in supply chains, or customers with loans) to support programmes such as LEAD. An example of this is the Santander Breakthrough Programme (2014).

This illustrates the emergence of a quasi demand-led approach in terms of policy where there is much less reliance on government-sponsored initiatives that have largely been sporadic and patchy in impact (Perren et al., 2002) and very hard to find, with the financial tap being turned off.

In its place, private sector initiatives are the new green shoots of an alternative policy for the development of SMEs. These initiatives are likely to be much more hard-nosed in terms of return on investment (ROI), and the link with universities to provide robust evaluation is common to both of the above examples.

We see the role of government is to make such initiatives much more prevalent, much more the norm. The old adage "that there is no such thing as a free lunch" suggests that the key will be evaluation and examination of the ROI. This leads us into the next ambitious group: the ambitions of the leadership development practitioners.

HOW AMBITIOUS ARE LEADERSHIP DEVELOPMENT PRACTITIONERS?

Can the leadership development industry respond to this emerging opportunity in this ambitious vision of transforming owner/manager development to enable growth? It seems very odd to wonder whether this might be problematic. After all the supply side has been shown to be most extensive and most flexible in terms of responding to a myriad of initiatives. Furthermore, the skill set is advanced in terms of the Zeitgeist process of coaching, along with action learning as well as delivering training sessions on prescribed approaches with great emotional affect.

However, the evidence from our research, from the other evaluations of LEAD and from the Northern Leadership Academy (Thorpe et al., 2008) is a fundamental philosphical orientation to create a situated programme that embraces the development of the three capitals we have outlined: human capital, social capital and institutional capital.

Human capital development is the most common orientation of the leadership development industry. It suits the extensive literature base (both academic and airport books) of the development of leaders. Favoured approaches are often applied like a form of alchemy that can transform an individual. Bluntly this alone is of little value and arguably often very dangerous to the complex ecosytem that is the relationship of the owner/ manager with their business.

Reflecting back to the structural disadvantage of the owner/manager context, new ideas packaged elegantly can be readily consumed and applied, regardless of context. Furthermore, the primary need for human capital development is a nurturing of "becoming": observing others and linking such observations with experiments in context, travelling towards a new sense of identity formed in conjunction with colleagues in the business. In this way careful alignment of human and social capital development is vital. The designed programme must place emphasis on mechanisms that achieve this.

Finally, both human and social capital needs to be fused with the institutional capital – the creation and development of a social group of learners – travelling a journey together, sharing insights, challenges and solutions applied to their respective businesses. The institutional capital has a collective responsibility to each other and as a consequence is a most valuable resource that enables the development of both human and social capital. This of course is the essence of LEAD. The stories of Freddie, Jane and Bill have given insight into how the development of the three capitals becomes manifest.

It is uncommon for such a focus. For example when LEAD was rolled out across the North West of England to eight providers, the training was most complex. Not in terms of the different elements. The providers were, for example, comfortable with coaching, action learning and masterclasses, perhaps less with shadowing and exchanges. The big challenge was seeking to get across the philosophy of integration. Returning to our earlier discussion on marbles and the bird's nest in theory sandwich 10 – the marbles approach dominated. Arguably there was little success in imbuing the concept of the bird's nest. There was much wonderful shining of marbles – accentuating delivery of elements that were strengths of the respective delivery partner. Evaluation was oriented to each respective element, thereby furthering disintegration.

The notion of identity shift, enhanced salience of leadership and processes of vicarious learning through observation and participation were difficult to assimilate. The experience suggests that it is a bigger challenge to embrace this form of development than envisioned. With hindsight this may reflect that leadership learning is less about explicit knowledge and much more about tacit knowing that emerges in an invisible manner through interactions and participations with others: leadership learning as a process of becoming.

From a pedagogic perspective the fundamental shift required of the leadership development industry is wonderfully captured by Day: "It means helping people to learn from their work rather than taking them away from their work to learn" (2000, p. 586). By this Day is suggesting that there is too little attention paid to the complex, emergent and relational dynamics that form the social capital, and only through enabling full recognition of integrating learning that directly engages in this "work" can the learning be effective for the everyday practices of the owner/manager and the employees.

The form of development programme outlined in this book addresses this call. Furthermore the approach outlined herein addresses three questions offered by Kempster (2009a) as challenges that must be addressed if leadership development programmes are to be more than an act of faith:

1. Can interventions span sufficient time to allow naturalistic experiences to take effect?
2. In terms of efficacy, can outcomes be measured in relation to designed inputs?
3. In essence, can naturalistic development be controlled and accelerated if a significant part of leadership learning occurs through repeating routines and socialization over extended periods [drawn from unexpected events in complex situations]?

The evaluations say these questions have been answered (Wren and Jones, 2006, 2012; Gill and Harris, 2014). Nevertheless this is challenging for many as it feels like an act of faith – "trust the process", the evidence says it works. There is a deep irony in this issue of an act of faith as for so long the industry has been characterized as being an act of faith (Burgoyne, 2001). There has been too little evidence of what works (Thorpe et al., 2008).

So when we speak of how ambitious is the leadership development industry to embrace this approach the answer may be much less certain than might be expected. We hope not. However, this is not as important as the final group: the ambitious owner/managers.

HOW AMBITIOUS ARE THE OWNER/MANAGERS FOR GROWTH THROUGH LEADERSHIP LEARNING?

First, we wish to stress that economies owe a great debt of gratitude to owner/managers for taking on such a burden of risk and responsibility to establish and build their businesses, to create employment and wealth. Second, that by taking such responsibility owner/managers provide leadership. In a sense, with leadership as a social process of influence it must be ever present. Such leadership is an integral part of the relational fabric that is the business. So when we speak of leadership learning it is building on what has been learnt through embracing connectivity to what has gone before rather than imposing a prescriptive solution on to it.

The ambitious aspect we are speaking of then is related to embracing new learning and change in practice that speaks to a sense of redistributing power and control. Early in the book (theory sandwich 1) we drew on the work of Cope et al. (2011), who argue that distributed forms of leadership are important to growth as they allow for a greater array of talents, resources and networks to be brought into play within the business. Without such distribution it does appear that growth is constrained. This is not a new assertion. Greiner in 1972 outlined a stage model of business growth, which has been much cited, applauded and recently criticized for its successive process when aspects of the various crisis could occur in combinations or in different sequences (Levie and Lichtenstein, 2010).

Nevertheless, Greiner's work remains a most influential sensemaking model to issues impacting on growth. He argued that organizations grow through a series of stages punctuated by a crisis – that triggers the next growth stage. The first stage was called the "crisis of leadership". The essence of this crisis reflects the inability for the owner/manager to control everything. At start-up such control is fundamental, blended with astonishing levels of commitment and total investment of the owner/manager – in more than capital but also "blood, sweat and tears".

It is most understandable, perhaps even fundamentally natural, not to wish to let go of the controls – after all the success has been because of such control. Yet letting go in an appropriate way is necessary. Very much like a parent letting go of their children. Letting them take risks and allowing them to grow in the full sense of the word. So it is natural in not wishing to let go, and yet it is also a natural requirement to let go. Continuing on the metaphor of the parent, this is scary, but reassuring when discussing with others who have shared the same experience and now speak of the considerable growth and development in their relationship with their children. We have stretched this metaphor probably to its limit but we hope it helpfully illuminates the very natural issues that are to be overcome.

Issues of letting go also apply to processes of learning. Velsor and Guthrie make this point most clearly: "To learn, managers needed to let go of their current strengths long enough to acquire new ones. They must be strong and secure enough to make themselves vulnerable to the stresses and setbacks in the learning process" (1998, p. 242).

We have seen through the book that the ambitious stance for owner/ managers seeking the growth that we as a society so want from them is not without considerable personal challenge. It is vital that support is readily available: support that is both from peers experiencing similar challenges and also aligned professional support. This dual support attuned to enabling change to leadership practice is appropriate to the delicate and complex historic relationships of the business.

The case examples of Freddie, Jane and Bill have illustrated that they possess very complex skill-sets that have been developed over long careers and honed by challenges in a wide variety of contexts. Throughout their professional lives they have each been faced with and overcome a huge range of problems and from each of these they have learned valuable lessons. While none had made any systematic study of leadership in an academic sense, in general they had reached the same conclusions as the researchers and experts whose views and prescriptions were discussed earlier. Owner/managers learn as and when they require knowledge and they have a preference for experiential learning (Cope, 2003).

In this way the demand-led aspect of policy reflects the need for leadership development to be experiential for the demand to become realized. We would of course suggest by necessity that designs should be evidence based. Equally designs need to be offered that fundamentally have a sensitivity and deep empathy to the complex owner/manager context.

Finally, it is clear that academics and educators have a lot to learn from people such as Freddie, Jane and Bill, and the interviews have only scratched the surface of the huge reservoir of experience that each carries with them. There is a major task ahead in developing a richer understanding of the meta-skills that each possesses, and the means by which these have been developed, before using this knowledge to inform the content of future education and training programmes.

Epilogue – Turning LEAD into GOLD to GAIN: business alchemy and Work Based Learning

The three delegates meet to discuss and reflect forward on what they wish to do next to continue to develop their leadership learning journey.

With the snow falling and the wind gusting, Freddie, Jane and Bill were huddled together in the soft leather seats beside the window in a local coffee shop. The new year had barely begun and Freddie was keen to meet up with the other two to hear their thoughts on "*What next?*" – the subject of the email from Jane that had brought the three together.

"There is 'Life after LEAD' as we all have made it here," joked Freddie, clasping a warm cup of heavily sweetened coffee.

"It's good to see you both," smiled Jane.

"Yes, meeting again is most timely," acknowledged Bill. "During the seasonal break I wondered if anyone would want to keep together and keep learning. So chatting to you both about whether we should or could carry on post-LEAD will be time well spent."

"Indeed, and whether to work with David and Ann again or someone else, or not do any more at this stage," observed Jane.

"I have been reflecting too," said Freddie. "We know that LEAD is a journey. I have had a picture in my head that my journey was one in a hot air balloon, a LEAD Balloon, which goes up and up, as opposed to a lead balloon which, per the old saying, sinks without a trace.

"The image of going up in a LEAD Balloon works for me. On LEAD, I came to recognize the value of counter-intuitive ways, for example focus on the top 20 per cent of employees rather than the bottom 20 per cent to drive change and improvements. I know many business people who believe it is right to run their companies by being anchored to their desks and are slaves to doing tasks 'in' the business. They are actually being weighed down, or using my metaphor, they are *going down like a lead balloon*. I know I made the right choice a year ago as me and my business have soared."

"We all made the right choice then," said Jane. "Let's hope more business leaders follow our lead and do the same for the good of the local economy. We can be advocates and play our part in raising awareness of LEAD and its benefits.

"The question for today is *what next*?" asked Jane.

"Well, there was that LEAD–GOLD–GAIN *thing* that David and Ann mentioned when we were last together," said Bill.

"Yes that thing and somehow we can get a Master's degree. Hard to believe but rather tempting," said Freddie with a childish grin. "My family will be astonished."

"Yes," agreed Bill. "I like the option that we can choose how far we want to proceed. We don't need to do GOLD[21] or GAIN[22]."

"Just reflecting on what I said a few minutes ago," said Freddie. "It is as if there is a form of business alchemy underway transforming lead into gold or, in our language, LEAD into GOLD for GAIN – both personal and business gains."

Jane and Bill laughed before Bill spoke.

"We have all gained so much from LEAD."

"I agree," nodded Jane. "It feels right that our learning is recognized and accredited through Work Based Learning."

"Exactly! Why would we not do it? We have done the hard work on LEAD," said Bill.

"Good point," acknowledged Freddie. "Who would have thought we'd be able to receive a Postgraduate Certificate for demonstrating our learning on a practical leadership programme that was designed to help us in the first place?"

"I have no business qualifications so part of the appeal is being able to obtain professional recognition," said Jane. "Not only is our learning on LEAD at Master's level, we can then participate on the subsequent GOLD and GAIN programmes where our learning can be accredited at Diploma level and ultimately we can receive a Master's degree. In essence, we can get a Master's degree for running our own company! So, not only do you benefit from the practical programmes, you can obtain academic recognition."

"Work Based Learning sounds challenging," said Bill.

"Yes," noted Jane, "but we all have plenty of evidence of tools, techniques and models obtained in Masterclasses and Action Learning Sets that we have applied to develop ourselves and our businesses."

Freddie paused. "Bill, you will have no problem in critically reflecting

---

[21] Research-led programme developed by the Institute for Entrepreneurship and Enterprise Development within Lancaster University Management School.

[22] Research-led programme on the leadership of innovation created by QuoLux.

on your own learning. You have so many examples of reflecting *on action* and *in action*, generating learning which you took forward into future action. We all saw an abundance of that on LEAD which is why you won the Leadership Improvement Award."

"That's kind of you to say that, Freddie," smiled Bill. "I am still flattered with that recognition. It meant a lot to me and my family."

"It was well-deserved," said Jane. "Of course we will need to communicate clear, focused, coherent and well-reasoned judgements about our own experiential learning in both oral and written form to demonstrate our Master's level learning."

"You're right. I think we can all be confident going into the Work Based Learning programme. We have done the work on LEAD, we now must evidence it," stated Bill.

"So we will all do Work Based Learning?" asked Jane. Freddie and Bill nodded.

"That's another five months together," laughed Bill.

"I enjoyed working with David and Ann," said Freddie, "and I can see the benefits of GOLD. For example, working in each other's organizations through a mixture of simulated Board meetings and Masterclasses with a focus on strategic leadership, change management, decision making processes and culture change. But, I would like to implement some of my LEAD learning before I join GOLD."

"I must be more of a *business alchemist* than you Freddie," teased Jane. "I plan to turn LEAD into GOLD! What it has to offer directly affects me and my interactions with my Board. I know I need to become more of a strategic leader so I plan to enrol when I complete Work Based Learning."

"I am not sure what I will do," said Bill. "In my long-term personal plan I would like to be a Non-Executive Director (NED) and may at some stage consider having a NED on the Board of my company. I'll *do* Work Based Learning first then *review, plan* my next steps then *do* just as Sammy said at the Overnight Experiential all those months ago."

The friends laughed, grabbed their jackets and scarves, got up to leave and ventured out into the fading afternoon light on their next steps on their very personal leadership journeys, confident in the knowledge that they had made real, practical progress.

* * * * *

References

Alvesson, M. and Willmott, H. (1996), *Making Sense of Management: A Critical Introduction*, London: Sage Publications.

Alvesson, M. and Sveningsson, S. (2003), 'The great disappearing act: Difficulties in doing "Leadership"', *The Leadership Quarterly*, **14**(3), 359–81.

Anderson, L. (2006), 'Analytic autoethnography', *Journal of Contemporary Ethnography*, **35**(4), 373–95.

Anderson, L. and Gold, J. (2009), 'Conversations outside the comfort zone: Identity formation in SME manager action learning', *Action Learning: Research and Practice*, **6**(3), 229–42.

Anderson, L.E. (2010), *Social Capital in Developing Democracies: Nicaragua and Argentina Compared*, Cambridge: Cambridge University Press.

Anderson, S. (2002), 'Joining entrepreneurs in their world: Improving entrepreneurship, management and leadership in SMEs', London: Council for Excellence in Management and Leadership.

Anderson, S.M. and Cole, S.T. (1990), 'Do I know you? The role of significant others in general social perception', *Journal of Personality and Social Psychology*, **59**(3), 384–99.

Argyris, C. and Schön, D.A. (1978), *Organizational Learning: A Theory of Action Perspective*, Reading, MA: Addison Wesley.

Arvey, R.D., Rotund, M., Johnson, W., Zhang, Z. and McGue, M. (2006), 'The determinants of leadership role occupancy: Genetic and personality factors', *Leadership Quarterly*, **17**, 1–20.

Atkinson, P.A., Coffey, A. and Delamont, S. (2003), *Key Themes in Qualitative Research: Continuities and Change*, Walnut Creek, CA: AltaMira Press.

Avolio, B. and Luthans, F. (2006), *The High Impact Leader: Moments Matter in Accelerating Authentic Leadership Development*, New York: McGraw-Hill.

Bandura, A. (1977), *Social Learning Theory*, Englewood Cliffs, NJ: Prentice-Hall.

Bandura, A. (1986), *Social Foundations of Thought and Action: A Social Cognitive Theory*, Englewood Cliffs, NJ: Prentice-Hall.

Bandura, A. (1997), *Self-efficacy: The Exercise of Control*, New York: Freeman.

Barling, J. (2014), *The Science of Leadership: Lessons from Research for Organizational Leaders*, New York: Oxford University Press.

Bass, B.M. (1990), *Bass and Stogdill's Handbook of Leadership*, New York: Free Press.

Bateson, G. (1973), *Step to an Ecology of Mind*, New York: Ballantine Books.

Beaty, L., Cousin, G. and Hodgson, V. (2010), 'Revisiting the e-quality in networked learning manifesto', paper presented at the *7th International Conference on Networked Learning*, Aalborg, Denmark, 3–4 May, 2010, available at: http://www.lancs.ac.uk/fss/organisations/netlc/past/nlc2010/abstracts/Hodgson.html.

Bennis, W. (1989), *On Becoming a Leader*, Reading, MA: Addison-Wesley.

Bennis, W.G. and Thomas, R.G. (2002), 'Crucibles of leadership', *Harvard Business Review*, **80**(9), 39–46.

BIS (Department for Business, Innovation and Skills) (2014), available at: https://www.gov.uk/government/statistics/business-population-estimates-2014

Bolden, R.R. (2011), 'Distributed leadership in organizations: A review of theory and research', *International Journal of Management Reviews*, **13**(3), 251–69.

Bolton, G. (2010), *Reflective Practice, Writing and Professional Development*, 3rd edn, Thousand Oaks, CA: Sage Publications.

Bosworth, D.L., Davies, R. and Wilson, R.A. (2002), 'Skills, high level work practices and enterprise performance', IER Research Report, University of Warwick.

Boud, D., Keogh, R. and Walker, D. (1994), *Reflection: Turning Experience into Learning*, London: Kogan Page.

Bowman, C. (1995), 'Strategy workshops and top team commitment to strategic change', *Journal of Managerial Psychology*, **10**, 42–50.

Boyle, M. and Parry, K.W. (2007), 'Telling the whole story: The case for organizational autoethnography', *Culture and Organization Journal*, **13**(3), 185–90.

Bryman, A.S. (1996), 'The importance of context: Qualitative research and the study of leadership', *Leadership Quarterly*, **7**(3), 353–70.

Bryman, A.S. (2004), 'Qualitative research on leadership: A critical but appreciative review', *Leadership Quarterly*, **15**(6), 729–69.

Burgoyne, J.G. (2001), 'Tester of faith', *People Management*, **7**(4), 33–4.

Burgoyne, J.G. and Stewart, R. (1977), 'Implicit learning theories as determinants of the effect of management development programmes', *Personnel Review*, **6**(2), 5–14.

Burgoyne, J.G. and Hodgson, V.E. (1983), 'Natural learning and managerial action: A phenomenological study in the field setting', *Journal of Management Studies*, **20**(3), 387–99.

Burns, P. (2007), *Entrepreneurship and Small Business*, New York: Palgrave Macmillan.

Carroll, B., Levy, L. and Richmond, D. (2008), 'Leadership as practice: Challenging the competency paradigm', *Leadership*, **4**(4), 363–79.

Carter, S. and Jones-Evans, R. (2006), *Enterprise and Small Business: Principles, Practice and Policy*, Harlow: Pearson Education Limited.

Catrambone, R. and Markus, H. (1987), 'The role of self-schemas in going beyond the information given', *Social Cognition*, **5**(4), 349–68.

Chartered Institute of Personnel and Development (2008), *Training and Development 2008: Annual Survey Report*, London: CIPD.

Checkland, P. and Scholes, J. (1999), *Soft Systems Methodology in Action*, Chichester: John Wiley and Sons.

Chia, R. and MacKay, B. (2007), 'Post-processual challenges for the emerging strategy-as-practice perspective: Discovering strategy in the logic of practice', *Human Relations*, **60**(1), 217–42.

Cohen, W.M. and Levinthal, D.A. (1990), 'Absorptive capacity: A new perspective on learning and innovation', *Administrative Science Quarterly*, **35** (March), 128–52.

Conger, J.A. (2004), 'Developing leadership capability: What's inside the black box?' *Academy of Management Executive*, **18**(3), 136–9.

Cope, J. (2003), 'Entrepreneurial learning and critical reflection: Discontinuous events for "higher level" learning', *Management Learning*, **34**(4), 429–50.

Cope, J., Kempster, S. and Parry, K. (2011), 'Exploring distributed leadership in the small business context', *International Journal of Management Reviews*, **13**(3), 270–85.

Cox, C.J. and Cooper, C.L. (1989), 'The making of the British CEO: Childhood, work experience, personality and management style', *The Academy of Management Executive*, **3**(3), 241–5.

Cunliffe, A.L. (2004), 'On becoming a critically reflexive practitioner', *Journal of Management Education*, **28**(4), 407–26.

Daudelin, M.W. (1996), 'Learning from experience through reflection', *Organizational Dynamics*, **24**(3), 36–48.

Davies, J. and Easterby-Smith, M. (1984), 'Learning and developing from managerial work experience', *Journal of Management Studies*, **21**(2), 169–83.

Day, D. (2000), 'Leadership development in the context of ongoing work', *Leadership Quarterly*, **11**(4), 581–613.

Denzin, N.K. (1997), *Interpretive Ethnography: Ethnographic Practices for the Twenty-First Century*, Newbury Park, CA: Sage Publications.

DeRue, D.S. and Ashford, S.J. (2010), 'Who will lead and who will follow? A social process of leadership identity construction in organizations', *Academy of Management Review*, **35**, 627–47.

DfES (2003), 'The government's White Paper on the future of higher education', available at: http://www.dfes.gov.uk/highereducation/hestrategy/.

Dick, F.W. (2010), *Winning Matters*, Abingdon Management Company.

Drath, W.H., McCauley, C.D., Palus, C.J., Van Velsor, E., O'Connor, P.M.G. and McGuire, J.B. (2008), 'Direction, alignment, commitment: Toward a more integrative ontology of leadership', *The Leadership Quarterly*, **19**(6), 635–53.

Du Toit, A. and Reissner, S. (2012), 'Experiences of coaching in team learning', *International Journal of Mentoring and Coaching in Education*, **1**(3), 177–90.

Elliott, C. (2008), 'Emancipating assessment: Assessment assumptions and critical alternatives in an experience-based programme', *Management Learning*, **39**(3), 271–93.

Ellis, C. (2004), *The Ethnographic I: A Methodological Novel about Autoethnography*, Walnut Creek, CA: AltaMira Press.

Ellis, C. and Bochner, A. (2000), 'Autoethnography, personal narratives, reflexivity: Researcher as subject', in N. Denzin and Y. Lincoln (eds), *Handbook of Qualitative Research*, 3rd edn, London: Sage Publications, pp. 1–32.

Ely, R.J., Ibarra, H. and Kolb, D. (2011), 'Taking gender into account: Theory and design for women's leadership development programs', *Academy of Management Learning & Education*, **10**(3), 474–93.

E-Quality Network (2002), 'E-quality in e-learning Manifesto', presented at the Networked Learning 2002 conference, Sheffield, available at: http://csalt.lancs.ac.uk/esrc/.

Ezzy, D. (1998), 'Theorizing narrative identity: Symbolic interactionism and hermeneutics', *The Sociological Quarterly*, **39**(2), 239–52.

Framework for Regional Employment and Skills Action (2002), 'Productivity through employability', available at: http://www.network-foreurope.eu/files/File/downloads/FRESA%202004.pdf.

Garvey, B., Stokes, P. and Megginson, D. (2009), *Coaching and Mentoring: Theory and Practice*, London: Sage Publications.

Gaskill, L.R., Van Auken, H.E. and Manning, R.A. (1993), 'A factor analytic study of the perceived causes of small business failure', *Journal of Small Business Management*, **31**(4), 18–31.

Gemmill, G. and Oakley, J. (1992), 'Leadership: An alienating social myth?' *Human Relations*, **45**, 953–75.

Gergen, K.J. (1971), *The Self Concept*, London: Holt, Rinehart and Winston.

Gibb, A. (2009), 'Meeting the development needs of owner managed small enterprise: A discussion of the centrality of action learning', *Action Learning: Research and Practice*, **6**(3), 209–27.

Gibson, D.E. (2003), 'Developing the professional self-concept: Role model construals in early, middle and late career stages', *Organization Science*, **14**(5), 591–610.

Gibson, D.E. (2004), 'Role models in career development: New directions for theory and research', *Journal of Vocational Behavior*, **65**(1), 134–56.

Gill, A. and Harris, G. (2014), 'Evaluation and impact of the LEAD programme on owner/managers of small- and medium-sized enterprises in South West England from 2011–2014 using mixed methods', Cheltenham: GillFoxJames Ltd, unpublished.

Gioia, D.A. (1986), 'Conclusion: The state of the art in organizational social cognition: A personal view', in H.P. Sims and D.A. Gioia (eds), *The Thinking Organisation: Dynamics of Organizational Social Cognition*, San Francisco, CA: Jossey-Bass.

Goldratt, E. (1994), *It's Not Luck*, Aldershot: Gower.

Goldratt, E. and Cox, J. (2004), *The Goal: The Process of On-going Improvement*, 3rd edn, Aldershot: North River Press.

Goleman, D., Boyatzis, R. and McKee, A. (2002), *The New Leaders: Transforming the Art of Leadership into the Science of Results*, London: Little, Brown.

Graen, G.B. and Uhl-Bien, M. (1991), 'The transformation of work-group professionals into self-managing and partially self-designing contributors: Toward a theory of leadership-making', *Journal of Management Systems*, **3**(3), 33–48.

Graya, D.E., Ekincib, Y. and Goregaokara, H. (2011), 'Coaching SME managers: Business development or personal therapy? A mixed methods study', *The International Journal of Human Resource Management*, **22**(4), February, 863–82.

Greiner, L.E. (1972), 'Evolution and revolution as organizations grow', *Harvard Business Review*, **50**, 37–46.

Guthey, E. (2005), 'Management studies, cultural criticism and American dreams', *Journal of Management Studies*, **42**(2), 451–65.

Guthey, E. (2013), 'The production of leadership fashions', *The Academy of Management Proceedings*, Meeting Abstract Supplement, doi: 10.5465/AMBPP.2013.12214abstract.

Habermas, J. (1971), *Knowledge and Human Interest*, Boston, MA: Beacon Press.

Hall, R.J. and Lord, R.G. (1995), 'Multilevel information processing explanations of followers' leadership perceptions', *The Leadership Quarterly*, **6**(3), 265–87.

Hill, L.A. (2003), *Becoming a Manager: How New Managers Master the Challenges of Leadership*, Boston, MA: Harvard Business School Press.

Hoyt, C.L. and Simon, S. (2011), 'Female leaders: Injurious or inspiring role models for women?', *Psychology of Women Quarterly*, **35**(1), 143–57.

Ibarra, H. (1999), 'Provisional selves: Experimenting with image and identity in professional adaptation', *Administrative Science Quarterly*, **44**(4), 764–92.

Jackson, B. and Parry, K. (2011), *A Very Short, Fairly Interesting and Reasonably Cheap Book about Studying Leadership*, 2nd edn, London: Sage Publications.

Jackson, P.Z. and McKergow, M. (2007), *The Solutions Focus: The SIMPLE Way to Positive Change*, 2nd edn, London: Nicholas Brealey.

Janson, A. (2008), 'Extracting leadership knowledge from formative experiences', *Leadership*, **4**(1), 73–94.

Jarvis, P. (1987), 'Meaningful and meaningless experience: Towards an analysis of learning life', *Adult Education Quarterly*, **37**(3), 164–72.

Jones, O., Macpherson, A. and Thorpe, R. (2010), 'Learning in owner-managed small firms: Mediating artefacts and strategic space', *Entrepreneurship and Regional Development*, **22**(7/8), 649–763.

Jones, O., Macpherson, A., Thorpe, R. and Ghecham, A. (2007), 'The evolution of business knowledge in SMEs: Conceptualizing strategic space', *Strategic Change*, **16**(6), 281–94.

Kempster, S. (2005), 'Examining how managers learn to lead', PhD thesis, University of Gloucestershire.

Kempster, S. (2006), 'Leadership learning through lived experience: A process of apprenticeship?', *Journal of Management and Organization*, **12**, 4–22.

Kempster, S. (2009a), *How Managers Have Learnt to Lead: Exploring the Development of Leadership Practice*, Basingstoke: Palgrave Macmillan.

Kempster, S. (2009b), 'Observing the invisible: Examining the role of observational learning in the development of leadership practice', *Journal of Management Development*, **28**(5), 439–56.

Kempster, S. and Watts, G. (2002), 'The entrepreneur as a leader: An exploration of leadership development amongst small business owner-managers', Proceedings of the 25th Annual Conference of the Institute for Small Business and Entrepreneurship.

Kempster, S. and Cope, J. (2010), 'Learning to lead in the entrepreneurial context', *International Journal of Entrepreneurial Behaviour and Research*, **16**(1), 6–35.

Kempster, S. and Stewart, J. (2010), 'Becoming a leader: A co-produced autoethnographic exploration of situated learning of leadership practice', *Management Learning*, **41**(2), 205–19.

Kempster, S. and Jackson, B. (2011), 'Leadership as purpose: Exploring the role of purpose in leadership practice', *Leadership*, **7**(3), 317–34.

Kempster, S. and Iszatt-White, M. (2012), 'Towards co-constructed coaching: Exploring the integration of coaching and co-constructed autoethnography in leadership development', *Management Learning*, **44**, 319–36.

Kempster, S. and Parry, K. (2013), 'Exploring observational learning in leadership development for managers', *Journal of Management Development*, **33**(3), 164–81.

Kempster, S. and Smith, S. (2014), 'Becoming a leader through becoming a delegate: Leadership development as a community of practice through a situated curriculum', *Lancaster University Working Papers Series*.

Kempster, S., Smith, S. and Barnes, S. (in press), 'A review of entrepreneurial leadership learning: A three dimensional explanation that draws on human, social and institutional capitals', in C.M. Leitch and R.T Harrison (eds), *Research Handbook on Entrepreneurship and Leadership*, Cheltenham, UK and Northampton, MA, USA: Edward Elgar Publishing.

Kim, D.H. (1993), 'The link between individual and organizational learning', *Sloan Management Review* (Fall), 37–50.

Kolb, D. (1984), *Experiential Learning*, London: Prentice-Hall.

Lave, J. and Wenger, E. (1991), *Situated Learning: Legitimate Peripheral Participation*, Cambridge: Cambridge University Press.

Leitch, C.M., McMullan, C. and Harrison, R.T. (2013), 'The development of entrepreneurial leadership: The role of human, social and institutional capital', *British Journal of Management*, **24**, 347–66.

Levie, J. and Lichtenstein, B.B. (2010), 'A terminal assessment of stages theory: Introducing a dynamic states approach to entrepreneurship', *Entrepreneurship: Theory and Practice*, **34**, 317–50.

Ling, Y., Simsek, Z., Lubatkin, M.H. and Veiga, J.F. (2008), 'The impact of transformational CEOs on the performance of small- to medium-size firms: Does organizational context matter?', *Journal of Applied Psychology*, **93**, 923–34.

Lord, R.G. and Emrich, C.G. (2001), 'Thinking outside the box by looking inside the box: Extending the cognitive revolution in leadership research', *The Leadership Quarterly*, **12**(3), 551–79.

Lord, R.G., Brown, D.J., Harvey, J.L. and Hall, R.J. (2001), 'Contextual constraints on prototype generation and their multilevel consequences for leadership perceptions', *The Leadership Quarterly*, **12**(3), 311–38.

Macleod, D. and Clarke, N. (2009), 'Engaging for success: Enhancing performance through employee engagement', available at: Department of Business, Enterprise and Regulatory Reform, www.berr.gov.uk/files/file52215.pdf.

Majumdar, S. (2008), 'Modelling growth strategy in small entrepreneurial business organisations', *Journal of Entrepreneurship*, **17**, 157.

Markus, H. and Nurius, P.S. (1986), 'Possible selves', *American Psychologist*, **41**, 954–69.

Markus, H. and Wurf, E. (1987), 'The dynamic self-concept: A social psychological perspective', *Annual Review of Psychology*, **38**, 299–337.

Marserick, V.J. and Watkins, K.E. (1990), *Informal and Incidental Learning in the Workplace*, London: Routledge.

McCall, M.W. (1998), *High Flyers: Developing the Next Generation of Leaders*, Boston, MA: Harvard Business School.

McCall, M.W. (2004), 'Leadership development through experience', *Academy of Management Executive*, **18**(3), 127–30.

McCall, M.W., Lombardo, M.M. and Morrison, A. (1988), *The Lessons of Experience*, Lexington, MA: Lexington.

McCauley, C.D. and Brutus, S. (1998), *Management Development Through Job Experience: An Annotated Bibliography*, Greensboro, NC: Center for Creative Leadership.

McDonald, M. and Wilson, H. (2011), *Marketing Plans: How to Prepare Them, How to Use Them*, 7th edn, Chichester: Wiley.

Meindl, J.R. (1995), 'The romance of leadership as a follower centric theory: A social constructionist approach', *The Leadership Quarterly*, **6**, 329–41.

Mezirow, J. (1985), 'A critical theory of self-directed learning', in S. Brookfield (ed.), *Self-Directed Learning: From Theory to Practice*, San Francisco, CA: Jossey-Bass, pp. 17–30.

Mezirow, J. (1991), *Transformative Dimensions of Adult Learning*, San Francisco, CA: Jossey-Bass.

Mezirow, J. (1997), 'Transformative learning: Theory to practice', *New Directions for Adult and Continuing Education*, **74**(7), 41–50.

Mischel, W. (2004), 'Toward an integrated science of the person', *Annual Review of Psychology*, **55**, 1–22.

Neale, S., Spencer-Arnell, L. and Wilson, L. (2009), *Emotional Intelligence Coaching: Improving Performance for Leaders, Coaches and the Individual*, London: Kogan Page.

Nonaka, I. and Takeuchi, H. (1995), *The Knowledge-Creating Company*, Oxford: Oxford University Press.

North West Development Agency (2010), 'High growth programme', available at: http://www.edocr.com/doc/63/nwda-high-growth-programme-criteria.

Oliver, J.J. (2001), *The Team Enterprise Solution: A Step-by-Step Guide to Business Transformation*, Cork: Oak Tree Press.

Oliver, J.J. and Memmott, C. (2006), *Growing Your Own Heroes: The Common Sense Way to Improve Business Performance*, Cork: Oak Tree Press.

Parry, K.W. (1998), 'Grounded theory and social process: A new direction for leadership research', *Leadership Quarterly*, **9**(1), 85–105.

Pedler, M., Burgoyne, J. and Brook, C. (2005), 'What has action learning learned to become?', *Action Learning: Research and Practice*, **2**(1), 49–68.

Peel, D. (2004), 'Coaching and mentoring in small to medium sized enterprises in the UK – Factors that affect success and a possible solution', *International Journal of Evidence-Based Coaching and Mentoring*, **2**(1), 46–56.

Perren, L. and Grant, P. (2001), *Management and Leadership in UK SMEs: Witness Testimonies from the World of Entrepreneurs and SME Managers*, London: Council for Excellence in Management and Leadership.

Perren, L., Davis, M. and Kroessin, R. (2002), *Mapping of UK SME Management and Leadership Development Provision*, London: Council for Excellence in Management and Leadership.

Phelps, R., Adams, R. and Bessant, J. (2007), 'Life cycles of growing organizations: A review with implications for knowledge and learning', *International Journal of Management Reviews*, **9**(1), 1–30.

Pittaway, L., Missing, C., Hudson, N. and Maragh, D. (2009), 'Entrepreneurial learning through action: A case study of the Six-Squared program', *Action Learning: Research and Practice*, **6**(3), 265–88.

Polanyi, M. (1966), *The Tacit Dimension*, London: Routledge.

Pye, A. (2005), 'Leadership and organizing: sense-making in action', *Leadership*, **1**(1), 31–50.

Rae, D. (2009), 'Connecting entrepreneurial and action learning in student initiated new business ventures: The case of SPEED', *Action Learning: Research and Practice*, **6**(3), 289–303.

Raelin, J. (2011), 'From leadership-as-practice to leaderful practice', *Leadership*, **7**(2), 195–211.

Revans, R.W. (1982), 'What is action learning?', *Journal of Management Development*, **1**(3), 64–75.

Revans, R. (1983), *The ABC of Action Learning*, Bromley: Chartwell-Bratt.

Revans, R. (2011), *ABC of Action Learning*, Farnham: Gower.

Reynolds, M. (1998), 'Reflection and critical reflection in management learning', *Management Learning*, **29**(2), 183–200.

Reynolds, M. (1999a), 'Grasping the nettle: Possibilities and pitfalls of a critical management pedagogy', *British Journal of Management*, **10**(2), 171–84.

Reynolds, M. (1999b), 'Critical reflection and management education: Rehabilitating less hierarchical approaches', *Journal of Management Education*, **23**(5), October, 537–53.

Reynolds, M. and Vince, R. (2004), 'Critical management education and action-based learning: Synergies and contradictions', *Academy of Management Learning and Education*, **3**(4), 442–56.

Robinson, S. (2007), '*Relational Learning: Towards a Model of Owner-manager Development*', Proceedings of the HRD Conference, London, April.

Rogers, C.R. (1980), *A Way of Being*, New York: Mariner Books.

Santander Breakthrough Programme (2014), http://www.santanderbreak-through.co.uk/.

Schein, E.H. (1992), *Organizational Culture and Leadership*, 2nd edn, San Francisco, CA: Jossey-Bass.

Schön, D.A. (1983), *The Reflective Practitioner: How Professionals Think in Action*, New York: Basic Books.

Shotter, J. (1993), 'Becoming someone: identity and belonging', in N. Coupland and J.F. Nussbaum (eds), *Discourse and Lifespan Identity: Language and Language Behaviors*, Thousand Oaks, CA: Sage Publications, pp. 5–27.

Smallbone, D., Kitching, J., Blackburn, R. and Mosavi, S. (2015), 'Anchor institutions and small firms in the UK: A review of the literature on anchor institutions and their role in developing management and leadership skills in small firms', UKCES (UK Commission for Employment and Skills), available at: https://www.gov.uk/government/uploads/system/uploads/attachment_data/file/414390/Anchor_institutions_and_small_firms.pdf

Smirich, C. and Morgan, G. (1982), 'Leadership: The management of meaning', *The Journal of Applied Behavioural Science*, **18**(3), 257–73.

Smith, A.J., Whittaker, J., Loan-Clarke, J. and Boocock, J.G. (1999), 'Management training and development in small and medium-sized enterprises: An assessment of the effectiveness of Training and Enterprise Councils in the East Midlands', *Journal of Small Business and Enterprise Development*, **6**(2), 178–90.

Smith, L. (2009), 'Experiences of action learning in two SME business support programmes', *Action Learning: Research and Practice*, **6**(3), 335–41.

Smith, L. and Peters, S. (2006), 'Leading by design: The case of LEAD', *Symposium: Entrepreneurial Leadership Learning*, Belfast, British Academy of Management, September.

Smith, S. (2011), 'How do small business owner-managers learn leadership through networked learning?', in L. Dirckinck-Holmfeld, V. Hodgson and D. McConnell (eds), *Exploring the Theory, Pedagogy and Practice of Networked Learning*, New York: Springer, pp. 221–36.

Stake, R.E. (2005), 'Case Studies', in N.K. Denzin and Y.S. Lincoln (eds), *Handbook of Qualitative Research*, 3rd edn, Thousand Oaks, CA: Sage Publications, pp. 236–47.

Stewart, J. and Alexander, G. (2006), 'Virtual action learning: Experiences from a study of an SME e-learning programme', *Action Learning: Research and Practice*, **3**(2), 141–59.

Storey, D.J. (1994), *Understanding the Small Business Sector*, London: Thomson Learning.

Stryker, S. and Statham, A. (1985), 'Symbolic interaction and role theory', in G. Lindzey and E. Aronson (eds), *Handbook of Social Psychology*, 3rd edn, New York: Random House, pp. 311–78.

Sveningsson, S.F. and Larsson, M. (2006), 'Fantasies of leadership: Identity work', *Leadership*, **2**(2), 203–24.

Thorpe, R., Cope, J., Ram, M. and Pedler, M. (2009), 'Leadership development in small and medium-sized enterprises: The case for action learning', *Action Learning: Research and Practice*, **6**(3), 201–208.

Thorpe, R., Gold, J., Anderson, L., Burgoyne, J., Wilkinson, D. and Malby, B. (2008), *Towards 'Leaderful' Communities in the North of England*, Cork: Oak Tree Press.

Tsoukas, H. and Chia, R. (2002), 'On organizational becoming: Rethinking organizational change', *Organization Science*, **13**(5), 567–82.

Uhl-Bien, M. (2003), 'Relationship development as a key ingredient for leadership development', in S. Murphy and R. Riggio (eds), *The Future Leadership Development*, Mahwah, NJ: Lawrence Erlbaum Associates, pp. 129–45.

Usher, R.S. (1985), 'Beyond the anecdotal: Adult learning and the use of experience', *Studies in the Education of Adults*, **17**(1), 59–74.

Van Maanen, J. (2011), 'Ethnography as work: Some rules of engagement', *Journal of Management Studies*, **48**(1), 218–34.

Velsor, E. and Guthrie, V.A. (1998), 'Enhancing the ability to learn from experience', in C.D. McCauley, R.S. Moxley and E. Van Velsor (eds),

Handbook of Leadership Development, San Francisco, CA: Jossey-Bass, pp. 242–61.

Wenger, E. (1998), *Communities of Practice: Learning, Meaning, and Identity*, Cambridge: Cambridge University Press.

Wenger, E. (2000), 'Communities of practice and social learning systems', *Organization*, **7**(2), 225–46.

Wenger, E., McDermott, R. and Snyder, W.M. (2002), *Cultivating Communities of Practice*, Boston, MA: Harvard Business School Press.

Whitmore, J. (2002), *Coaching for Performance: GROWing People, Performance and Purpose*, London: Nicholas Brealey.

Wood, R. and Bandura, A. (1989), 'Social cognitive theory of organizational management', *Academy of Management Review*, **14**(3), 361–84.

Wren, C. and Jones, J. (2006), 'Ex-Post evaluation of the LEAD programme', University of Newcastle Upon Tyne: Newcastle, available at: http://www.lums.ac.uk/leaddeval.

Wren, C. and Jones, J. (2012), 'Quantitative evaluation of the LEAD Programme, 2004–11', University of Newcastle Upon Tyne: Newcastle, available at: http://www.ncl.ac.uk/nubs/research/publication/192709.

Index